D1590870

# THE JAPANESE AUTOMOBILE INDUSTRY

# The Japanese Automobile Industry

## A Business History

KOICHI SHIMOKAWA

THE ATHLONE PRESS
London and Atlantic Highlands, NJ

HD
9710
J32
S514
1994

First published 1994 by
THE ATHLONE PRESS
1 Park Drive, London NW11 7SG
and 165 First Avenue,
Atlantic Highlands, NJ 07716

© *Koichi Shimokawa 1994*

British Library Cataloguing in Publication Data
*A catalogue record for this book is available
from the British Library*

ISBN 0 485 11270 1

Library of Congress Cataloging in Publication Data
Shimokawa, Kōichi, 1930–
    The Japanese automobile industry : a business history /
Koichi Shimokawa.
        p.    cm.
    Includes bibliographical references and index.
    ISBN 0-485-11270-1 (lib) : $85.00
    1. Automobile industry and trade--Japan--History.    I. Title.
HD9710.J32S514    1994
338.4'7004'0952--dc20                                        94-18947

Typeset by
*Bibloset, Chester*

Printed and bound in Great Britain by the
*University Press, Cambridge*

# Contents

To

The late Professor W.J. Abernathy
My Teacher the late Professor Katsuzo Baba
Professor T.C. Barker
Professor Alfred D. Chandler
My late father and my wife

# *Foreword*

The Japanese automobile industry is moving into a new era of internationalization. Compared with the late 1940s when just 20,000 units or so a year were produced in Japan – mainly small and medium-sized trucks – the output, mostly of automobiles, surpassed 13 million in 1991 for the third year in succession, making it the largest in the world. Japanese automakers are also based in forty countries overseas. In North America, Japan's largest overseas market, more than ten plants have been set up, and in Europe as many as seven. In Asian countries too, the production of automobiles is being promoted by Japanese automakers and parts manufacturers. The rise in the international status of the Japanese automobile industry has caused some friction with countries such as the USA and Europe. The Japanese automobile industry is currently involved in the reorganization and reconstruction of automobile industries throughout the world.

The Japanese automobile industry began to emerge internationally after 1980 when the US automobile industry began to lose its competitiveness and went into decline, after the second oil crises. Japan, the latecomer among OECD countries, took advantage of this situation, and proceeded to establish its superiority, mainly in compact cars, both in cost and quality. The internationalization of the Japanese automobile industry was helped along by the appreciation of the yen after the G–5 meeting in September 1985.

The rapid increase in the international competitiveness of the Japanese automobile industry since 1950 is an outstanding achievement. The postwar world economy saw the expansion of international trade and the growth of the OECD economies. It was not long before Japan achieved high economic growth, and began to benefit from a domestic automobile market that expanded rapidly. It was fortunate that Japanese automakers produced mainly compact cars, due largely to the Japanese dependency on other countries for petroleum. As a result they were able to adapt themselves successfully to changes in the demand structure after the oil-price crises. Although these events were favourable to Japanese automakers, what is important is how they reacted to them. This book offers an account and an analysis of what took place.

The Japanese automobile industry also owes its rapid development to the performance of the supplying industries – such as the steel, rubber, plastic, machine tools and parts industries. Other elements in the development of the industry include: a dynamic and competitive structure (unlike that in the USA and European countries where oligopoly prevailed); the establishment of a co-operative relationship between automakers and parts manufacturers; good labour–management relationships encouraging the improvement of productivity, distribution of corporate accomplishments and participation in corporate management and the development of new production systems such as QC (Quality Control) circle activities and the 'just-in-time' method of production. All ensured high standards of productivity and quality. Focusing on the conditions that enabled the development of the Japanese automobile industry, this book analyses historical developments and the characteristics of labour/management relations, the business relations and structure of the parts industry and automobile sales and distribution. In addition to these general features of the industry, the book also looks at the histories and recent experiences of the eleven principal Japanese automakers. It takes an overview of developments in the new era of internationalization.

This book was first planned in 1983. I was given a publishing project by The Athlone Press, on the recommendation of Professor T.C. Barker of the University of London with whom I was associated as a student. The publisher then suggested that the study should be done in collaboration with an English-speaking student who was interested in the Japanese automobile industry. Professor W.J. Abernathy of Harvard Business School, who was a friend of mine at school, agreed to co-author the book, and prepare an outline for it. Unfortunately Professor Abernathy died at the end of 1983. Many of the ideas from his writings such as *Productivity Dilemma* (M.I.R. Press, 1977) and *Industrial Renaissance* (Harvard University Press, 1982 ) are contained in this book. Tracing the challenge of the Japanese automobile industry objectively, Professor Abernathy probed deeply into main difficulties that the US automobile industry was at that time confronted with, and insisted on the USA learning how to benefit form Japan's experiences.

Fortunately, Mr Paul Summerville, economist of Jardine Fleming Securities Ltd., Tokyo branch, then agreed to help with the book. He assisted with one third of the original text. Finally, I received considerable collaboration in the translation from Union Service Co., its president, Mr Hajimu Ikeda, and its editor, Howard Mulvey. This book owes much to the great assistance received from these people. Also included in this book are my findings from joint research into the international automobile industry in the 'International Motor Vehicle Program' at the Massachusetts Institute of Technology, which I have participated in since 1981. The above-mentioned Professor T.C. Barker, and Mr Brian Southam, director of The Athlone Press, gave me helpful advice. I heartily thank these persons and parties concerned for their kindness.

It will be gratifying if the book presents students of the automobile industry and automobile industrialists with an overall historical view of the Japanese automobile industry and will help them to foresee the prospects of the industry as well as the role the Japanese automobile industry will play in the future.

Koichi Shimokawa

# Introduction

The world automobile industry underwent tremendous structural changes from the late 1970s up until 1983: there was the decline of the Detroit manufacturers, who had been the top auto-producers in the world for over sixty years, and the rapid development in the international competitiveness of the Japanese automobile industry.[1] This also had a great impact on the European automobile industry, which has been in decline since the first oil crisis in 1973. The decline of both the US and European automobile industries coupled with the rapid penetration of their markets by the Japanese led to increasingly strong governmental restrictions against Japanese exports in general and Japanese automotive exports in particular.

Since 1983, however, Detroit has made a recovery. Increased automobile demand in the USA coupled with improved productivity and investment in new production capacity has made the Detroit manufacturers more profitable and as greatly reduced their break-even lines of production; they made a US$6 billion profit in 1983, which offset the losses of the four previous years, and, in 1984, they made record profits of almost US$9 billion. While the second oil crisis revealed a startling decline of the Detroit producers, their subsequent return to profitability has been spectacular. One key question posed by this revival is how it will affect the competitive position of the Japanese manufacturers.[2] Moreover, following the G–5 meeting in September 1985, broader political pressures have produced a revaluation of the yen against the US dollar and many other currencies. The revival of Detroit together with the ever strengthening yen is affecting the international competitive position of the Japanese. It remains an open question how the competitive rivalry in the production of automobiles will develop, particularly as the international trading regime evolves to limit the competitive position of the Japanese automobile manufacturers. Given the key position of the automobile industry in Japan, the US and major European countries, it has become symptomatic of the problems and changes occurring in the international economy. The Japanese automobile industry has become a target for broader complaints concerning the impact of the Japanese economy on its trading partners, particularly the USA.

The decline and recovery of Detroit can also be seen as typical of the changes and problems that the automobile industry faced as a whole. Consider the automobile crisis of the early 1980s which led to the near bankruptcy of Chrysler. In Detroit, close to one million people were unemployed in the automotive and related industries and there were record losses by Detroit manufacturers. However, government aid was given to Detroit, followed by investment in new plants and equipment, and, along with the scrapping of old plants, there was the introduction of robotics, and a new strategy by the United Auto Workers (UAW) union, based on wage concessions and increased co-operation with management; all of these factors combined to ensure the revival of the industry. Since 1982, Chrysler has been brought back to life, repaying government money before it was due and making record profits (the result of higher productivity due to high investment in new technology and a reduction in the number of employees). 1984 also saw a revival of the US market for large cars. In short, in less than six years, the American automobile manufacturers made a series of radical changes at a time of depression, followed by a rapid improvement and record profits.[3]

The European automobile industry did not go through quite the same dramatic cycle. The Europeans experienced a longer period of gradual decline that began after the first oil crisis in 1973–4. With more than 20 per cent overcapacity, a surplus workforce and a production system set up for full-line production, the European manufacturers suffered steady losses and declining international competitiveness. More recently however, the European industry has been adopting a strategy based on inter-firm collaboration, including links with producers in other countries: for example, joint production of engines and components. This has been accompanied by huge investments in new technology. Thus, as in the USA, the Europeans are now using more and more robots and computers.[4]

Among the European manufacturers, the producers of luxury cars, such as Daimler–Benz and Volvo, have maintained a stable profit profile despite a decreasing volume of production and market share. It was the full-line producers, such as Volkswagen, Renault, Peugeot,

Fiat and British Leyland, who faced the task of maintaining profitability and, in some cases, even staving off bankruptcy itself. These companies had been plagued by poor management/labour relations. The historical legacy of the European trade union movement has reinforced suspicion between management and labour in many European automobile firms. This problem was exacerbated as management tried to reduce the number of employees and increase automation at a time of recession. In addition, questionable strategic decisions to build overseas production facilities in the USA and South America did not remedy the poor profit performance of many of the European manufacturers.[5]

Thus, the dramatic change that the American automobile industry (and, to a lesser degree, the European automobile industry) has been through since the early 1980s is characterized by a survival strategy based on increased productivity through the modernization of production facilities and the rationalization of production systems. The driving force behind this adjustment – which is now beginning to have an impact on the structure of the automobile industry internationally – was the international competitiveness of the Japanese automobile industry, which rose quickly to the status of world leader. Why did this happen in the way that it did? What is the nature of the so-called 'Japanese challenge'? What lesson can we learn from it all?

In assessing the international competitiveness of the Japanese automobile industry, some fundamental questions must be asked. Firstly, in comparison with the industrial practices of leading Western producers, what accounts for the international success of the Japanese industry? Secondly, to what extent did management and production technology contribute to the efficiency of the Japanese production system? Thirdly, to what extent did stable management/labour relations contribute to high productivity and high quality production? An appraisal has to be made of Quality Control (QC) activities, the consultative systems between management and labour and the emergence of company-based unions. Fourthly, to what extent did the structure of the Japanese automobile industry, in terms of the relationship between automobile assemblers and their suppliers, contribute to the success of the industry's competitive manufacturers? We will outline the vertical division of labour in the Japanese component of parts manufacturing supply system, the group-oriented structure of co-operative assembler/supplier relations, the long-term contract supply system, designed to ensure high quality through supplier quality guarantees, the continual innovation in product design and the production system throughout the Japanese automobile industry, particularly in the case of the suppliers, and the Japanese approach to rationalization in the parts industry. Finally, there is the role of Japan's domestic economy, in terms of the importance of other industries (such as steel, plastic, rubber and glass, electronics and machine tools) in the competitiveness of the Japanese automobile industry.

The 'Japanese challenge' is based on the redefinition of the conventional rules of product design and production systems. The Japanese challenged many industrial 'rules' which had emerged from over a half century of American can European automobile production. In particular, the Japanese introduced a quality-focused system of production, extending from the design stage to the final assemble of the vehicle and through to distribution and after service. The essential difference is that the Japanese made quality production profitable, undermining sixty years of American thinking that increased quality could only decrease profits. The Japanese-style system emphasized process technology, stable and co-operative management/labour relations and a well-organized component supply system, designed to face the constant challenge of smoothly introducing new technological innovations, such as robot and electronic technologies.

Change is part and parcel of the Japanese system and innovation is the driving force. The 'Japanese challenge' represents a new age of innovation in what had previously been considered a mature industry. The commitment to innovation by the Japanese has ended the myth that the industry could only be run on the basis of high volume and high-speed production in order to benefit from economies of scale. At the same time, however, the appreciation of the yen and the growing protectionist attitude in Japan's major export markets have given the Japanese manufacturers new and perhaps even more difficult conditions in which to operate. The industry in Japan is now entering a new phase of internationalization by building production facilities in its major export markets and farming out highly labour intensive parts production to neighbouring low-wage Asian countries, such as Taiwan, Thailand, Malaysia and soon South Korea.

# CHAPTER 1

# The Japanese Automobile Industry: A Brief History

The Japanese automobile industry began in 1902 when Shintaro Yoshida and Komanosuke Uchiyama, partners in a small business called the 'Automobile Company' (Otomobiru Shokai), produced a trial car with a two-cylinder, 12-horsepower American engine. In 1904 Torao Yamaba produced a two-cylinder steam automobile in Okayama. In 1912 Kaishinsha, a company created by Masujiro Hashimoto, produced a car called the Dattogo. These were all trial models. Various other pioneers continued to experiment until, in 1920, Hakuyosha produced the Otomogo automobile; 250 of these cars were made in 1923, the largest output of any make in Japan in those early years.[1]

In Japan, these early trials did not begin until much later than they had in America and Europe. However, despite the emergence of many manufacturers in Japan, it was not until much later that the volume of production became large enough to be profitable. The chief reason for this was that domestic cars, produced in small numbers, could not compete with the cars that were being imported, especially from the USA, just after the Tokyo earthquake of 1923. After the earthquake, the Tokyo city government bought T Fords and rebuilt them as buses (popularly known as Entaro buses), which became the new form of transport in the city. With their superior production techniques, marketing and service systems, Ford and General Motors set up subsidiary companies in Japan in 1925–6 and started assembling trucks and cars from imported parts. The Japanese market was then completely swamped by foreign automobiles. While the number of imported cars had reached 15–16,000 a year by 1929,[2] it was not until 1933 that the annual domestic production reached the one thousand mark.

The Japanese automobile industry was soon left behind by the US and European manufacturers and this can be attributed mainly to the under-developed and imbalanced state of Japan's industrial technology at the time, bearing in mind that automotive manufacturing involves almost all sections of the machine-tool industry. There were problems at all stages from the low quality of basic materials, such as steel plates and special steels, to poor techniques in stamping, casting, forging, machining, electroplating, painting and other operations. Most of the advanced areas of Japanese industrial technology were linked to military production and the country fell short of the overall technological standards required for auto-manufacturing. This made automotive production a risky business and even well-established 'Zaibatsu', financial groups, such as Mitsui and Mitsubishi, were reluctant to make commitments to automobile manufacturing, despite pressure by the Japanese military authorities for the development of domestic production after World War I.[3]

Before World War II, the Japanese automotive industry, under government direction, concentrated on producing military trucks. The Japanese military authorities were aware of the value of motor vehicles during World War I and this led to the Military Vehicle Subsidy Law (Gun'yo Jidosha Hojo Ho) in 1918, to promote the development of truck production technology. At the beginning of the Showa period, in 1926, domestic automobile production was promoted in the light of the international political situation. Even though the established 'Zaibatsu' were still hesitant about entering into the industry, new manufacturers appeared and took up automobile production, despite many technological difficulties. Among these were Nissan Motor and Toyota Motor Corporation. Nissan, formerly the automotive division of the Tobata Foundry Company, obtained the patent for the Datto vehicle and in 1933 became a part of the new Nissan 'Zaibatsu'. Toyota as established in 1933 as the automobile department of Toyoda Automatic Loom Works, and became an independent company in 1936. These two companies were licensed as authorized companies in accordance with the Automotive Manufacturing Industries Law (Jidosha Seizo Jigyo Ho) of 1935. This act was aimed mainly at protecting an promoting domestic automobile production by providing favourable tax treatment and other incentives as well as by restricting the activities of foreign automobile manufacturers. As Japan's economy moved into wartime, foreign car manufacturers became subject to strict regulations, which led to the end of their operations in Japan by 1940. Domestic manufacturers produced medium-sized trucks in accordance with the military's industrial plans, and at the same time worked to improve the underdeveloped spare parts industry. Diesel Jidosha Kogyo, successor to Tokyo Jidosha Kogyo (now Isuzu Motors), was later added as an authorized manufacturer, primarily engaged in the production of diesel trucks and buses.[4]

Following the start of World War II, the domestic manufacturers (including the addition of Mitsubishi Heavy Industries and Hino Motors) made substantial contributions to the production of military trucks and weapons. After the war, the Occupation authorities allowed these manufacturers to continue limited production, principally of trucks, in order to improve the domestic transport system, but total production in the first year only amounted to abut 20,000 units. An opportunity to recover was provided by the military procurements boom during the Korean War and manufacturers started to produce passenger cars in 1952. In the beginning, most of the demand was from the taxi trade, the demand from private individuals being minimal. Around this time the major manufacturers began to look for technical associations with European automobile manufacturers to improve their manufacturing technology; for example, affiliations such as Nissan–Austin, Hino–Renault and Isuzu–Hillman. The transfer of technology from European automakers extended as far as the parts manufacturers, in order to improve both the engineering of components and the basic technology relating the the design and production of cars. However, these ties between Japanese and European manufacturers were temporary and were also limited to the transfer of technology concerning small cars. Some domestic manufacturers, such as Toyota and Prince Motors, made their own way. Also around this time, the Japanese government, led by the Ministry of International Trade and Industry (MITI), began to support and protect its own domestic industry. Although no direct financial assistance was made, MITI sought to ensure favourable allocations of foreign currency for the development of new technology, to restrict vehicle imports and foreign investment, and to help the parts industry with technical assistance and advice.[5]

After 1960, with the Japanese economy in a new period of liberalized trade and high growth, the domestic production of cars increased at an unprecedented rate. A wave of motorization began to sweep the country and several new manufacturers joined the original three car makers of the prewar days. These included Mitsubishi, which had produced trucks during the war and after the war had been split into three companies, two of which had started manufacturing motor vehicles and later remerged; Hino, which had originally manufactured diesel trucks; Fuji Heavy Industries (maker of the Subaru), which had been an aircraft manufacturer; and Prince. Others included Toyo Kogyo Company (now Mazda), the Daihatsu Motor Company and the Honda Motor Company, which had formerly made machinery, three-wheeled cars and motor cycles. Many new factories were built for the manufacture of cars, with production capacities reaching 100,000 units a year. The parts industry went through a process of integration and concentration resulting in the formation of an organized subcontracting system. Nationwide sales networks were strengthened. At the same time, Toyota and Nissan adopted a full-product line policy in response to the widening range of demand. They also took the lead in developing strategic models such as the Crown, Cedric, Corona and Bluebird, all of which were suited to high-volume production. These strategies proved successful and Toyota and Nissan began to emerge as the giants of the modern Japanese automotive industry.[6]

After 1965, with the liberalization of capital movement, the industry entered a new period. To prepare for the inflow of foreign capital – led by America's big three automakers – MITI launched a carefully-planned campaign to promote the reorganization of the automobile industry. In 1961 MITI had already announced a plan to strengthen this vital industrial sector by integrating and reorganizing the domestic automobile manufacturers into three groups – producers of mass-production passenger cars, producers of 'specialty' vehicles (commercial vehicles etc.), and producers of minicars. However, despite MITI's efforts, due to the differing opinions and expectations on the part of the companies involved, the reorganization was not carried out in the way originally intended. Some mergers and formations of new business groups did take place: Toyota made agreements with Hino and Daihatsu and created its own group; Nissan absorbed Prince in 1966 and, in a tie with Fuji Heavy Industries, formed the Nissan Group. These two groups came to hold 60 per cent of the market, a strong oligopolistic outcome. Other manufacturers began to seek links with foreign manufacturers, partly due to the advice of their banks. Mitsubishi entered into capital and operational ties with Chrysler in 1969. This was followed by a capital tie between Isuzu and General Motors in 1971, and sales and operational ties between Toyo Kogyo (now Mazda) and Ford in the same year.[7]

As a result of these developments, a new structure emerged in the industry consisting of three groups of manufacturers – one group containing the two major domestic manufacturers and their affiliates; another group containing the three companies associated with US manufacturers, and a third group containing two other independent manufacturers. These last two were Honda, the world-famous manufacturer of motor cycles which moved into the small car market, and Suzuki, which specialized in motor cycles and minicars.

Around 1968, Toyota and Nissan rapidly increased their exports of automobile and light trucks. By 1975, they were joined by the expanding Honda company as well as the manufacturers associated with US firms.

The Japanese industry's competitive strength in world markets can be attributed to several factors, including increases in the scale of production, improvements in technology due to the introduction of automation and computers, relatively low labour coasts *vis-à-vis* total production costs, and the rising technological levels in the manufacture of car parts. Japanese cars established a reputation abroad for their high quality and ease of maintenance. Furthermore, since the industry in Japan concentrated on the production of small, fuel-efficient cars (a result of the country's road conditions and the high cost of gasoline), the Japanese car proved well suited to the needs of the US market, where a growing demand for second and third cars coincided with the need to conserve fuel in the wake of the two oil crises of the 1970s.[8]

In 1977, the two largest producers in Japan each produced over two million vehicles, and in 1980 Toyota exceeded three million; both companies exported close to 50 per cent of their production. The industry as a whole depended heavily on exports, sending abroad 51 per cent of its total output in 1977 and 54 per cent in 1980. However, the steep rise in exports led to the threat of import restrictions by countries seeking to protect their own foreign balance of payments. Since 1985, the competitive edge has been eroded by the appreciation of the yen and the development of small cars by US manufacturers, who have to comply with US government fuel economy standards. This has all contributed to a decrease in Japanese car exports, and several Japanese companies now produce cars in the USA itself.

In just twenty-five years, the Japanese automobile industry increased its annual production one hundredfold – from 111,000 units (including trucks and buses) in 1956 to 11,043,000 units in 1980. The automobile industry accounted for 10 per cent of Japan's total manufacturing output in 1977, and, in terms of output, followed the food industry and the electrical appliances industry as the third largest. Automobile manufacturing employment (including parts) totalled 653,000. When employment in related occupations is included, the total came to about 4,500,000, or 10 per cent of the country's entire workforce. (This continues to be the case in the early 1990s. Japan Automobile Manufacturing Association figures for 1989, as shown in Table 4, put the total number of employees in motor-vehicle-related industries at 5,523,000, out of a total labour force of 54,370,000.)

**Table 1**   Motor Vehicle Production in Japan, 1975–91

| Year | Cars | %Chg | Trucks | %Chg | Buses | %Chg | Total | %Chg |
|------|------|------|--------|------|-------|------|-------|------|
| 1991 | 9,753,069 | −2.0 | 3,447,914 | −1.4 | 44,449 | 10.6 | 13,245,432 | −1.8 |
| 1990 | 9,947,972 | 9.9 | 3,498,639 | −11.0 | 40,185 | −4.5 | 13,486,796 | 3.5 |
| 1989 | 9,052,406 | 10.4 | 3,931,255 | −11.5 | 42,074 | 26.7 | 13,025,735 | 2.6 |
| 1988 | 8,198,400 | 3.9 | 4,443,994 | 3.2 | 57,413 | 14.9 | 12,699,807 | 3.7 |
| 1987 | 7,891,087 | 1.0 | 4,308,100 | −2.3 | 49,987 | 18.1 | 12,249,174 | −0.1 |
| 1986 | 7,809,809 | 2.1 | 4,407,666 | −3.0 | 42,342 | −46.8 | 12,259,817 | −0.1 |
| 1985 | 7,646,816 | 8.1 | 4,544,688 | 5.2 | 79,591 | 10.2 | 12,271,095 | 7.0 |
| 1984 | 7,073,173 | −1.1 | 4,319,538 | 10.6 | 72,209 | 29.1 | 11,464,920 | 3.2 |
| 1983 | 7,151,888 | 3.9 | 3,903,823 | 3.2 | 55,948 | −16.5 | 11,111,659 | 3.5 |
| 1982 | 6,881,586 | −1.3 | 3,783,218 | −7.8 | 66,990 | −34.9 | 10,731,794 | −4.0 |
| 1981 | 6,974,131 | −0.9 | 4,102,996 | 4.9 | 102,835 | 12.3 | 11,179,962 | 1.2 |
| 1980 | 7,038,108 | 14.0 | 3,913,188 | 15.2 | 91,588 | 46.4 | 11,042,884 | 14.6 |
| 1979 | 6,175,771 | 3.3 | 3,397,214 | 4.9 | 62,561 | 11.5 | 9,635,546 | 4.0 |
| 1978 | 5,975,968 | 10.0 | 3,237,066 | 6.7 | 56,119 | 15.7 | 9,269,153 | 8.9 |
| 1977 | 5,431,045 | 8.0 | 3,034,981 | 9.5 | 48,496 | 15.1 | 8,514,552 | 8.6 |
| 1976 | 5,027,792 | 10.1 | 2,771,516 | 18.6 | 42,139 | 16.7 | 7,841,447 | 13.0 |
| 1975 | 4,567,845 | 16.2 | 2,337,632 | −9.2 | 36,105 | −21.2 | 6,941,591 | 5.9 |

*Source*: Japan Automobile Manufacturers' Association (JAMA), *The Motor Industry of Japan*, 1992.
*Note*: %Chg represents the change from the preceding year.

There were several reasons for this considerable growth, the most important being: the quick and effective adoption of new technology; the good working relations between automobile producers, parts workers and repair and maintenance personnel; the stable labour/management relations along with the existence of a skilled labour pool; a well-developed marketing system, with close co-operation between producers and dealers; effective government regulation coupled with general government guidance and support.[9]

In the 1970s, the social environment of the Japanese automobile industry underwent rapid changes; there was the establishment of a recall system to improve auto safety, and the enactment of laws to deal with the pollution of metropolitan areas from exhaust fumes. The industry responded effectively to the problems of pollution control and safety, partly because of the strictness of pollution regulations and also the supervision by government agencies of the recall system. It also dealt with the issue of fuel efficiency by concentrating on the production of small, energy-saving cars, partly in response to the imposition of a

**Figure 1**   Trends in Motor Vehicle Production, 1982–91

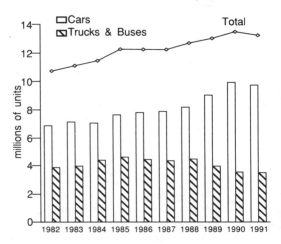

*Source*: JAMA, *The Motor Industry of Japan*, 1992.

**Figure 2**   Motor Vehicle Exports, 1975–91

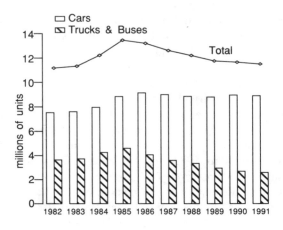

*Source*: JAMA, *The Motor Industry of Japan*, 1992.

**Table 2**  Motor Vehicle Exports, 1975–91

| Year | Cars | %Chg | Trucks | %Chg | Buses | %Chg | Total | %Chg |
|------|------|------|--------|------|-------|------|-------|------|
| 1991 | 4,452,233 | −0.7 | 1,247,263 | −4.7 | 53,883 | 34.8 | 5,753,379 | −1.3 |
| 1990 | 4,482,130 | 1.8 | 1,309,121 | −9.4 | 39,961 | 13.7 | 5,831,212 | −0.9 |
| 1989 | 4,403,060 | −0.7 | 1,445,694 | −11.1 | 35,149 | −23.1 | 5,883,903 | −3.6 |
| 1988 | 4,431,887 | −1.7 | 1,626,576 | −7.7 | 45,688 | 29.9 | 6,104,151 | −3.2 |
| 1987 | 4,507,530 | −1.4 | 1,762,220 | −12.1 | 35,168 | 28.4 | 6,304,918 | −4.5 |
| 1986 | 4,572,791 | 3.3 | 2,004,733 | −10.4 | 27,399 | −58.2 | 6,604,923 | −1.9 |
| 1985 | 4,426,762 | 11.2 | 2,238,104 | 8.0 | 65,606 | 16.7 | 6,730,472 | 10.2 |
| 1984 | 3,980,619 | 4.6 | 2,072,325 | 13.7 | 56,240 | 38.2 | 6,109,184 | 7.8 |
| 1983 | 3,806,396 | 1.0 | 1,822,429 | 2.8 | 40,685 | −13.3 | 5,669,510 | 1.4 |
| 1982 | 3,770,036 | −4.5 | 1,773,547 | −12.1 | 46,930 | −44.4 | 5,590,513 | −7.6 |
| 1981 | 3,946,542 | 0.0 | 2,017,521 | 3.3 | 84,384 | 27.6 | 6,048,447 | 1.4 |
| 1980 | 3,947,160 | 27.2 | 1,953,685 | 37.2 | 66,116 | 79.4 | 5,966,961 | 30.8 |
| 1979 | 3,101,990 | 2.0 | 1,423,930 | −6.8 | 36,861 | 21.0 | 4,562,781 | −0.8 |
| 1978 | 3,042,237 | 2.8 | 1,528,045 | 11.5 | 30,453 | 26.8 | 4,600,735 | 5.7 |
| 1977 | 2,958,879 | 16.5 | 1,369,917 | 18.8 | 24,021 | 34.3 | 4,352,817 | 17.3 |
| 1976 | 2,538,919 | 38.9 | 1,152,807 | 38.3 | 17,882 | 7.4 | 3,709,608 | 38.5 |
| 1975 | 1,827,286 | 5.8 | 833,672 | −4.7 | 16,654 | 4.3 | 2,677,612 | 2.3 |

*Source*: JAMA, *The Motor Industry of Japan*, 1992.
*Note*: %Chg represents the change from the preceding year.

steep tax on petrol. Yet, as Japan enters a new era of public awareness regarding the use of resources and energy, the automobile industry will have to make further technological innovations. It must also be clear about the role of the automobile in both the nation's transport system and the economy as a whole. The industry must move away from simple quantitative growth towards qualitative improvements.

The second oil crisis in 1979–80 brought about a new phase in the Japanese automobile industry. This reflected the fact that the Japanese automobile industry was spotlighted in the US market just as the 'big three' of Detroit were switching to a compact car strategy in response to the restriction on energy consumption, following the rapid rise in oil prices. From 1980 to 1983, the US automobile market saw a radical shift in demand in favour of fuel-efficient, compact cars; the large cars lost their dominance in the market. While the structure of market demand changed in this way and total demand also fell (Detroit suffering two-digit inflation and high rates of interest for about three years from 1980), Japanese cars actually increased their share of the US market from 15 to about 25 per cent. As a result of such a serious

**Table 3**   Export Destinations

|               | 1988        | 1989        | 1990        | 1991        |
|---------------|-------------|-------------|-------------|-------------|
| Asia          | 473,749     | 512,540     | 569,143     | 565,933     |
| Middle East   | 225,483     | 222,977     | 283,866     | 377,483     |
| Europe        | 1,705,363   | 1,708,934   | 1,750,497   | ,1709,474   |
| (EC)          | (1,212,794) | (1,237,190) | (1,256,328) | (1,263,999) |
| North America | 2,978,818   | 2,725,167   | 2,521,823   | 2,363,184   |
| (USA)         | (2,695,835) | (2,430,259) | (2,236,988) | (2,075,523) |
| Latin America | 203,506     | 194,230     | 216,375     | 273,288     |
| Africa        | 230,275     | 119,655     | 129,278     | 138,162     |
| Oceania       | 265,484     | 382,493     | 344,236     | 308,942     |
| Others        | 21,473      | 17,907      | 15,994      | 16,913      |
| Total         | 6,104,151   | 5,883,903   | 5,831,212   | 5,753,379   |

*Source*: JAMA, *The Motor Industry of Japan*, 1992.

slump, the worst unemployment since the 1929 financial crisis and the near bankruptcy of Chrysler, the share of Japanese-made cars rapidly expanded, thereby worsening trade frictions. In 1981, the Japanese government decided on a self-imposed restriction of their export of passenger cars to the USA, setting the limit at 1,680,000 cars per year. Each automaker was allotted a share of this total in proportion to its export accomplishments. This self-restriction on the export of passenger cars to the USA is still in action today, in 1993. From 1985 to 1991 the limit was increased to 2.3 million passenger cars, but it should be noted that exports consistently fell short of this limit, with the exception of 1986 (as shown in the breakdown of export figures in Table 5). For the fiscal year 1992, due largely to increased transplant production, the limit was cut ot a maximum of 1.65 million cars.

From 1981, when the self-restriction on exports to the USA was established, through to 1985, when the G–5 (the Minister-of-Finance Convention of the Five Major Countries) was held, the value of the dollar continued to weaken against the yen, and Japanese automakers increased the number of highly-valued compact cars due to the limited number of units for export, which allowed Japanese automakers to gain large profits from exports to the USA. On the other hand, the Japanese market steadily matured, the demand ranging from 5.3 million to 5.6

**Table 4**    Employees in Motor Vehicle-Related Industries

| | |
|---|---:|
| Total Labour Force of Japan | 54,370,000 |
| Motor Vehicle-Related Industries | 5,523,000 |
| Automobile Manufacturing Sector | 746,000 |
|    Automobile mfrs. | 190,000 |
|    Automobile parts & accessories mfrs. | 505,000 |
|    Automobile body & related mfrs. | 51,000 |
| Material Supply Sector | 498,000 |
|    Steel mfrs. | 45,000 |
|    Non-ferrous metal mfrs. | 14,000 |
|    Tyre & tube mfrs. | 26,000 |
|    Glass & glassware mfrs. | 13,000 |
|    Others (plastics, textiles, paint, battery, beating mfrs. etc.) | 400,000 |
| Supporting Sector | 547,000 |
|    Petroleum refineries | 4,000 |
|    Lubricant & grease mfrs. | 3,000 |
|    Gasoline stations | 257,000 |
|    Petroleum wholesalers | 18,000 |
|    Insurance agents, etc. | 98,000 |
|    Others (advertising, printing, tyre retailers, etc.) | 167,000 |
| Sales & Maintenance Sector | 1,127,000 |
|    Automobile dealers | 529,000 |
|    Motor-cycle retailers | 84,000 |
|    Automobile wholesalers | 110,000 |
|    Auto-parts & accessories wholesalers | 85,000 |
|    Automobile maintenance shops | 319,000 |
| Utilizing Sector | 2,605,000 |
|    Road-passenger transport | 689,000 |
|    Road-freight transport | 1,130,000 |
|    Automobile rental & lease services | 18,000 |
|    Parking lots | 69,000 |
|    Transport-related services | 399,000 |
|    Others (chauffeurs, etc.) | 300,000 |

*Source*: JAMA, *The Motor Industry of Japan*, 1989
*Note*: Number of employees in material supply sector, et al. is estimated according to the percentage of automotive-related production.

**Table 5**   Japanese Vehicle Exports to the USA by Category

| Year | Passenger cars* | Commercial vehicles |
|------|-----------------|---------------------|
| 1985 | 2,216,000 | 916,000 |
| 1986 | 2,348,000 | 1,096,000 |
| 1987 | 2,205,000 | 880,000 |
| 1988 | 2,051,000 | 645,000 |
| 1989 | 1,944,000 | 485,000 |
| 1990 | 1,876,000 | 361,000 |
| 1991 | 1,763,000 | 312,000 |

* Voluntary Export Restraint agreements apply only to passenger cars.
*Source*: Nissan Motor Co., Ltd., *Jidosha Sangyo Handbook 1990*, September 1990, 396.
    Nissan Motor Co., Ltd., *Jidosha Sangyo Handbook 1992/1993*, September 1992, 395.

million cars per year from the late 1970s to the early 1980s. In the early 1980s, the industry owed most of its profit to exports, thanks to the high valuation of the dollar, and generally did not profit from the domestic market due to maturity and severe competition among automakers. All the manufacturers used much of their export profits to automate their plants, renew facilities and develop the standards of production technology. A huge investment was made into the research and development of establishing the R & D system of technological innovation in the late 1980s.

While trade frictions continued, the Japanese began building plants in the USA. In 1981, Honda built an assembly plant in Ohio and Nissan a plant in Tennessee in 1982. In 1984, Toyota started a joint venture with GM in California and in 1987 set up a plant for sole entry in Kentucky. Mazda built a plant in Michigan in 1987, and Mitsubishi set up local manufacturing facilities in Illinois on a joint management basis with Chrysler. Suzuki also built a plant in Ontario, Canada, in joint management with GM. Isuzu and Fuji Juko worked together on a plant in Indiana.

The G–5 meeting in September 1985 marked a turning point for the Japanese industry. The age of internationalization began when the appreciation of the yen made exports more difficult and further rationalization imperative. The exchange rate fell from ¥240 to ¥130 per dollar in about one year after September 1985, and this quickly reduced the volume of exports to the USA, forcing the Japanese to raise prices several times. They tried to offset events by further differentiating their export models, but this was not entirely successful and exports fell below the 'permitted' number of 2.3 million. At the same time, locally-based Japanese production in America rose to about 1.2 million units per year, including the OEM (Original Equipment Manufacturing) supplies by those tied up with the 'big three'.

Japanese automakers set about rationalization in order to counteract the rise in the value of the yen. This time, they did more than simply repeat Japanese-style rationalization by eliminating waste and loss as they had done immediately after the first oil crisis, they made use of new computer and communication technology for production planning and promoted a well-systematized rationalization of parts makers. By the end of 1987, they had created a system that enabled a sufficient reduction in material and energy costs to offset the appreciation of the yen.

In the meantime, the domestic automobile market in Japan expanded rapidly, the number of units sold increasing from 5.7 million in 1986 to 6.02 million in 1987 and the 6.72 million in 1988. The domestic market then peaked at just under 7.78 million vehicles in 1990 before falling back slightly in 1991 to 7.52 million to end a decade-long period of expansion. (These figures are for vehicle registrations and include registrations of foreign cars.) This expansion featured extensive modification to existing models and an increase in the number of high-class, large cars in addition to the increase in the total number of units. The automakers reduced product-planning 'lead time' for the introduction of new and deluxe models. Some companies began producing larger cars with an 8-cylinder engine for the first time and in 1989 the abolition of the commodity tax made it easy to mark down the price of high-class cars and thereby increase their sales. The upgrading market also permitted an increase in the number of imported cars, from 50,000 units a year in 1985 to 130,000 units in 1988 and a peak of 220,000 in 1990. The number of imported cars registered in 1991, however, fell back by 11 per cent to just under 200,000.

Thus, the appreciation of the yen reduced the dependency of the Japanese industry on exports and enabled the industry to profit from its own domestic market, thereby shifting the profit-gaining structure of Japanese automakers. Also the appreciation of the yen accelerated the promotion of locally-based production and an international division of labour in developing countries, such as Asia and the Pan-Pacific areas, as well as in advanced countries. As a result, exports of KD (knock-down) sets to both advanced and developing countries increased from 1 million units in 1985 to 1.81 million in 1987. Japan has now linked up with many developing countries, such as Thailand, Malaysia, Indonesia and the Philippines, and NIES countries such as South Korea and Taiwan. This development was initially in the form of technological transfers by Japanese automakers for use in home production. A complementary international division of labour between production bases is also being created. In this way, the Japanese industry is becoming internationally stronger and a global view of overseas strategies is emerging as a key problem. While on the one hand Japanese automakers compete fiercely with those in Europe and the USA, on the other hand they are also strengthening their relations with foreign automakers in the form of business partnerships, joint management and technical co-operation.

# CHAPTER 2

## *The Structure of the Industry*

In 1991, Japan produced 13,245,000 passenger cars, trucks and buses and remained the world's top automotive producing country for the twelfth consecutive year since it overtook the USA in terms of production in 1980. Over the last decade Japanese production has consistently accounted for roughly one third of world production (about 44 million vehicles in 1991, over 85 per cent of which comes from the major OECD countries: namely Japan, the USA and Canada, 8,810,000 and 1,875,000 vehicles respectively in 1991, and the leading members of the European Community: Germany 5,015,000; France 3,610,000; Spain 2,080,000; Italy 1,880,000; Belgium 1,150,000 and UK 1,450,000 vehicles in 1991).

At the end of World War II, the Japanese automobile industry produced just 20,000 units, made up entirely of trucks and buses. Within thirty-five years production had increased over five hundred times. This growth is unprecedented in the history of the automobile industry. In the postwar period, Japanese production has grown steadily almost every year, experiencing slight decreases on five occasions: in 1974, following the 1973–4 oil crisis, in 1982 as a consequence of the self-imposed restriction on exports to the North American market, in 1986 and 1987 following the leap in value of the yen and in 1991. The upward trend of Japanese production contrasts with the records of many other major automobile-producing countries, where production levels have tended to experience roller-coaster fluctuations due to the impact of domestic and international economic changes.

By any measure, the automobile industry plays a strategic role in the Japanese economy and is perhaps the single most important industry. In 1990, total earnings in the industry (cars, trucks, buses motor cycles, parts and accessories) were estimated by the Ministry of International Trade and Industry (MITI) at approximately 42,400 billion yen, representing about 13 per cent of the total Japanese industrial production. The industry is also Japan's biggest exporter, totalling US$64.5 billion in 1990 and US$69.5 billion in 1991 (of which motor cycles and motor-cycle parts accounted for about US$9 billion), the figure for 1991 representing 22 per cent of the total value of Japanese exports.[1]

The strategic role of the automobile industry in any economy of an automobile producing country is due principally to the nature of automobile design, production, distribution and method of transport. The industry requires support from a myriad of parts and component suppliers, as well as general material suppliers. The automobile represents the latest in design, materials construction and machine and electronic technologies. Every automobile is a testimony to the latest developments throughout industry in general; the automobile industry can use everything that technology for product design and production systems has to offer. At the same time, the industry requires extensive distribution networks and support services for the sale and maintenance of automobiles. Moreover, the automobile is used to transport goods as well as people. The accounts for the vast number of people employed in the industry and related industries (around 10 per cent of the Japanese workforce, as mentioned in chapter 1).[2]

AUTOMOBILE MANUFACTURERS

There are many features that are unique to the Japanese automobile industry when compared to the industries of America or Europe. The main difference is the relatively high degree of oligopoly in both the USA and Europe, in contrast to the competitive structure of the Japanese industry. Japan has nine passenger-car companies that also produce trucks together with two other truck specialists. In the USA, just three companies – General Motors, Ford and Chrysler – control virtually all new car and truck sales. With the exception of Germany, which has three mass production companies – VW, BMW and Daimler–Benz – every other European country with an automobile industry has centralized production to one or two companies, sometimes publicly owned. France has Renault and Peugeot–Citroen; Italy has Fiat and Alfa Romeo in addition to some speciality sports car makers; Britain has the Rover Group and some European subsidiaries of the major American and Japanese companies.[3]

The contrast with Japan is startling, where even the two biggest companies, Toyota and Nissan, accounted for only 48 per cent of the total Japanese production in 1991. In that year, Toyota produced 4.05 million units (30.8 per cent) and Nissan produced 2.32 million units (17.7 per cent). Under the top producers is a second level, comprising the three automobile firms, Mitsubishi, Mazda and Honda which in 1991 produced 1.41 million units, 1.38 million units and 1.33 million units respectively. The bottom tier of Japanese automotive producers is made up of four companies – Suzuki, principally a minicar manufacturer, Daihatsu, Fujijuko (Fuji Heavy Industries, the so-called 'Subaru') and Isuzu. In 1991, these four firms produced 858,000 units, 670,000 units, 528,000 units and 471,000 units respectively. In addition, there are two heavy-duty truck specialists, Hino, which produced 90,000 units in 1991, and Nissan Diesel, producer of 61,000 units in the same year. Minicar production of cars with engine displacements of 660 cc and under (550 cc and under prior to 1990) which qualify for reduced automobile tax rates in undertaken, in decreasing order of volume according to 1991 production figure, by Suzuki (251,000), Daihatsu, Mitsubishi, Honda, Fuji Heavy Industry and Mazda (56,000).

Apart from minicars, there are three broad, unofficial passenger car classifications – the large-sized car (over 2500 cc), the compact car (between 1600 cc and 2500 cc) and the sub-compact or popular car (between 1000 cc and 1600 cc). Until 1985, only Toyota and Nissan produced all three sizes. In 1985, however, Honda, Mitsubishi and Mazda announced plans to expand into the big car market, which has meant more competition in this area recently.

The key structural feature of the Japanese automobile industry is the coexistence of eleven automotive firms known as the 'competitive coexistence'. Despite intense competition, a strategic path of collaboration or grouping either with other Japanese companies or with American car producers is being made for survival, but without consolidation or mergers. The one attempt by MITI to consolidate the Japanese automobile industry in the 1960s was defeated by the fierce resistance of the industry and the appearance of a new competitor as Honda expanded from motor-cycle to automobile production. The only merger in the postwar history of the Japanese automobile industry was the absorption of Prince by Nissan in 1966.[4]

Closer links with other companies have taken place within a group structure or in collaboration with American car producers. For example, Toyota brought both Daihatsu and Hino into its group, and Nissan has done the same with Fuji Heavy Industries and Nissan Diesel. The independent identity of each company in the Toyota and Nissan groups is maintained; there is no consolidation. Each company, however, conducts its product planning on a group footing, which is made easier by the mobility of top management between the member companies. Each company will sometimes try to get another member to produce a particular popular car or truck. This arrangement makes for competition within the group while providing the benefit of being part of the same group.

In contrast with the other Japanese manufacturers, Mazda, Mitsubishi, Isuzu and Suzuki all have some of their equity held by the three major Detroit automobile manufacturers. As of March 1992, Ford had a 24.4 per-cent stake in Mazda, Chrysler a 6.3 per-cent stake in Mitsubishi (now zero per-cent) and General Motors a 37.5 per-cent stake in Isuzu and a 3.5 per-cent stake in Suzuki. All three American manufacturers send representatives to the board meetings of their associated companies, with the exception of Suzuki. American capital first appeared in the Japanese automobile industry soon after 1969, following capital liberalization and the re-organization of the industry in Japan, and it was the American companies who took the initiative in this direction.

In time, as the Japanese industry began to become competitively stronger, the importance of these equities to the American producers increased as Mazda, Mitsubishi, Isuzu and Suzuki all began to produce small cars to expand the product lines of their American partners. The Japanese have also done some consignment production of components such as transaxles and small-car engines. Honda is the exception to all this, as it is independent of both other Japanese and foreign companies.[5]

Why did the Japanese automobile industry not experience the consolidation which is so typical of this industry in other countries and of mature industries in general? Despite joining up in groups, the Japanese automakers have retained a fierce independence. Each has a distinctive corporate culture which is reinforced by the 'lifetime employment system'. Many Japanese managers recognize that any attempt to unify companies would be institutionally difficult. Also the advantages of large-scale production through consolidation are not all that important to the Japanese companies. The smaller Japanese car makers have learned to flourish with a production of just 500,000 vehicles a year, based on high productivity and the subcontracting of parts production. This has greatly reduced the breakeven point for the Japanese automotive producers.[6]

From a macro-economic perspective, it is important to note that since the early 1950s the Japanese automobile industry has never suffered a prolonged depression, but has enjoyed steady and sometimes very high growth, although it has faced some problems with the economic

downturn of the early 1990s. With the exception of the acquisition
of Prince Motors by Nissan in 1966, there has not been a single
consolidation in the Japanese automobile industry.

### THE VERTICAL DIVISION OF LABOUR

Another key characteristic of the Japanese automobile industry is its
efficiency in the organization of the parts and components supply
system. A very large number of parts are used in the production of
an automobile and co-ordination of design, production and assembly
of parts is a crucial managerial task. One important feature which
distinguishes the Japanese automobile industry from its North American
and European counterparts is the facility of 'in-house' production of
parts and components: in Japan, only about 30–40 per cent of parts
are 'in-house'. In North America and Europe up until the early 1980s,
the rate of in-house parts production was 60 to 70 per cent, but in
recent years there has been a tendency to increase reliance on outside
parts manufacturers to Japanese levels (Chrysler, for instance, now only
makes about 30 per cent of its parts in-house, although for General
Motors the figure is still high, at about 60 per cent). In addition, there
is a vertical division of labour in the Japanese automobile industry which
features close and co-operative relationships between the assemblers and
suppliers, designed to introduce and reinforce efficiencies. 'In-house'
production in the North American and European automobile industries
was intended to ensure a stable supply of pars and their mass production
to benefit from economies of scale. One important theme in the history
of the Western automotive industry is that of consolidation and the
acquisition of major parts makers by assemblers.[7]

'In-house' production of parts is not as extensive in Europe as it has
been in North America and the European parts makers enjoy a position
of autonomy. They often supply many different car producers and the
division of labour is horizontal. In North America too, the parts makers
are usually independent and deal with many car makers. Consequently,
the relationship between the assembler and parts suppliers tends to be
rather fragile.

The nature of the relationship between the assembler and supplier
in the Japanese automobile industry is quite different. The Japanese
automobile industry is like a pyramid, with a vertical division of
labour, divided into three tiers of suppliers, centered around the seven
main assembly groups or single assemblers – Toyota–Daihatsu–Hino,

Nissan–Fuji Heavy Industries–Nissan Diesel, Honda, Mazda, Mitsubishi, Isuzu and Suzuki. Each assembler has its own parts association. For example, Toyota's Kyouhoukai and Nissan's Takrakai are designed to maintain close relations with the parts makers and to provide an exchange of information. There are some Japanese companies who are part of one group but still supply assemblers outside the group. Moreover, some companies belong to more than one parts association. Nippon Denso, Japan's top manufacturer of car electronics and electronic parts, is a leading member of Toyota's parts association and a company in which Toyota is the major stockholder; nevertheless, it supplies components to many other Japanese companies (with the exception of Nissan) as well as North American manufacturers. Some of the major parts makers supply the entire Japanese automobile industry: for example, Nippon Hatsujo, Japan's biggest suspension and car-spring maker; Akebono Brake, a general brake manufacturer; NOK, a famous oil-seal maker; and Nippontokushutogyou, a spark-plug maker. These are, however, exceptions to the rule that the Japanese parts makers are divided into assembler-affiliated groups. The close relationship between assemblers and suppliers is particularly evident in the case of the first-tier suppliers, who provide key strategic parts and pre-assembled parts. The relationship between the assembler and the supplier is often decided by way of an equity holding as well as two-way exchanges of personnel.[8]

TIE-UPS WITH PARTS MANUFACTURERS

An important factor in the competitive success of the Japanese automobile industry has been the ability of assemblers to relate closely with their suppliers; this is enhanced by the degree to which the Japanese affiliated parts suppliers have evolved as the technological leaders in their field. In the beginning, in the 1950s, the relationship between the assembler and the parts maker was such that the supplier acted simply as a subcontractor, controlled by the assembler who exerted pressures on the supplier to maintain low prices. In addition, the supplier had to meet tight production schedules and quality requirements. Sales were settled by long-term promissory notes from the assembler. In short, the Japanese parts makers bore a great deal of the cost-reduction burden.

Today, in the early 1990s, while some of these features still exist, there have been improvements, especially for the major suppliers. For one thing, suppliers have developed independent engineering capabilities and this has had a great impact on product design and production systems.[9] The assemblers recognized that if they did not support their suppliers with engineering and management expertise, these suppliers would not be able to contribute to the growth and development of the industry. Thus, by means of an intra-group transfer of technological and management skills, the group structure of the industry became a strategic factor in assisting the development of affiliated parts makers. There was a synergy of interests, whereby the assemblers co-operated to make their parts suppliers more competitive and the parts suppliers, anxious to profit from this development, follow the assemblers' lead. This allowed the parts makers to count on stable business, and the assembler to count . on the supplier.

In addition to stabilizing parts supply and assisting in intra-group transfers of technology and management expertise, the group structure of relations enabled the suppliers to make plans for new plants and equipment more assuredly, while allowing co-ordination in research and development. The supplier was now involved in the production of new models from the design stage to the actual production. This working arrangement also gave the suppliers' bankers less to worry about, since in many cases the assembler would guarantee new loans. Moreover, the transfer of management personnel for engineering guidance and management assistance gave the assemblers an inside view of their suppliers while promoting the exchange of new ideas and information. This type of relationship was often extended even to independent parts makers to ensure that the impetus of technological change was maintained throughout the industry.[10]

While the benefits from such a design and planning perspective are somewhat self-evident, this type of relationship contributed a great deal to the highly efficient production system which characterizes the Japanese automobile industry. In particular, it allowed for a high degree of flexibility in the production process in an industry noted for its difficulties in responding to changes in consumer demand. The Japanese automobile industry is characterized by a multiple product-focus production philosophy, which is based on low volumes, tightly linked to changes in market structure. The demand for frequent design change, linked to the dynamics inherent in new technologies and innovation, as well as new market demand, has been well handled by the assembler/supplier structure. The assemblers (in tandem with their suppliers) are geared to respond to the changes in market demand during the production cycle of any model and have also reduced the 'lead time' for introducing new models.

It is important to note that these relationships exist not only on an assembler/supplier basis but also on a supplier/supplier basis. First-tier suppliers also require parts from second and third-tier suppliers as they often pre-assemble parts for final assembly. Inter-supplier relations are similar to the relationship described above – containing technological and management transfers and stable, long-term commitments. It is interesting that in some respects the European industries are the same; but in their case, the parts makers are much more independent, consequently blunting the positive aspects of any close relationship.

## LABOUR RELATIONS

During the postwar period of both dynamic and stable economic growth in Japan, relations between management and labour have been relatively stable. The automobile industry has been no exception and has, in fact, set a pattern for industrial relations in Japan. Management and labour have established a form of relationship which is at the heart of a system whose main objectives are greater productivity and higher quality. The one outstanding feature of the structure of industrial relations in the automobile sector has been the use of company unions rather than a nationwide or industrial union. This emerged from the serious labour troubles that Toyota suffered in 1950 and Nissan in 1953. At that time, large and potentially threatening strikes occurred at these companies, principally due to impending redundancies. Both companies were on the brink of bankruptcy, in part because of problems between management and labour.[11] A variety of systems, based on the concepts of a company union and much closer management/labour relations were tried at this time in order to avoid further labour disputes.

## PRECONSULTATION BY MANAGEMENT

One of the unique practices in the Japanese automobile industry is that of preconsultation in order to maintain stable labour relations. As a matter of routine, management now consults its company union on general business planning, investment schedules, preliminary production schedules and even key strategic initiatives.[12]

These consultations are taken seriously by both sides as an opportunity not only to voice objections and offer different points of view but also to discuss new ideas and propose suggestions. One of the main objectives of this process is to decide on the most efficient plan possible, and management/labour consultation is essential to this goal. Adequate time is given for labour's contribution to the process and where serious differences emerge, time is allowed for further discussion and concessions. In addition to the overall plan of the company, this process of consultation covers day-to-day concerns, such as shop-floor working conditions and the introduction of new machines and systems of work. Consultation will also include matters such as changing the allocation of workers to match fluctuating production volumes, training programmes, promotion, new assignments and rationalization measures. The obvious strength of this system is that it provides a forum for resolving management and labour conflict, without upsetting ongoing production. Thus, not only are future problems avoided but the efficiency of the production system is also maintained. Changing labour conditions which are the consequence of market forces and personnel changes – the human element in an production system – are simultaneously managed in a non-confrontational manner. Problem solving is done in a regular and routine fashion, with opportunity given for opinions to be expressed and exchanged. Finally, not only are management and labour views brought together but there is the added possibility that the marriage of different perspectives will produce better answers to both broad strategic and day-to-day problems in the factory.[13]

In contrast to the Japanese system, management and labour relations in North America and Europe tend to be based on the premise that there are no mutual or common interests between management and labour, and the outcome is distrust. Preconsultation is difficult to arrange because overtures by management are viewed with suspicion, particularly on issues such as productivity and production cuts. Until the late 1980s there was little incentive for change, but the experience of Japanese labour relations and the establishment of Japanese production facilities overseas have made Western managers more aware of the value of a much better relationship between management and labour. The antagonistic element in American and European labour/management relations is exacerbated by fluctuating market forces.

In addition to the merits noted above, perhaps the key advantage to a system of preconsultation is that it allows a quick response to the introduction of new production systems. The most recent example is the introduction of robotics. Viewed as a process of replacing labour, consultation between management and labour established the use of robots as a means of improving working conditions by replacing workers for mundane and dangerous jobs with machines and allowing greater discretion to on-line workers in the control of production. In North

America and Europe strict contractual agreements between management and labour make the introduction of new production processes difficult and time-consuming. At the workshop level many issues that can be resolved by consultation and dialogue require elaborate negotiations and new contracts. This slows down the process of adapting new technology into production systems. At its best, Japanese preconsultation permits almost day-to-day improvements to the production process. From a competitive point of view, regular model changes and the system of small-lot production arise from the nature of market demand, which is constantly changing. The ability of the Japanese automakers to respond to these changes is a result of stable and good management/labour relations.[14]

The focus of North American and European trade unions has been on labour conditions, wage levels, pension schemes holidays and unemployment benefits; management has done little to encourage the involvement of unions in either broad planning or even workshop improvements. Until the late 1980s, issues such as productivity and training were not viewed as matters about which labour should be consulted. This made it difficult to generate any interest in innovation and the introduction of new equipment. The different response to Quality Control (QC) circles in Japanese and North American factories is a case in point. Clearly, when issues like planning, productivity and training are viewed solely as management matters, labour unions will view any innovation with suspicion. The realities of the market and new technologies do not become part and parcel of the factory as a unit of enterprise.

QUALITY CONTROL CIRCLES

Due to the success the Japanese have had with QC circles, the United Automobile Workers of America (UAW) has adopted the introduction of Quality of Working Life (QWL), also sometimes referred to as Employee Involvement (EI).

In the North American factories of Japanese producers, Japanese-style QC circles have become more and more acceptable. In Japan, QC circles are seen as contributing to the production of defect-free automobiles. The key to the mater is the hands-on role of labour and co-ordination between management and labour in order to ensure not only that defects are identified but also that quality problems are properly reported. Workers have an interest in quality and are properly reported. Workers have an interest in quality and are encouraged to communicate about it with management. QC circles also play a role in rationalizing production processes. While QC circles are outside the scope of union activities, they are generally supported by labour. Active QC circles, soon led to better working conditions as well as a labour input into production engineering. For example, workers suggest changes to the machines they operate, leading to a safer and more efficient workplace and therefore a more contented workforce.[15]

In North America, quality control was carried out not by the workers but by managers who set up a special line or layer of quality control personnel who had no hands-on contact with either the product or the production system. The result was constant friction between on-line labour and quality control officials. The Japanese approach to quality control has been to bring both the manager and worker at the shop-floor level into a single entity, in contrast to the North American system of creating another division of labour. With the support of the company union, the Japanese system not only ensures product quality but reinforces labour stability.

MUTUAL TRUST

By and large the existence of company unions in the Japanese automobile industry has not undermined the ability of labour to have an important impact on management. In seeking consensus before decisions are carried and communicating about working conditions, a strong foundation of mutual trust has been built up. Although there have been times when management has had to force the hand of labour, this only happens after enormous efforts at reconciliation have been made.

Unquestionably, the prosperity that the industry enjoyed from the early 1960s gave management the opportunity to set up these co-operative systems. But even from the early postwar years, the industry tried to avoid redundancies, keeping the numbers of employees fairly stable, maintaining high wages and good working conditions. This was rewarded by improved labour productivity. The effort made to promote stable labour relations and to bring management and labour together was accompanied by cost reduction and quality improvement and so ensured the industry's international competitiveness. Given the success of the Japanese automobile industry since the 1970s, it is perhaps not too much of an exaggeration to say that the special nature of labour/management relations, given the complicated production process that is necessary in the construction of automobiles, is the foundation for quality improvement.[16]

INTERNATIONAL PRODUCTIVITY

There is intense competition between the Japanese automobile companies. For each of them, there is close co-operation between the assemblers and their parts makers, as well as between management and labour. The structure of the industry as created the conditions for constant technological improvement and stable production. The Japanese automobile industry quickly became the world's most productive, setting high standards in both production engineering and product development.

It has been claimed that in the early 1980s Japan had a cost advantage over US producers of as much as US$1,600 in the 1500 cc subcompact class of vehicle, although by the early 1990s this gap had closed so as to be virtually non-existent due to the appreciation of the yen, increasing labour costs, huge investment into R & D and new facilities and a tendency towards greater efficiency by US manufacturers.

A startling illustration of Japan's productivity is its volume in terms of relative plant capacity. In the case of Toyota and Nissan, Japan's only full-line automobile producers, their assets are only a quarter the size of General Motors'. After adjusting for different ratios of in-house parts manufacturing and car size, the Japanese assemblers could still produce the same number of cars as their American competitors, but using only half the plant capacity. The appreciation of the yen since September 1985 has eroded Japanese competitiveness, but on a man-hours basis, Japan is still out in front.

Not only is Japanese productivity outstanding but so is the quality of production. In all aspects of the car's performance – from sophisticated ignition and braking systems to simple wear and tear of the car's interior and exterior – Japanese-made cars have redefined and upgraded quality standards. Until the automobile crisis of 1980–1, it was though that too much attention to quality would harm productivity, upsetting the high-speed philosophy of the North American automobile industry since the early days of Henry Ford. The Japanese automobile makers argued that high quality was compatible with high productivity; these were not competing but complementary objectives.[17]

OTHER FACTORS

In addition to the structure of the industry, the nature of the relationship between automobile manufacturers and auto parts suppliers, stable management/labour relations, and the attention paid to productivity and product quality, are three other factors that account for the postwar success of the Japanese automobile industry.

Firstly, the Japanese had the benefit of rebuilding their automobile industry almost from scratch following its destruction during the war and in this way enjoyed the benefits of being a 'latecomer' to the industry in such ways as having the latest in production facilities, production technology, parts technology and previous patent licences. Secondly, the Japanese automobile industry took advantage of the remarkable growth of the Japanese economy as a whole from the mid-1950s to the first oil shock. In many way, of course, the success of the Japanese automobile industry reflects the success of the Japanese economy itself. Only three times has car production actually declined from the previous year (1986, 1987 and 1991). The steady success of the industry, however, masks the fact that there were three distinct product strategies, as well as market targets. In the first period of reconstruction up to about 1960, the industry concentrated on small trucks, whose market was the business world. From 1960 to 1973, the industry switched its attention to passenger cars, as the growth of the economy was manifested in consumer spending on durables. With pressure in the mid-1970s to produce more environmentally acceptable automobiles (as well as the switch to replacement demand sales) the industry redesigned the automobile. Responding to criticisms about the automobile and stressing the newest technologies in materials, electronics and design, the Japanese automobile makers produced a car that was both practical and stylish. This set the stage for the Japanese penetration of the markets of the North American and European manufacturers, and relieved some of the problems arising out of a maturing home market. Finally, the Japanese automobile industry benefited form the highly-competitive industries in other sectors of the Japanese economy. These included traditional material industries such as steel, aluminium, rubber, plastic and glass. The automobile is the product not only of the company that assembles it but also of the companies that supply the materials and parts that go to make it up. It is in the interest of the assembler, therefore, to raise the standards of all its component suppliers. The industrial conditions for the world's most competitive automobile producers were well established by the early 1960s, and have since improved in every sector of the economy, particularly in electronics. Thus emerged the world's most dangerous automobile competitors.[18]

# CHAPTER 3

# *Labour Relations and Worker Participation*

INTRODUCTION

There are some special features of labour union leadership in Japan. In general, Japanese labour relations are stable and have contributed greatly to Japan's economic prosperity, especially since the 1973–4 oil crisis. One reason for this stability is the way in which Japanese labour unions are organized. The automobile industry is a typical new industry in Japan, and the latest comer to the world auto-producer scene. The industry's rapid growth has contributed much to Japan's economic prosperity. Although there are many factors that account for the success of the Japanese automobile industry, good labour relations is an important one.

The stable labour relations in the industry helped to develop worker participation, for example, QC circle activities and the 'just-in-time' (Kanban) system.[1] Although the unions supported 'worker participation', it was not organized by any union but by the workers themselves.

In the recent history of the Japanese automobile industry, there were two big strikes, at Toyota in 1950 and at Nissan in 1953, but since then there have been no strikes. In the major Japanese industries there have been few strikes since the end of the war. What is the reason for such a long period without strikes in the Japanese automobile industry? The reason might be its stable labour relations. If so, it is relevant to ask: how have the stable labour relations been created? Why are they well organized? Why are they still functioning so well?

In this chapter I will initially describe the special features of Japanese labour relations in general, and show the differences between labour relations in Western countries and Japan. Then I will introduce the factors explaining how stable labour relations have been rooted in the Japanese automobile industry.

How has worker participation been organized along with company union shop-floor activities, and has it contributed to the competitiveness

**Table 6** Unions and Union Membership, 1947–91

| | Number of unions | Union membership (000's) | Japanese workforce (000's) | membership ratio (%) |
|---|---|---|---|---|
| 1947 | 23,323 | – | 12,560 | 45.3 |
| 1950 | 29,144 | – | 12,510 | 46.2 |
| 1955 | 32,012 | 6,286 | 16,620 | 37.8 |
| 1960 | 41,561 | 7,662 | 22,690 | 33.8 |
| 1965 | 52,879 | 10,147 | 29,140 | 34.8 |
| 1970 | 60,954 | 11,605 | 32,770 | 35.4 |
| 1971 | 62,428 | 11,798 | 33,830 | 34.9 |
| 1972 | 63,718 | 11,889 | 34,570 | 34.4 |
| 1973 | 65,448 | 12,098 | 36,390 | 33.2 |
| 1974 | 67,829 | 12,462 | 36,490 | 34.2 |
| 1975 | 69,333 | 12,590 | 36,280 | 34.7 |
| 1976 | 70,039 | 12,509 | 37,100 | 33.7 |
| 1977 | 70,625 | 12,437 | 37,460 | 33.2 |
| 1978 | 70,868 | 12,383 | 37,960 | 32.6 |
| 1979 | 71,780 | 12,309 | 38,990 | 31.6 |
| 1980 | 72,693 | 12,369 | 40,120 | 30.8 |
| 1981 | 73,694 | 12,471 | 40,550 | 30.8 |
| 1982 | 74,091 | 12,526 | 41,020 | 30.5 |
| 1983 | 74,486 | 12,520 | 42,090 | 29.7 |
| 1984 | 74,579 | 12,464 | 42,820 | 29.1 |
| 1985 | 74,499 | 12,418 | 43,010 | 28.9 |
| 1986 | 74,183 | 12,343 | 43,830 | 28.2 |
| 1987 | 73,138 | 12,272 | 44,480 | 27.6 |
| 1988 | 72,792 | 12,227 | 45,650 | 26.8 |
| 1989 | 72,605 | 12,227 | 47,210 | 25.9 |
| 1990 | 72,202 | 12,265 | 48,750 | 25.2 |
| 1991 | 71,685 | 12,397 | 50,620 | 24.5 |

*Source*: Taishiro Shirai, *Kigyobetsukumiai, (The Company Union)*, 49.
Rododaijin Kanbo, *Rodokumiaikihonchosahokoku, (Basic Research Report on Labour Unions)*, 1992.

of the industry? These key points relate to the characteristics of the company union and its shop-floor activities in conjunction with the workers' participation.

LABOUR RELATIONS

Many people are familiar with the fact that labour relations are an important concern of Japanese-style management, in relation to lifetime employment, the wage structure, on-the-job training, communication between labour and management and the welfare system. A key factor, however, is the way in which company unions are organized.

In general, company unions are organized by their members and limited to the company's employees (except for temporary workers). Regardless of their job or rank, employees are organized according to shop agreements applicable to all employees,[2] both blue-collar and white-collar. Nevertheless, there are conflicting interests within the unions, for example, between lower management and shop-floor workers, the well educated and the lesser educated, senior workers and junior workers, male workers and female workers.

A second feature of the Japanese company union is the union officers' background. Union officers are elected from company employees and only very rarely are non-company employees elected. Therefore, a union officer, even if he has been chosen, maintains his company employee status. There are no professional union leaders in the company union, only semi- or non-professional union leaders.[3]

The company union is also fully autonomous and has independent financial control over membership fees, though the company supports the union by deducting union fees from employee salaries.[4] The company union has control over most of the assets, revenue and expenditure of the union.[5] Though a company union is part of a federal union of the industry, control of union finances rests solely with the company union.

What are the features of labour relations in Japan compared with Western countries? While there are different forms of union organization in Western countries, namely trade unions and industrial unions, most unions are organized along horizontal lines, running across companies, and union membership is not based on company employment.[6] Even if union members are fired or leave a company, they do not lose their union membership. In Japan, if company employees leave the company, they not only lose status but also union membership, even if they are a union leader.[7] Union leaders in Western countries consist of non-company employees and company employees. The former are elected as union officers and the latter are usually appointed as union officials, including shop stewards. In Japan, both officers and officials are usually company employees. A Japanese union, if it is participating in a federal union organization for a specific industry, is basically organized as a company union and in material form is a loosely gathered body.

How do these differences reflect on union activities and functions? In the early days, Japanese unions had little bargaining power on account of their company base.[8] The company unions of big companies and major industries tend to be powerful and competitive; but in small companies and declining industries, the company unions tend to be rather weak. A company union will also tend to make compromises in favour of the company. As a result, until a period of high economic growth, Japanese unions could do little about the wide disparity in wages and welfare levels between large and small businesses. However, the high economic growth during the 1960s created a labour shortage; consequently, wage levels rose in small businesses and government regulations for a minimum wage level were introduced.

In general, the unions failed to raise their share of the national income, but wages did rise at a pace more or less equal to economic growth. This can be explained in terms of the company unions' weak bargaining power and their policy of going for step-by-step wage increases. There is a choice between increasing wages without reference to the company's income and raising the company's profitability to permit gradual increases in wags and welfare levels. This demonstrates that the key issues are the size of the pie versus the distribution of the pie.

Despite their company base, Japanese unions cover workers nation-wide and industry-wide, with a higher overall membership ratio than in Western countries. The company union is also keen to promote consultation and negotiation on a day-to-day basis at the factory or place of work. In Japan, these approaches are the most important and significant union activities. In Western countries, there are few shop-floor negotiating arrangements. In addition, the Japanese union is made up of a wide variety of workers, it has a more 'intellectual'; leadership, and has better access to business information.[9]

Why did the company union become the dominant type of organiza-tion in Japan? After World War II, the Occupation authorities introduced severe regulations concerning labour unions and these came mainly from American 'New Deal' advisers who expected Japanese labour to be organized into industrial unions, a principle supported by Japanese economists and academics. In general, however, since Japanese workers were more familiar and attached to their companies, they preferred company unions to industrial ones.

The company was seen as committed to holding on to its workers. Before World War II, some big companies in Japan had a lifetime employment arrangement under a paternalistic system. Thus, the new unionized workers tended to choose the company union principle. They

**Table 7** Percentage of Workers Unionized, 1970–91

|  | *1970* | *1975* | *1979* | *1981* | *1983* | *1985* | *1987* | *1989* | *1991* |
|---|---|---|---|---|---|---|---|---|---|
| All Industries | 35.4 | 34.7 | 31.6 | 30.8 | 29.7 | 28.9 | 27.6 | 25.9 | 24.5 |
| Agriculture | 22.5 | }23.8 | 21.1 | 18.9 | 16.4 | 17.2 | 14.5 | 11.3 | 11.2 |
| Fishing | 29.5 | | | | | | | | |
| Mining | 72.2 | 50.4 | 45.5 | 49.7 | 41.7 | 48.7 | 38.2 | 51.1 | 42.2 |
| Construction | 24.9 | 18.1 | 16.8 | 17.2 | 18.6 | 19.7 | 18.2 | 17.5 | 17.3 |
| Manufacturing | 38.7 | 41.1 | 36.0 | 34.9 | 35.8 | 33.7 | 34.2 | 30.9 | 29.9 |
| Wholesale | 8.5 | 10.1 | 9.6 | 9.5 | 9.5 | 9.3 | 8.8 | 9.0 | 8.8 |
| Retail | 68.3 | 59.7 | 60.8 | 54.4 | 49.5 | – | – | – | – |
| Transport & communications | 65.0 | 65.3 | 61.0 | – | 59.6 | 57.9 | 56.5 | 50.1 | 46.1 |
| Electricity, gas and water | 77.5 | 73.7 | 73.1 | – | 64.0 | 67.9 | 66.7 | 71.4 | 60.9 |
| Services | 23.9 | 23.4 | 21.5 | 21.0 | 18.8 | 18.2 | 16.7 | 15.5 | 14.1 |
| Public Sector | 71.4 | 68.6 | 73.1 | 75.8 | 73.8 | 76.4 | 72.4 | 76.9 | 72.6 |

*Source*: Taishiro Shirai, *Kigyobetsukumiai*, 83.
 Rododaijin Kanbo, *Rodokumiaikihonchosahokoku*, 1992.

preferred the guarantee of lifetime employment to union industrial power.[10]

COMPANY UNIONS

After World War II, government regulation of unions was gradually relaxed and new company unions were formed in the Japanese automobile industry: unions at Toyota, Nissan and Isuzu started at almost the same time. The new car union leaders had no union experience, and they were quite radical, but times were often quite hard. There was high inflation in the immediate postwar years and a depression in 1950, when many Japanese companies, both large and small, came close to bankruptcy.

Toyota would have become bankrupt were it not for a bank syndicate rescue organized by the Bank of Japan. At this time, the bank syndicate asked Toyota to reduce its number of employees[11] and Mr Kiichiro Toyoda, the founder of Toyota Motors, resisted it, but finally could not refuse the bank's demand. In general, big labour disputes in Japan were mainly due to large-scale redundancies. If such redundancies occurred, the employees' proclamation was that the loyalty of 1,500 employees would be lost. Toyota's case was typical. After the company's announcement of lay-offs, a big strike was called.[12]

The company was faced with the choice of fighting it out until it went bankrupt or reaching a compromise. After three weeks of the strike, they arrived at a compromise. The union agreed to the lay-offs and changed to a more co-operative policy; Kiichiro Toyoda took responsibility for the strike, resigned and retired. There was no winner in this dispute.[13]

In Nissan's case, the circumstances were a little different. Until the big strike in 1953, the Nissan union had been radical and left-wing. Though organized as a company union, it behaved as an industrial union. In the 1953 recession, the union planned a big strike for a wage increase. Nissan was faced with near bankruptcy. In the end, the Nissan union broke up and another break-away union was formed. Many of the original union activists were dismissed or had to resign from the company. Eventually, the Nissan union came round to a much more co-operative relationship with the company.[14]

Another case was Mazda in 1974. It made a mistake in increasing the production of rotary engine cars just after the oil crisis and the company came near to bankruptcy. Even though the Mazda union was radical, it decided to compromise: to avoid lay-offs, it accepted a proposal to move surplus workers from the shop-floor to auto dealers as salesmen, and over a period of three years, about 1,500 workers were transferred. This saved the day for Mazda and even led to a stronger sales force.[15]

Japanese automobile company unions eventually settled for a consensus approach (especially on the shop-floor) with the aim of raising wages and welfare levels within the limit of the company's growth.

Toyota's experience is worth noting. After the labour dispute in 1950, rationalization of plant operations was required, and Toyota held a series of unofficial discussions with its workers and drew on its experience of co-operation between management and labour. In 1951, the labour agreement which had been in effect was abolished and was not replaced until 1974. During this time, however, Toyota upheld practices that were agreed upon at management and labour council meetings (see Table 8). Whenever problems arose about production, Toyota held discussions with their workers which reflected the actual circumstances of production operations. They standardized the practices that were developed from these discussions and the problems regarding the relationship between management and labour were solved through council meetings, under the principle of discussion, rather than through the notion of collective bargaining.[16] Although there is a formal Management–Labour Conference and a Production Subcommittee, discussions concerning production problems are usually held at informal gatherings, called

**Table 8** Procedures for 'Establishing a Mutual Consensus' at Toyota

**1  Listening to the Membership**

The union holds a wide variety of meetings designed to elicit opinions, demands, complaints, etc. from the members:

\*Shop meetings
\*Meetings of shop stewards
\*Meetings of chiefs of shop stewards
\*Hearings, sponsored by the executive committee, to grasp complaints and grievances
\*"Talk & touch activities" — designed to improve communication between the executive committee and the shop stewards

**2  Communicating between the Membership and the Management**

It is the union executive's job to communicate the membership's views and demands to the company and, in the other direction, to keep union members informed of developments in company policy.

▶ **Labor-Management Councils (Bargaining Sessions)**

| Council Name | Main items negotiated | Members |
|---|---|---|
| Spring Labor-Management Council | Wage hikes, reduction in working hours ('89 ~ ), lump sum allowances ('91 ~ )* | (Representing the union:) All executive committee members (with all chiefs of shop stewards attending as observers) |
| Autumn Labor-Management Council | Fringe benefits | (Representing management:) Chairman, president, and all directors (with all department managers and assistant department managers attending as observers) |

*From 1991, wage hikes, reduction in working hours, and lump sum allowances are to be negotiated concurrently in the Spring Labor-Management Council.

● **Specialized Committees**

The details of the above items are discussed, as the occasion may demand, in the Specialized Committees on;
① Production, ② Health and Safety, ③ Employees' Welfare, ④ Employees' Wages, and ⑤ Personnel Matters.

▶ **Joint Round-Table Conference**

| Joint Labor-Management Round-Table Conference |
|---|

● Held:        Generally three times a year
● Participants:  (Union)    Entire executive committee
              (Company)  Chairman, President, and all of Board of Directors
● Discusses:   Management's proposals for investment, production, recruitment, etc.
              Economic situation, union policies, and union activities

| Plant-level joint round-table conference |
|---|

● Held:        Generally four times a year
● Participants:  (Union)    Top union officers, regional directors, chief shop stewards
              (Company)  Plant manager, departmental managers, and assistant departmental managers
● Discusses:   Problems arising at the plant level with regard to production, safety, health, working environment, etc.

| Shop-level joint round-table conference |
|---|

● Held:        Generally once a month
● Participants:  (Union)    Regional director, chief shop steward, councillors, and shop stewards
              (Company)  Departmental manager, assistant departmental manager, and section managers
● Discusses:   Problems arising at the shop level with regard to working environment, work organization, etc.

*Source*: Extract from *Union Activities: Basic Concepts, Organization, Activities* Federation of all Toyota Workers' Union, 1991, 14

Management and Labour Meetings and, under, them, Plant Meetings and Shop Meetings that are organized according to job units.[17] The Shop Meetings, in particular, serve as a channel of communication by involving everyone on the job. They work in conjunction with QC circles and the views of rank-and-file workers are taken into account.[18] QC circles are voluntary and different from formal union activities, but the meetings also help to create team spirit. According to the type of problems, the participants in these meetings range from rank-and-file workers to assistant foremen, foremen, supervisors and section managers who are working members at the production site and, at times, department managers and other managerial and executive personnel.

Assistant foremen, foremen and supervisors who are managerial personnel at the production site, are all members of the trade union. It is a feature of Japanese union organization that white-collar and blue-collar workers are not separated. This leads to better communication and co-operation of the production site personnel; the one who holds the key to the operations is the foreman, who is responsible for coasts and the volume of output in his unit of operation. At election time for union committees, there is a tendency to choose assistant foremen and foremen who are resourceful. The principle of solving problems related to production is to encourage workers to find the solutions. Situations are made known to top management in realistic terms and, in turn, management has ample opportunity to explain in advance its plans to the union and rank-and-file workers at the production site. Management provides information concerning problems such as the rationalization of production and tries to ensure that its proposals are well understood. Detailed discussion at various levels makes for an exchange of information on each particular point. At the same time, the opportunity to solve problems is given to the shop floor and to individual workers, thereby forestalling problems and ensuring direct feedback before a problem is likely to occur. As for discussions on rationalization of production, the guiding principle is to identify potential problems before they occur.[19]

Since discussions are directly concerned with the circumstances of the production line, the grievance committee between management and labour has little to do, and indeed discussions at the shop-floor level make it easier to deal with problems as they arise. This has contributed to good and stable labour relations, making for more efficient production in terms of productivity and quality.

The Toyota plant has the famous 'just-in-time' or 'Kanban' production system. This ensures that parts are supplied in accordance with the required volume and time at each step of the assembly process, thus minimizing the stock of parts held at each work station in the plant.[20] An accumulation of stock can cover up the existence of problems; an alternative way of reducing stock was to shift from lot production, which could result in the accumulation of work-in-process inventory, to smooth production. Keeping stock down at each station and having a worker handle just a few stations were closely interrelated factors, and by proceeding to make workers versatile enough to handle a few stations, in line with the sequence of operations, the flow of production was greatly facilitated and, at the same time, accumulation of inventory at each station was lessened.[21]

The 'Kanban' system was not introduced at all stations of production at the same time, neither was it introduced to all of Toyota's plants. Its introduction was subject to agreements between management and labour, starting with stations that could cope with the system more easily. For example, multiple station handling started at the machining shop. The system required parts and components to be delivered at a predetermined time and place, matching the production flow of the assembly plant. Since it was up to the assemblers themselves to deal with the obstacles in the way of stock reduction, they did not pressure the parts suppliers to reduce stocks. Results emerged only after lengthy discussions between management and labour at meetings and QC circle activities, and these led on to Toyota's Total Quality Control (TQC) campaign.[22]

With the first oil crisis at the end of 1973, domestic demand began to shrink and Toyota set out to create an organizational structure that could cope with a reduction of up to 30 per cent in the plant operation rate. For this, the 'Kanban' system and TQC proved useful. Both were introduced not only into Toyota's factories but also into its related parts and components suppliers on a large scale. In addition to Toyota, other Japanese automakers also introduced the 'just-in-time' system and, with their own methods of utilizing it, generated favourable results. Of course in these stable labour relations were always a key factor in the success of the system.[23]

At this stage, Toyota tried to put the relocation of workers in its factories and shops within factories into operation: the practice of lending a hand in order to minimize the imbalance of production volume generated by changes in demand and product diversification. Toyota

**Table 9**  The Toyota Workers' 'Flexible and Constructive Approach to Production'

■ **Flexible Approach to Production Issues**

1. The lack of a layoff system in Japan severely limits the company's flexibility with respect to manning levels.
   The union acknowledges this fact and so is forced to respond, within limits, to company demands to do overtime work – whether it be after-hours or on regularly scheduled days off – and to "help out" by shifting to other job areas.

2. However, the union will not allow management to attempt to exploit our acceptance by keeping manning levels and production capacity at low levels and then expecting the workers to make up the difference when demand exceeds this minimum production capacity. Such an approach may seem like an easy way to cut costs, but only leads to chronic overwork deleterious to both the worker's health and family life.

3. To strike a balance, therefore, the union meets monthly with management to hear the company's production plans, how it plans to assign personnel, how much overtime will be required, and the company's reasons for requesting overtime.

4. To provide the production flexibility required in such a business environment, union members are willing to lend a hand in areas normal considered outside their job classification. They do not do this because they are ordered to, but because all such job transfers take place within a framework of strict guidelines agreed upon, in advance, by both labor and management.
   The same sort of framework exists for deciding on the necessity of overtime work.

By "lending a hand," we refer to the situation where a certain section — an assembly line, for example — finds that a sudden increase in production will leave it short of manpower and requires assistance from other manufacturing or non-manufacturing sections. It has absolutely no connection with job rotation whatsoever.

▶ **Understanding Concerning Such Assistance**

Such temporary loans of personnel from the non-manufacturing sector into the manufacturing one are subject to three stringent restrictions:
- The basic term is three (3) months.
- The basic principle shall be that a person may only be transferred for such a requirement twice a year, at the most, and the total transfer term shall be up to six (6) months.
- The full details of the transfer shall be submitted for union review at least five (5) working days before it is due to take effect.

▶ **Agreement Limiting Overtime Work**

|  | Work outside and in addition to regular working hours | | Work on scheduled holidays |
|---|---|---|---|
|  | Per day | Per month |  |
| Manufacturing sector | 4 hours | *50 hours | 2 times/month |

\* As from July, 1990

*Source*: Extracts from *Union Activities: Basic Concepts, Organization, Activities* Federation of all Toyota Workers' Union, 1991, 24, 26

also developed a working system to enable certain workers not only to handle a few machines or stations but to handle multiple jobs rather than just expanding their ability through job rotations within the factory. Although Toyota rarely relocates workers as a result of a large-scale change in facilities (except when a new factory is established) it has coped with demand changes and model changes by flexible removal and relocation of workers in response to the changing production system. No rule has been made by labour and management regarding relocation of workers. Although it is stipulated that the union must receive notification of the period and frequency of relocation of workers at least one week before execution, these procedures are normally facilitated by detailed consultation between union and management (see Table 9).

The development of a worker's ability to do different types of jobs was connected with promotion and forms part of 'on-the-job' training. Along with the development of the worker's ability,[24] efforts were also made to reduce the amount of work by improving tools and jigs.

WORKER PARTICIPATION

Toyota's system of consultative meetings was also found in Nissan and other Japanese automobile companies. There were some special features in Nissan where top executives and union leaders kept in touch through formal and informal channels. In informal discussions, Nissan's president relayed privileged information, such as management personnel changes and promotions, a practice not found in other automobile companies (though even Nissan has now stopped doing this). Other companies' top executives kept in touch with their union leaders but would only discuss general issues and kept to the boundaries of management and union affairs.

Worker participation, such as QC circles, was supported by the union through shop-floor negotiating activities. Worker participation itself was not part of union activities, nevertheless, the union helped to create the conditions for the development of worker participation, and this in turn promoted trust and communication between labour and management. A corporate identity had to be established, enabling workers to participate actively and usefully, and company unions have played their part in creating such a corporate identity.

How did the situation on the shop floor change as a result of worker participation? Workers sought new ways to improve their productivity while maintaining quality. In voluntary activities, such as QC circles,

**Table 10** Example of Nissan's New Technical Skill Standard (Sample Form)

Body Assembly Process

| Level | Job | Job Requirement | | |
|---|---|---|---|---|
| | | *Technical Skill* | *Direct Knowledge* | *Relative Knowledge* |
| Elementary class | Test assembly | 1. Ability to do unit operation of several work stations in each group within the standard time. 2. Ability to operate jig-setting. 3. .............. | 1. Understanding layout and jig structure of own working process, and surface accuracy standard. 2. .............. | 1. Part's name and relative working process. 2. .............. |

Step 1; Job Skills by Technical Standard of Job Content

| | | |
|---|---|---|
| 1 Spot welding | -------------------- | Necessary for test |
| 2 Special purpose multi-welding | | Automating equipment |
| 3 General purpose multi-welding | | Automating equipment |
| 4 Robot welding | ------------------- | Manpower-eliminating equipment and electronics etc. |
| 5 Gas welding | --------------------- | Necessary for test run |
| 6 Arc welding | --------------------- | Necessary for test run |
| 7 Test assembly | ------------------- | Mainly experience and know-how oriented job |
| 8 Solder finishing | ----------------- | Mainly experience and know-how oriented job |
| 9 Metal-work finishing | ----------- | Mainly experience and know-how oriented job |

Step 2; Each job skill classified in step 1 is integrated as required.

Innovation response ------------------ {
Special purpose multi-welding
General purpose multi-welding
Robot welding

Test development response ---------- {
Spot welding
Gas welding
Arc welding

Succeeding traditional skill
with experience and know-how ---- {
Test assembly
Solder finishing
Metal-work finishing

**Table 10** continued

Example of Mature Training in Body Assembly

| | Elementary level | Middle level | Upper level |
|---|---|---|---|
| Innovation response | Special purpose multi-welding<br>General Purpose multi-welding<br>Robot welding ⎬ a | $a_3$+one job skill within b.c | $a_2+b_1+c_1+\alpha$ |
| Test development response | Spot welding<br>Gas welding ⎬ b<br>Arc welding | $b_3$+one job skill within a.c | $a_1+b_2+c_1+\beta$ |
| Succeeding traditional skills with experience and know-how | Test assembly<br>Solder finishing ⎬ c<br>Metal-work finishing | $c_3$+one job skill within a.b | $a_1+b_1+c_2+\gamma$ |

*Source*: from Nissan company data with company permission.
*Note*: $\alpha$, $\beta$, $\gamma$ mean training experience in different working place.

workers co-operated with the foremen and managers.[25] Workers looked for new ways of solving problems in their work and by participating in workers' groups would discuss issues about working practices, many of which were consequently changed. In one case, workers became involved in reducing the time spent for die changes. In the die casting or press process, die changes were a hindrance to more flexible manufacturing, taking up to three or four hours to change a die. Workers reduced this time to a matter of minutes.[26]

Another example was the engine component machining process. Until 1965, each worker had specialized on one machine in order to allow line synchronization, but changes were made in favour of a modular type of production work and progressed to multiple and automatized machines. As a result, the efficiency of engine-machining work improved without any loss in the quality of the product. These improvements sometimes led to a fall in the number of workers. When quality control becomes part of the work process, there is less need for independent quality inspection of the work.[27]

Table 10 shows the skill training system and standard at Nissan on the introduction of robots. Figures 3 and 4 show the effect of robots on employment and work content in an auto company. We can see

**Figure 3**  Robots and Employment in a Large Welding Shop of a Car
Manufacturer

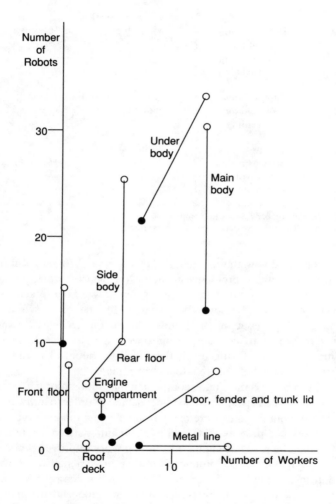

*Source*: Koyo Shokugyo Sogo Kenkyujo (Institute of Employment and Occupation) and
Mitsubishi Sogo Kenkyujo (Mitsubishi Institute), *Kigyo ni okeru Seisan System no Henka
to Koyo ni Kansuru Chosa Kenkyu (Research Report on the Changed Production System
and Employment in Firms)*, 2, September 1982, 74.

**Figure 4** Number of Welding Spots per Chassis and their Content

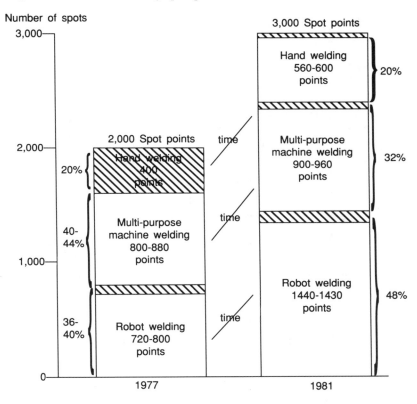

*Source*: Koyo Shokugyo Sogo Kenkyujo (Institute of Employment and Occupation) and Mitsubishi Sogo Kenkyujo (Mitsubishi Institute), *Kigyo ni okeru Seisan System no Henka to Koyo ni Kansuru Chosa Kenkyu (Research Report on the Changed Production System and Employment in Firms)*, 2, September 1982, 71.

how multi-skill training systems operate and the nature of change in the welding shop after robotization.

While worker participation has been supported by company unions, it is important to distinguish between union activities and worker activities. Though voluntary, QC circle and TQC activities call for good leadership by plant managers. Foremen and older workers have a key role in these groups, organizing and co-ordinating the voluntary activities of the participating workers. Worker participation in work

**Table 11**  Annual Wage Increases in Main Industrial Sectors, 1977–92

Increase in monthly pay in yen (% increase)

| | 1977 | 1978 | 1979 | 1980 | 1981 | 1982 | 1983 | 1984 |
|---|---|---|---|---|---|---|---|---|
| Metal-ore mining | 12,162( 8.8) | 6,000( 4.2) | 6,710(4.01) | 10,141(5.75) | 12,952(7.32) | 12,447(6.66) | 6,268(3.22) | 6,681(3.29) |
| Coal mining | 12,977( 8.9) | 5,258( 3.3) | | | | | | |
| Seafood & food | 15,174(10.0) | 12,014( 7.2) | 10,045(5.63) | 10,813(5.74) | 13,734(6.94) | 13,788(6.57) | 11,059(4.99) | 10,805(4.71) |
| Pulp & paper | 11,572( 8.1) | 7,403( 4.8) | 8,930(5.39) | 11,366(6.62) | 13,049(7.12) | 12,940(6.66) | 8,790(4.27) | 9,676(4.55) |
| Chemicals | 13,575( 9.1) | 9,466( 5.8) | 10,802(6.28) | 12,953(7.13) | 14,829(7.72) | 13,614(6.70) | 9,957(4.63) | 10,398(4.71) |
| Petroleum | 14,821( 9.3) | 13,369( 7.6) | 12,192(6.46) | 11,941(6.45) | 14,865(7.59) | 12,730(6.05) | 8,474(4.20) | 9,247(4.63) |
| Rubber | 12,254( 8.9) | 8,386( 5.6) | 9,124(5.38) | 11,556(6.45) | 13,603(7.19) | 13,380(6.66) | 8,881(4.35) | 9,304(4.21) |
| Cement | 12,096( 8.3) | 10,600( 6.9) | 10,600(6.37) | 10,924(6.19) | 14,000(7.72) | 13,600(6.95) | 8,505(4.14) | 8,700(4.09) |
| Iron & steel | 11,893( 8.5) | 6,106( 3.8) | 8,561(5.03) | 11,038(6.17) | 13,473(7.02) | 13,087(6.38) | 6,822(3.17) | 6,966(3.17) |
| Electrical wire | 11,964( 8.9) | 8,470( 5.8) | 9,096(5.90) | 10,589(6.52) | 12,920(7.56) | 12,739(7.03) | 7,939(4.13) | 8,201(4.15) |
| Nonferrous metals | | | | | | | | |
| General machinery | 12,730( 8.9) | 9,830( 6.3) | 10,108(6.09) | 12,023(6.82) | 14,034(7.62) | 13,638(7.00) | 9,293(4.51) | 9,622(4.50) |
| Electrical equipment | 12,116( 9.0) | 9,623( 6.6) | 9,943(6.65) | 11,419(7.2) | 13,496(8.06) | 13,223(7.47) | 9,106(4.91) | 9,585(5.01) |
| Shipbuilding | 13,100( 8.8) | 6,671( 4.1) | 5,600(3.26) | 9,902(5.56) | 13,647(7.22) | 13,100(6.56) | 6,800(3.21) | 7,000(3.21) |
| Rolling-stock etc. | 13,150( 9.3) | 9,500( 5.9) | 9,500(5.71) | 11,800(6.86) | 13,900(7.67) | 13,400(7.07) | 7,100(3.53) | 8,300(4.05) |
| Automobiles | 12,975( 9.9) | 11,299( 7.8) | 10,508(6.78) | 11,911(7.24) | 13,829(7.98) | 13,471(7.36) | 9,517(4.97) | 9,849(4.97) |
| Printing | 11,233( 8.9) | 8,752( 6.4) | 9,743(6.83) | 11,667(7.74) | 13,323(8.41) | 12,867(7.60) | 8,660(4.87) | 9,286(5.09) |
| Wholesale & retail | 14,893(11.5) | 13,143( 8.1) | 13,865(7.88) | 15,036(8.43) | 16,950(9.09) | 16,362(8.09) | 10,209(4.96) | 10,506(4.86) |
| Land transport | 13,289( 9.0) | 8,806( 5.4) | 9,581(5.67) | 12,015(6.78) | 14,619(7.79) | 14,354(7.13) | 9,803(4.59) | 10,340(4.68) |
| Electricity | 13,800( 8.2) | 9,922( 5.4) | 9,900(5.13) | 11,800(5.90) | 14,300(6.89) | 13,800(6.28) | 9,600(4.17) | 10,050(4.31) |
| Gas | 13,426( 8.8) | 8,800( 5.5) | 7,756(5.57) | 11,572(6.19) | 13,900(7.07) | 13,800(6.60) | 9,505(4.20) | 9,971(4.21) |
| Media | 15,537( 8.7) | 14,355( 7.6) | 14,870(7.53) | 17,237(8.13) | 19,238(8.58) | 18,510(7.51) | 14,727(5.49) | 15,113(5.32) |
| Textiles | 5,140( 4.4) | 3,662( 2.9) | 6,722(4.76) | 9,566(6.33) | 12,283(7.69) | 12,091(7.10) | 7,595(4.23) | 8,183(4.44) |
| Securities | – | 9,600( 7.4) | 9,235(6.82) | 11,127(7.46) | 13,033(8.14) | 13,936(7.83) | 10,459(5.76) | 9,083(4.78) |
| Average | 12,536( 8.8) | 9,218( 5.9) | 9,615(5.83) | 11,679(6.74) | 14,037(7.68) | 13,613(7.01) | 8,964(4.40) | 9,354(4.46) |
| Index of dispersion | <0.07> | <0.20> | <0.10> | <0.06> | <0.06> | <0.06> | <0.15> | <0.12> |
| Public corporations | 13,621(9.10) | 8,731(5.39) | 9,453(5.68) | 11,546(6.63) | 13,996(7.64) | 13,434(6.90) | 8,460(4.13) | 8,943(4.26) |

Increase in monthly pay in yen (% increase)

| | 1985 | 1986 | 1987 | 1988 | 1989 | 1990 | 1991 | 1992 |
|---|---|---|---|---|---|---|---|---|
| Metal-ore mining | 8,934(4.41) | 6,357(3.13) | 4,646(2.29) | 7,811(3.75) | 12,431(5.60) | 14,206(6.18) | – | – |
| Coal mining | 11,326(4.76) | 11,061(4.64) | 9,435(3.84) | 11,145(4.39) | 12,958(4.96) | 14,383(5.35) | 14,519(5.31) | 14,257(5.04) |
| Seafood & food | 11,354(5.16) | 10,673(4.68) | 7,774(3.29) | 10,463(4.36) | 12,664(5.12) | 13,965(5.48) | 13,693(5.20) | 13,000(4.78) |
| Pulp & paper | 12,001(5.27) | 11,348(4.81) | 9,334(3.85) | 11,644(4.83) | 13,907(5.49) | 15,535(6.01) | 15,441(5.65) | 14,144(5.01) |
| Chemicals | 9,826(4.76) | 10,260(4.51) | 7,148(2.95) | 9,762(4.12) | 10,887(4.81) | 12,591(5.41) | 12,325(5.15) | 12,007(4.90) |
| Petroleum | 11,098(4.80) | 10,067(4.20) | 7,257(2.95) | 9,800(3.90) | 12,235(4.74) | 14,408(5.42) | 14,158(5.17) | 12,952(4.59) |
| Rubber | 9,900(4.52) | 9,800(4.35) | 8,100(3.45) | 10,800(4.58) | 13,353(5.44) | 15,342(6.03) | 15,009(5.67) | 14,001(5.16) |
| Cement | 9,040(3.94) | 6,497(2.74) | 3,939(1.63) | 4,769(1.96) | 6,511(2.61) | 12,150(4.81) | 11,675(4.44) | 10,172(3.74) |
| Iron & steel | 9,443(4.65) | 8,923(4.27) | 7,178(3.33) | 9,534(4.33) | 11,929(5.26) | 13,636(5.83) | 13,529(5.63) | 11,890(4.83) |
| Electrical wire | | | | | | | | |
| Nonferrous metals | | | | | | | | |
| General machinery | 11,086(5.06) | 9,754(4.28) | 7,453(3.18) | 10,094(4.24) | 12,415(5.02) | 14,812(5.89) | 14,498(5.56) | 12,695(4.71) |
| Electrical equipment | 10,797(5.51) | 9,789(4.84) | 7,546(3.61) | 9,913(4.60) | 12,090(5.41) | 13,743(5.94) | 13,382(5.56) | 11,718(4.74) |
| Shipbuilding | 9,000(3.99) | 5,435(2.32) | 3,900(1.63) | 6,523(2.69) | 10,329(4.14) | 14,000(5.44) | 14,000(5.22) | 14,000(5.00) |
| Rolling-stock etc. | 10,300(4.87) | 7,200(3.26) | 5,395(2.46) | 9,210(4.11) | 12,000(5.15) | 14,500(5.96) | 14,581(5.87) | 13,500(5.21) |
| Automobiles | 11,543(5.55) | 10,248(4.73) | 7,501(3.35) | 9,645(4.18) | 12,377(5.17) | 14,471(5.97) | 14,370(5.58) | 13,005(4.84) |
| Printing | 10,592(5.41) | 11,562(5.09) | 12,538(4.70) | 14,125(5.23) | 17,085(6.07) | 19,377(6.65) | 17,606(5.96) | 16,108(5.90) |
| Wholesale & retail | 11,653(5.28) | 12,251(5.39) | 9,986(4.31) | 11,987(5.14) | 14,792(6.11) | 16,684(6.87) | 16,935(6.86) | 16,054(5.51) |
| Land transport | 12,039(5.26) | 11,536(4.85) | 9,669(3.94) | 11,014(4.47) | 13,420(5.27) | 16,054(6.01) | 16,234(5.80) | 15,531(5.29) |
| Electricity | 11,450(4.82) | 11,600(4.75) | 9,850(3.92) | 12,000(4.68) | 13,900(5.22) | 15,900(5.70) | 15,600(5.32) | 14,900(4.89) |
| Gas | 11,371(4.85) | 11,572(4.79) | 9,794(3.94) | 11,958(4.65) | 13,845(5.21) | 15,785(5.76) | 15,482(5.44) | 14,764(4.99) |
| Media | 15,497(5.24) | 13,046(5.75) | 11,527(4.85) | 14,083(5.65) | 14,194(5.42) | 17,012(6.37) | 17,009(6.03) | 14,860(5.01) |
| Textiles | 9,846(5.17) | 8,327(4.22) | 6,705(3.30) | 9,477(4.57) | 11,198(5.24) | 13,111(5.94) | 12,770(5.56) | 11,628(4.87) |
| Securities | 10,223(5.13) | 10,314(5.10) | 8,702(4.08) | – | – | – | – | – |
| Average | 10,871(5.03) | 10,146(4.55) | 8,275(3.56) | 10,573(4.43) | 12,747(5.17) | 15,026(5.94) | 14,911(5.65) | 13,662(4.95) |
| Index of dispersion | < 0.09 > | < 0.14 > | < 0.18 > | < 0.12 > | < 0.11 > | < 0.08 > | < 0.08 > | < 0.11 > |
| Public corporations | 10,550(4.91) | 9,531(4.34) | 7,872(3.51) | 9,907(4.36) | 12,000(5.14) | 14,275(5.92) | 14,122(5.64) | 13,137(5.07) |

Source: Rōdō hakusho (Labour White Paper), 1992.

Note: 1 In general the data base of this table is of companies with over one thousand employees and two billion yen capital.

2 Index of dispersion = (Third quartile – first quartile) / (2 × median)

48      *The Japanese Automobile Industry*

**Table 12**   Union Wage Claims and Increases in the Japanese Automobile
Industry, 1974–92

|      | Average age of members | Years worked | Average monthly wage (¥) | Claim (¥) | Settlement (¥) | Rate of increase (%) | Percentage of claim |
|------|------|------|--------|--------|--------|------|------|
| 1974 | 29.7 | 6.7  | 74,328  | 28,378 | 24,093 | 32.4 | 84.9 |
| 1975 | 30.4 | 7.0  | 95,820  | 27,508 | 13,733 | 14.3 | 49.9 |
| 1976 | 30.8 | 7.4  | 108,437 | 15,625 | 16,297 | 9.50 | 65.9 |
| 1977 | 31.4 | 8.2  | 118,458 | 17,823 | 11,635 | 9.82 | 65.3 |
| 1978 | 31.8 | 8.4  | 127,935 | 15,448 | 9,647  | 7.54 | 62.5 |
| 1979 | 32.0 | 8.7  | 135,516 | 10,873 | 9,239  | 6.82 | 85.0 |
| 1980 | 32.1 | 9.1  | 141,991 | 11,436 | 10,425 | 7.34 | 91.0 |
| 1981 | 32.3 | 9.3  | 149.748 | 15.051 | 11.918 | 7.96 | 79.0 |
| 1982 | 32.4 | 9.5  | 158,536 | 14,321 | 11,569 | 7.30 | 81.0 |
| 1983 | 32.5 | 9.7  | 166.897 | 11,701 | 8,005  | 4.80 | 68.4 |
| 1984 | 32.8 | 10.2 | 172,920 | 10,398 | 8,396  | 4.86 | 80.7 |
| 1985 | 33.0 | 10.4 | 177,821 | 12,464 | 9,756  | 5.48 | 78.3 |
| 1986 | 33.1 | 10.6 | 184,521 | 12,935 | 8,477  | 4.60 | 65.5 |
| 1987 | 33.0 | 10.6 | 188,240 | 9,555  | 6,338  | 3.37 | 66.3 |
| 1988 | 33.3 | 11.0 | 192,195 | 1,545  | 8,234  | 4.29 | 71.3 |
| 1989 | 33.6 | 11.4 | 197,840 | 13,862 | 10,514 | 5,33 | 75.8 |
| 1990 | 33.5 | 11.3 | 204,570 | 16,512 | 12,946 | 6.36 | 78.8 |
| 1991 | 33.3 | 11.1 | 212,579 | 17,099 | 12,575 | 5.95 | 74.4 |
| 1992 | 33.1 | 10.9 | 220,549 | 17,642 | 11,351 | 5.19 | 64.8 |

*Source*: JAW Research Division, 1992

processes promotes work skills, and this facilitates changes in the
production system, making it more flexible and automated.

CONCLUSION

As previously noted, the company union in the Japanese automobile
industry has contributed much to the company's prosperity, despite its
weak bargaining power. In short, the company union has bypassed this
weakness by improving welfare, and achieving increased salary levels
via company prosperity. (Table 11 shows the trends of annual wage
increases in the main industrial sectors. Table 12 shows union wage
claims and actual increases for workers in the automobile industry.
Table 13 gives details of labour conditions for the Japanese automobile
manufacturers.) What is the size and priority of distribution of the cake?
The strategy of Japanese unions in the automobile industry has been to

**Table 13** Workforce Details of Japanese Automobile Makers, 1992

| Company union | Number of union members | Working hours (annual) | | | Average monthly wage (¥) | | | Structure of the workforce | | | Percentage by sex | |
|---|---|---|---|---|---|---|---|---|---|---|---|---|
| | | Basic hours | Overtime | Total | Regular wage | On top of regular wage | Total | Average age | Years worked | Number of dependants | Male | Female |
| Nissan | 54,000 | 1960 | 350 | 2210 | 275,679 | 55,189 | 330,868 | 36.4 | 15.2 | 1.5 | 92.4 | 7.6 |
| Toyota | 66,637 | 1960 | 341 | 2301 | 287,371 | 69,433 | 356,804 | 33.6 | 12.7 | 1.2 | 88.5 | 11.5 |
| Mazda | 26,778 | 1960 | 381 | 2341 | 278,946 | 88,796 | 367,742 | 39.8 | 17.3 | 1.5 | 93.9 | 6.1 |
| Mitsubishi | 25,372 | 1960 | 450 | 2410 | 257,732 | 97,050 | 354,782 | 37.0 | 14.9 | 1.2 | 91.7 | 8.3 |
| Honda | 30,357 | 1960 | 83 | 2043 | 288,976 | 45,090 | 334,066 | 34.2 | 12.9 | 1.4 | 94.4 | 5.6 |
| Isuzu | 11,644 | 1960 | 398 | 2358 | 256,263 | 107,082 | 363,345 | 37.6 | 14.6 | 1.1 | 95.7 | 4.3 |
| Daihatsu | 11,118 | 1960 | 335 | 2295 | 261,852 | 70,587 | 332,439 | 36.0 | 15.5 | 1.2 | 96.1 | 5.9 |
| Fuji (Subaru) | 14,073 | 1976 | 353 | 2329 | 255,853 | 66,785 | 322,638 | 36.6 | 15.5 | 1.1 | 93.7 | 6.3 |
| Hino | 7,273 | 1960 | 447 | 2407 | 266,714 | 73,746 | 340,460 | 36.1 | 14.5 | 1.0 | 91.5 | 8.5 |
| Suzuki | 11,318 | 1976 | 377 | 2353 | 252,559 | 48,601 | 301,160 | 36.1 | 13.2 | 1.2 | 91.9 | 8.1 |
| Yamaha | 8,253 | 1968 | 198 | 2166 | 266,972 | 54,165 | 321,137 | 36.0 | 13.1 | 1.5 | 90.7 | 9.3 |
| Nissan Diesel | 6,014 | – | – | – | 269,358 | 62,411 | 331,769 | 36.9 | 15.2 | 1.4 | 96.9 | 5.1 |
| Nissan Body | 5,192 | – | – | – | 263,136 | 73,394 | 356,530 | 36.8 | 16.2 | 1.5 | 94.1 | 3.9 |
| Toyota Body | 7,085 | – | – | – | 272,668 | 144,813 | 417,481 | 34.7 | 13.7 | 1.3 | 93.4 | 6.6 |
| Kanto | 5,875 | – | – | – | 267,605 | 119,283 | 386,888 | 34.4 | 14.0 | 1.1 | 94.3 | 5.7 |

*Source*: JAW Research Division
*Note*: Regular wages exclude overtime and non-contractual payments.

improve welfare and wages by working to increase the overall size of the cake. As a result, wages increased year by year to become among the top wages in Japanese industry. Total working hours (including overtime) were about average, namely, forty-two hours a week.

There are the questions as to why company unions became established in Japan and why they work so well. The Japanese union has a historical background of being organized on a company base by the company employees themselves and not by union leaders or management.

Many of the larger Japanese companies, especially after World War II, accepted the need for lifetime employment and wage systems which favoured company union organization. An important factor, however, was the outlook of the union members themselves. As company employees, union members identify with the company and see the company as part of their community. This characteristic is typical of Japanese culture. Certainly, many people, including Japanese scholars, consider the company union as a specific Japanese phenomenon with a Japanese cultural foundation in terms of the co-operative activities of group behaviour.

Union activities that involve more in the way of day-to-day negotiation and consultation on the shop floor are an important kind of development in labour relations. If there is different union organization in each country, it will be possible to modify or refine their principles by considering increasing the amount of white-collar membership in their organization. In the automobile industry, this is crucial and is manifested in the new single union systems in Britain and in the new thinking and strategies of the automobile union in the USA.

However, it cannot be said that the Japanese unions do not have problems. It is necessary for them to make their organization more international in view of an emerging global automobile industry. They also have to see to the wage and welfare disparities between large automobile companies and small component or parts producers. In addition, they must take more account of retired workers.

# CHAPTER 4

# *The Automobile Parts Industry*

INTRODUCTION

Japanese parts makers played an important role in the development of the automobile industry in Japan, especially in raising productivity and quality standards. The competitiveness of Japanese automakers derives to a large extent from the way they fostered parts makers with high technical standards by working closely with them, as well as concentrating on their marketing product-planning capacities.

Parts makers are divided into two groups: the automaker-affiliated group and the independent group. The affiliated parts makers fall into three categories: the primary, secondary and tertiary, representing a vertical division of labour. They take charge of machining, plastic processing such as pressing and sheet metal processing, surface treatment such as plating and assembly. They produce a range of special parts and supply them to automakers and the spare-parts dealers. Although many independent parts makers have business relations with more than two assemblers, Japan's parts industry consists mainly of parts makers who are affiliated to major assemblers. These form the nucleus of co-operative organizations belonging to automakers and are very closely tied in with them through supply channels, investment, personnel exchange and technical guidance. In comparison with the contractual business relations in the USA and Europe, this bond between automakers and parts makers is often seen as peculiarly Japanese. This reflects Japan's social system and cultural structure and is a kind of 'parent–child' relationship. Automakers constantly press parts makers to reduce costs, supply secure low-priced parts and keep the industry highly competitive. This is especially so in regard to the smaller secondary and tertiary parts makers. In essence, Japanese automakers and parts makers have acted together to promote Japanese-style rationalization, symbolized by the 'Kanban' (just-in-time) system, by means of the development of the technical standards of parts makers. The automakers and parts manufacturers thereby co-operated in innovating process technology and achieving high standards in quality and productivity.

In this chapter, I will illustrate the ways in which a vertical division of labour and the affiliation between automakers and parts subcontractors have been organized through the development of rationalization policies by automakers. By shedding light on how the introduction and development of production technology by automakers has changed. I will discuss the role their affiliated relationship with parts makers consequently played. I will also introduce some cases for consideration concerning how the parts makers have contributed to the innovation of process technology by Japanese-style rationalization, or Japanese-style micro management, fostered by the affiliated relationship between automakers and parts makers in the perspective of technological innovation in the automobile industry. Relating the flexibility in production with innovation in process technology, we can see how the constant changes in automaker/parts-maker relations will probably be accompanied by future innovations in automobile technology.

THE STRUCTURE OF THE PARTS INDUSTRY

The automobile parts industry has a wide and diverse substructure. Car parts and accessories are numerous and versatile, and some of the manufacturing processes are extremely complicated. Apart from parts makers directly linked with a certain automaker, there are also independent parts makers with no fixed affiliations. At the bottom end of the second and third layers of parts makers are small and medium-sized producers with less than 30 employees. These producers make up about 86 per cent of the total number of companies.[1] Automaker A, in Table 14, has 47,300 subcontractors of parts, including 41,700 at tertiary level. These figures include the gross number of parts makers engaged in the manufacture of parts for the company and are adjusted to eliminate double-counting to give 4,700 secondary subcontractors and 31,600 subcontractors. The bottom end of this complex structure is made up of small and medium-sized parts makers, the statistics of which cannot be easily recorded.[2] The purchase of parts by Japanese automakers amounts to 60 or 70 per cent of their total costs and about 30 per cent of these expenses relate to the small tertiary subcontractors.[3]

Secondary subcontractors produce mechanical parts, electrical parts, parts of the drive, transmission and steering equipment, suspension and brake parts, chassis parts, body parts, and other accessories, while tertiary subcontractors are engaged in pressing, plating, grinding, the manufacture of springs and screws, casting and forging parts, plastic parts, machining specific parts and assembly.[4]

**Table 14** Division of Labour in the Automobile Industry

Passenger Car Manufacturer A

Number of plants undertaking subcontracts by type of parts

| | Engines | Electrical components | Drive transmission & steering parts | Suspension, brake devices & parts | Equipment | Chassis parts | Body parts | Others | Total |
|---|---|---|---|---|---|---|---|---|---|
| Primary subcontractors | 25 | 1 | 31 | 18 | 18 | 3 | 41 | 31 | 168 |
| Secondary subcontractors | 912 | 34 | 609 | 792 | 926 | 27 | 1,213 | 924 | 5,437 |
| Tertiary contractors | 4,960 | 352 | 7,354 | 6,204 | 5,936 | 85 | 8,221 | 8,591 | 41,703 |
| Total | 5,897 | 387 | 7,994 | 7,014 | 6,880 | 115 | 9,475 | 9,546 | 47,308 |
| Ratio of medium, small offices, by parts (%) | 97.6 | 89.8 | 96.5 | 96.7 | 96.7 | 93.9 | 97.0 | 93.7 | |

*Source:* Small & Medium Enterprises Agency, *A Fact-Finding Survey on the Structure of the Division of Labour*, 1977

*Note:* 1. Primary subcontractors are in actual figures while secondary and tertiary subcontractors are mixed. After offsetting some double counting, there are 4,700 secondary subcontractors and 31,600 plants in a co-operative relationship. The subcontractors' plants include factories under co-operative relationship.

**Figure 5** Automobile Production Structures

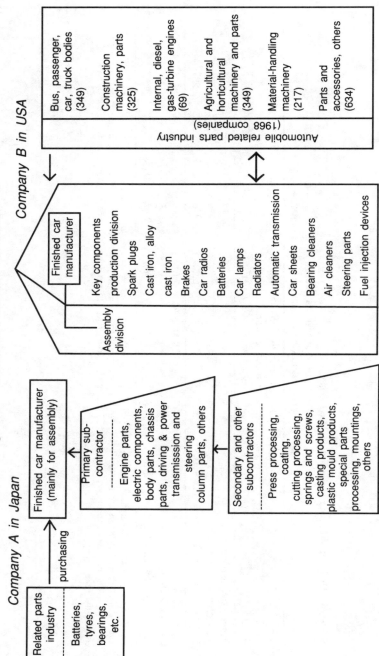

*Company A in Japan*

Related parts industry — Batteries, tyres, bearings, etc.

→ purchasing → Finished car manufacturer (mainly for assembly)

Primary sub-contractor

Engine parts, electric components, body parts, chassis parts, driving & power transmission and steering column parts, others

Secondary and other subcontractors

Press processing, coating, cutting processing, springs and screws, casting products, plastic mould products, special parts processing, mountings, others

*Company B in USA*

Finished car manufacturer

Assembly division

Key components production division — Spark plugs, Cast iron, alloy, cast iron, Brakes, Car radios, Batteries, Car lamps, Radiators, Automatic transmission, Car sheets, Bearing cleaners, Air cleaners, Steering parts, Fuel injection devices

Automobile related parts industry (1968 companies)

Bus, passenger, car, truck bodies (349)

Construction machinery, parts (325)

Internal, diesel, gas-turbine engines (69)

Agricultural and horticultural machinery and parts (349)

Material-handling machinery (217)

Parts and accessories, others (634)

*Source:* Small and Medium Enterprises Agency, *White Paper on Medium and Small Companies*, 1980.
*Note:* 1 In some cases primary subcontractors have more than one parent company.

Generally speaking, primary parts makers are in charge of important processes, requiring a high technical input, while secondary and tertiary parts makers are in charge of peripheral or specialized processes with a high labour input. Primary makers are closely affiliated to the automakers but independently linked to the secondary and tertiary parts makers. The production of automobile parts is shown in terms of a grand total of products by primary and independent parts makers. Between 1965 and 1980, the ratio of parts production as a percentage of all automobile production rose from 46 to 56 per cent, including fit-on parts which rose from 34 to 42 per cent. This shows that with an expansion of automobile production in Japan, the proportion of outside orders has been gradually increasing. In 1966, 1969, 1972 and 1973 the production of repair parts increased sharply by 20 to 30 per cent compared to the previous years, and by 56 per cent in 1979. This shows that, unlike general car parts, the increase of repair parts is easily affected by the market status and that the market trend in used cars is not uniform.

Primary and some secondary parts makers form the core of the parts industry, and are a kind of satellite for automakers in the organization. Many of these parts makers are organized into the Japan Auto Parts Industry Association – JAPIA.

The statistics in Table 16 for 474 members of JAPIA (310 in 1981) show that in 1991 small and medium-sized parts manufacturers, with capital of less than 100 million yen, accounted for only about 8 per cent of all production, but made up nearly 40 per cent of the number of companies. Those with less than 300 employees accounted for about 6 per cent of all production, making up about 43 per cent of the number of companies. While employment in the parts industry has risen by about 60 per cent over the last decade, production value has almost tripled. This shows how effective rationalization by the pars makers has been. The groundwork for this success was being laid back in the 1970s when, as shown in Table 17(i), parts makers invested heavily in production facilities and in research, increasing investment by three times between 1976 and 1981 (compared with two-and-a-half times by automakers). Over about the same period, the major parts makers steadily improved their profitability (see Figure 6), more than half of them enjoying the same profitability as the automakers, or, in some cases, even more.

**Table 15**  Automobile and Automobile Parts Production Value, 1965–91

(Production value in ¥ million)

| | | Automobiles | | | Auto parts (total) | | Parts for assembling | | | | Repair parts | | | Parts for 2 & 3 wheel vehicles | | | Parts for export | | |
|---|---|---|---|---|---|---|---|---|---|---|---|---|---|---|---|---|---|---|---|
| | Units produced | % of previous year | Production value | % of previous year | Production value | % of previous year | Production value | % of parts previous year | % of total prod value | % of total car prod value | Production | % of parts previous year | % of total prod value | Production value | % of parts previous year | % of total prod value | Export value | % of parts previous year | % of total prod value |
| 1965 | 1,937,908 | – | 836,786 | – | 391,554 | – | 280,790 | – | 71.8 | 33.6 | 59,545 | – | 15.2 | 45,696 | – | 11.6 | 5,511 | – | 1.4 |
| 1966 | 2,466,603 | 127.3 | 1,057,279 | 126.3 | 501,109 | 128.0 | 375,170 | 133.6 | 74.9 | 35.5 | 77,063 | 129.4 | 15.3 | 42,452 | 92.9 | 8.5 | 6,424 | 116.3 | 1.3 |
| 1967 | 3,406,265 | 138.1 | 1,421,190 | 134.4 | 667,536 | 133.2 | 530,613 | 141.4 | 79.6 | 37.2 | 90,661 | 117.6 | 13.5 | 37,307 | 87.9 | 5.6 | 8,955 | 139.4 | 1.3 |
| 1968 | 4,198,429 | 123.3 | 1,809,900 | 127.4 | 832,951 | 124.8 | 679,859 | 128.1 | 81.7 | 37.6 | 102,596 | 113.2 | 12.3 | 39,428 | 105.7 | 4.7 | 11,068 | 123.6 | 1.3 |
| 1969 | 4,850,151 | 115.5 | 2,124,722 | 117.4 | 986,603 | 118.4 | 793,215 | 116.7 | 80.5 | 37.3 | 133,779 | 130.4 | 13.5 | 49,260 | 117.3 | 4.7 | 13,349 | 120.6 | 1.3 |
| 1970 | 5,454,524 | 112.5 | 2,433,811 | 114.5 | 1,161,288 | 117.7 | 935,256 | 117.9 | 80.6 | 38.4 | 150,050 | 112.2 | 12.9 | 61,846 | 133.7 | 5.3 | 14,136 | 105.9 | 1.2 |
| 1971 | 5,883,562 | 107.9 | 2,709,984 | 111.3 | 1,315,330 | 113.3 | 1,059,047 | 113.2 | 80.6 | 39.1 | 160,414 | 106.9 | 12.2 | 76,838 | 124.4 | 5.8 | 19,031 | 134.6 | 1.4 |
| 1972 | 6,533,572 | 111.0 | 3,127,126 | 115.4 | 1,534,212 | 116.6 | 1,227,352 | 115.9 | 80.1 | 39.2 | 197,696 | 123.2 | 12.8 | 87,567 | 114.0 | 5.7 | 21,597 | 113.5 | 1.4 |
| 1973 | 6,994,515 | 107.1 | 3,604,739 | 115.3 | 2,006,702 | 130.8 | 1,610,379 | 131.2 | 80.3 | 44.7 | 260,159 | 131.6 | 13.0 | 112,182 | 128.1 | 5.5 | 23,982 | 111.0 | 1.2 |
| 1974 | 6,504,667 | 93.0 | 3,968,765 | 110.1 | 2,247,410 | 112.0 | 1,761,441 | 109.4 | 78.5 | 44.4 | 286,898 | 110.3 | 12.7 | 168,817 | 150.5 | 7.5 | 30,254 | 126.2 | 1.3 |
| 1975 | 7,130,999 | 109.6 | 4,739,197 | 119.4 | 2,495,310 | 111.0 | 1,985,303 | 112.7 | 79.6 | 41.9 | 341,709 | 119.1 | 13.7 | 138,494 | 82.0 | 5.5 | 29,804 | 98.5 | 1.2 |
| 1976 | 8,050,643 | 112.9 | 5,805,308 | 122.5 | 2,943,511 | 118.0 | 2,369,283 | 119.3 | 80.5 | 40.8 | 386,595 | 113.1 | 13.1 | 146,970 | 106.1 | 5.0 | 40,663 | 136.4 | 1.4 |
| 1977 | 8,777,279 | 109.0 | 6,670,126 | 114.9 | 3,399,695 | 115.5 | 2,718,378 | 114.7 | 80.0 | 40.8 | 445,265 | 115.2 | 13.1 | 181,191 | 123.3 | 5.3 | 54,861 | 134.9 | 1.6 |
| 1978 | 9,298,786 | 105.9 | 7,304,413 | 109.5 | 3,712,595 | 109.2 | 2,990,041 | 110.0 | 80.5 | 40.9 | 496,537 | 111.5 | 13.4 | 163,307 | 90.1 | 4.4 | 62,710 | 114.3 | 1.7 |
| 1979 | 10,065,643 | 108.2 | 8,064,102 | 110.4 | 4,373,499 | 117.8 | 3,325,678 | 111.2 | 76.0 | 41.2 | 778,198 | 156.7 | 17.8 | 204,388 | 125.2 | 4.7 | 65,235 | 104.0 | 1.5 |
| 1980 | 11,175,628 | 111.0 | 9,014,035 | 111.8 | 5,096,539 | 116.5 | 3,816,593 | 114.8 | 74.9 | 42.3 | 828,578 | 106.5 | 16.2 | 289,190 | 141.5 | 5.7 | 161,846** | 248.1 | 3.2 |
| 1981 | 11,114,478 | 99.4 | 9,646,777 | 107.0 | 5,277,943 | 103.6 | 4,086,197 | 107.1 | 77.4 | 42.4 | 644,200 | 77.7 | 12.2 | 318,205 | 110.0 | 6.0 | 229,341 | 141.1 | 4.3 |
| 1982 | 10,790,090 | 97.1 | 10,057,194 | 104.3 | 5,390,075 | 102.1 | 4,196,496 | 102.7 | 77.9 | 41.7 | 672,314 | 104.4 | 12.5 | 295,612 | 92.9 | 5.5 | 225,653 | 98.4 | 4.2 |
| 1983 | 11,206,579 | 103.9 | 10,800,191 | 107.4 | 6,138,283 | 113.9 | 4,852,619 | 115.6 | 78.7 | 44.9 | 739,103 | 109.9 | 12.0 | 269,053 | 91.0 | 4.4 | 277,508 | 123.0 | 4.5 |
| 1984 | 11,589,202 | 103.4 | 11,393,079 | 105.5 | 7,022,140 | 114.4 | 5,527,426 | 113.9 | 78.7 | 48.5 | 806,173 | 109.1 | 11.5 | 294,210 | 109.4 | 4.2 | 394,331 | 142.1 | 5.6 |
| 1985 | 12,416,741 | 107.1 | 12,415,248 | 109.0 | 7,946,186 | 113.2 | 6,276,285 | 113.5 | 79.0 | 50.7 | 872,301 | 108.2 | 11.0 | 318,730 | 108.3 | 4.0 | 478,870 | 121.4 | 6.0 |
| 1986 | 12,268,662 | 98.8 | 12,362,023 | 99.6 | 7,941,658 | 99.9 | 6,349,036 | 101.2 | 80.0 | 51.4 | 860,977 | 98.7 | 10.8 | 252,586 | 79.2 | 3.2 | 479,059 | 100.0 | 6.0 |
| 1987 | 12,349,472 | 100.7 | 13,384,618 | 108.3 | 8,491,817 | 106.9 | 6,635,231 | 104.5 | 78.1 | 49.6 | 1,075,551 | 124.9 | 12.7 | 247,581 | 98.0 | 2.9 | 533,454 | 111.4 | 6.3 |
| 1988 | 12,819,317 | 103.8 | 14,812,473 | 110.7 | 9,625,022 | 113.3 | 7,450,821 | 112.3 | 77.4 | 50.3 | 1,403,712 | 130.5 | 14.6 | 244,166 | 98.6 | 2.5 | 526,323 | 98.7 | 5.5 |
| 1989 | 12,953,790 | 101.0 | 15,870,972 | 107.1 | 11,886,358 | 123.5 | 9,244,025 | 124.1 | 77.8 | 58.2 | 1,822,689 | 129.8 | 15.3 | 268,497 | 110.0 | 2.3 | 551,147 | 104.7 | 4.6 |
| 1990 | 13,591,709 | 104.9 | 17,158,338 | 108.1 | 13,259,230 | 111.5 | 10,195,319 | 110.3 | 76.9 | 59.4 | 2,198,457 | 120.6 | 16.6 | 298,906 | 111.3 | 2.2 | 566,548 | 102.8 | 4.3 |
| 1991 | 13,145,742 | 96.7 | 20,129,560 | 117.3 | 14,678,419 | 110.7 | 11,494,068*** | 112.7 | 78.3 | 57.1 | 2,276,454 | 103.5 | 15.5 | 317,415 | 106.2 | 2.2 | 590,482 | 104.2 | 4.0 |

\* Automobile production figures exclude KD sets from 1979.     \*\* Export figures include repair parts from 1980 onwards.     \*\*\* Includes items for export.

*Source:* Automobile production figures are from *Machine Statistics* and *Automobile Annual Statistics*, MITI.

Figures for parts production value are from *Survey on Car Parts Production Trend*, JAPIA.

**Table 16**   The Size of Companies in the Automobile Parts Industry 1981/1991
(JAPIA companies)

i) Companies by capital and production value

| Capital (¥) | No. of companies (Percentage of total in brackets) | | Production value (¥ million) (Percentage of total in brackets) | |
|---|---|---|---|---|
| | 1981 | 1991 | 1981 | 1991 |
| Over 10 billion | | 44(9.3) | | 5,313,061(36.2) |
| 5 billion–10 billion | | 34(7.2) | | 2,186,826(14.9) |
| 2 billion–5 billion | | 44(9.3) | | 2,440,531(16.6) |
| (Over 2 billion for 1981) | 42(13.5) | | 2,223,552(43.7) | |
| 1 billion–2 billion | 27 (8.7) | 39.8.2) | 844,871(16.6) | 1,230,307 (8.4) |
| 0.5 billion–1 billion | 36(11.6) | 19(4.0) | 729,947(14.3) | 498,696 (3.4) |
| 100 million–0.5 billion | 84(27.1) | 110(23.2) | 771,136(15.1) | 1,768,944(12.1) |
| Less than 100 million (Small + Medium-size companies) | 121(39.1) | 184(38.8) | 527,033(10.3) | 1,240,054 (8.4) |
| Total | 310 | 474 | 5,096,539 | 14,678,419 |

ii) Companies by number of employees and production value

| Capital (¥) | No. of companies (Percentage of total in brackets) | | Production value (¥ million) (Percentage of total in brackets) | |
|---|---|---|---|---|
| | 1981 | 1991 | 1981 | 1991 |
| Over 2000 | 35(11.3) | 54(11.4) | 2,642,110(51.8) | 7,992,392(54.4) |
| 1,001–2,000 | 37(11.9) | 64(13.5) | 1,053,080(20.7) | 3,083,138(21.0) |
| 501–1,000 | 64(20.6) | 79(16.6) | 803,491(15.8) | 1,938,820(13.2) |
| 301–500 | 47(15.2) | 73(15.4) | 311,888 (6.1) | 834,132 (5.7) |
| 101–300 | 87(28.1) | 124(26.2) | 256,795 (5.0) | 733,277 (5.0) |
| Less than 100 | 40(12.9) | 80(16.9) | 29,175 (0.6) | 96,660 (0.7) |
| Total | 310 | 474 | 5,096,539 | 14,678,419 |

iii) Total no. of employees in JAPIA-affiliated companies, 1976/81/91*

| | 1976 | 1981 | 1991 |
|---|---|---|---|
| No. of employees | 243,224 | 274,430 | 445,919 |

* As of March of each year.

*Source*: JAPIA, *Survey of Auto Parts Production*, 1982, 1992.

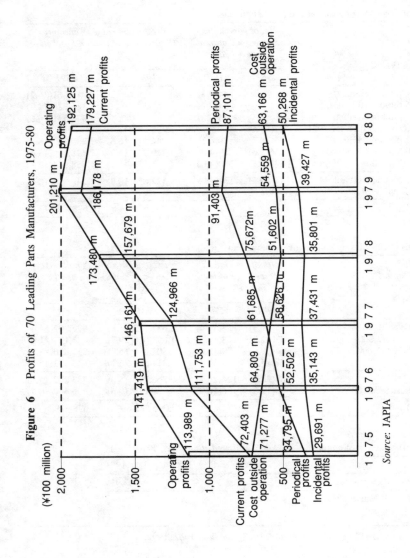

**Figure 6** Profits of 70 Leading Parts Manufacturers, 1975-80

(¥100 million)

Operating profits

Current profits

Periodical profits

Cost outside operation

Incidental profits

Operating profits
Current profits
Cost outside operation
Periodical profits
Incidental profits

2,000
1,500
1,000
500

1975 1976 1977 1978 1979 1980

201,210 m
192,125 m
179,227 m
186,178 m
173,480 m
157,679 m
146,161 m
141,419 m
124,966 m
113,989 m
111,753 m
91,403 m
87,101 m
75,672m
64,809 m
72,403 m
71,277 m
63,166 m
61,685 m
54,559 m
51,602 m
50,268 m
58,626 m
52,502 m
39,427 m
37,431 m
35,801 m
35,143 m
37,795 m
29,691 m

*Source:* JAPIA

By and large, Japanese automobile parts makers go for in-house production or integrated production within the group of companies in order to meet delivery dates, maintain quality and improve the standard of production technology, while making a point of placing some outside orders to ensure competition and efficiency.

GROUP ORGANIZATION

One of the motives for group organization among parts manufacturers stems from their past experience when the automobile industry in Japan was still underdeveloped. When automakers began full-scale production of passenger cars in 1953,[5] they saw the need to foster and organize parts manufacturers and create group links themselves. The technology of the industry at that time was based on the 'all-around' working system, based on multiple-use machines. This was particularly so in the case of small and medium-sized companies. Standards for casting, forging and metal finishing were low and product quality was variable. Therefore, when automakers planned to move to mass production, there were no parts manufacturers who could meet their new requirements. The automakers had little or no choice but to organize and develop the parts manufacturers themselves.

But why should automakers not go in for parts production of their own? The answer is that they gave priority to establishing mass production lines for the assembly of components rather than the production of the components themselves. Manufacturers in the 1950s did not have the capacity in their factories to produce thousands of parts, and also the extra cost would have been too great to yield much, if any, profit. In other words, it was better for automakers to get parts from specialist manufacturers on low-volume, small-batch production while controlling delivery times and ensuring product quality. Although the situation changed in the late 1960s, the wages paid by small and medium-sized manufacturers were low, and thus automakers were able to offer a low unit price for subcontract work by taking advantage of the strong competition among the parts manufacturers.[6]

These factors influenced automakers in the organization of the parts manufacturers into groups. In addition, the merits of vertically-integrated groups were demonstrated by the ability to adjust production technology and management, to set up an efficient system of mass production and to improve technological standards. Group organiza-

**Figure 7**   Distribution of 70 Companies by Profit, 1975–80

Operating profit as % of total sales turnover

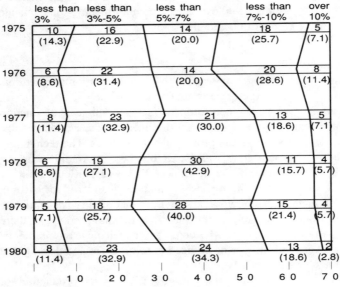

Current profit as % of total sales turnover

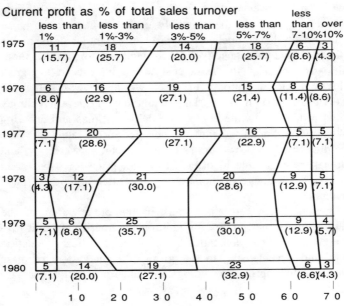

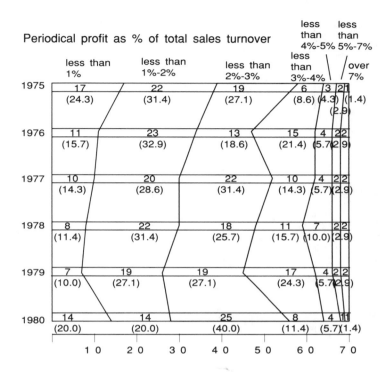

Figures in brackets are % distribution of the number of companies.

Operating profit = Total profit − (Production cost + Sales and Administration charge)
Current profit = (Operating profit + Incidental profit) − Cost outside operation
Periodical profit = Current profit − Company tax

*Source*: JAPIA

tion was crucial to automakers for the promotion of technological improvements and rationalization policies throughout the industry. Moreover, the division of labour in parts production allowed for more economies of scale and for the flexibility required to change design in cars or components. It also helped to introduce new production technology.

What were the benefits to parts manufacturers of being organized into groups? Firstly, a parts manufacturer was able to obtain secure

**Table 17** Investment by Major Automobile parts Manufacturers and Related Industries, 1976–91
i) 1976–81

(¥100 million)

| Year | 1976 | 1977 | 1978 | 1979 | 1980 | 1981 |
|---|---|---|---|---|---|---|
| *Parts Manufacturers* | | | | | | |
| No. of companies surveyed | 45 | 45 | 48 | 53 | 59 | 58 |
| Total investment | 777 | 1,120 | 1,223 | 1,397 | 2,168 | 2,503 |
| (% increast over previous year) | (33.5) | (44.1) | (9.2) | (14.2) | (55.2) | (15.5) |
| Investment breakdown | | | | | | |
| Production facilities | 641 | 960 | 1,084 | 1,233 | 1,838 | 2,176 |
| Research facilities | 35 | 43 | 54 | 64 | 101 | 104 |
| Welfare facilities | 36 | 38 | 38 | 33 | 68 | 67 |
| Distribution facilities | 11 | 9 | 10 | 14 | 15 | 14 |
| Other | 54 | 70 | 37 | 53 | 146 | 142 |
| *Related Industries* | | | | | | |
| Automobiles | | | | | | |
| No. of companies surveyed | 14 | 14 | 13 | 13 | 13 | 13 |
| Total investment | 3,561 | 4,841 | 4,664 | 5,076 | 8,133 | 8,498 |
| (% increase over previous year) | (36.9) | (35.9) | (−3.7) | (8.8) | (41.2) | (4.5) |
| Car bodies | | | | | | |
| No. of companies surveyed | 18 | 18 | 17 | 18 | 18 | 16 |
| Total investment | 232 | 371 | 361 | 513 | 540 | 718 |
| (% increase over previous year) | (24.7) | (59.9) | (−2.8) | (42.1) | (5.3) | (33.0) |

*Source: A survey by the Automobile Department of the Machinery Information Industries Bureau, MITI.*

ii) 1982–91

(¥100 million)

| Year | 1982 | 1983 | 1984 | 1985 | 1986 | 1987 | 1988 | 1989 | 1990 | 1991 |
|---|---|---|---|---|---|---|---|---|---|---|
| **Parts Manufacturers** | | | | | | | | | | |
| No. of companies surveyed | 53 | 61 | 57 | 45 | 54 | 52 | 44 | 55 | 71 | 66 |
| Total investment | 1,389 | 2,110 | 2,326 | 2,859 | 2,943 | 2,651 | 2,823 | 4,209 | 5,920 | 5,967 |
| (% increase over previous year) | (−44.5) | (51.9) | (10.2) | (22.9) | (2.9) | (−9.9) | (6.5) | (49.1) | (40.7) | (0.8) |
| **Automobiles** | | | | | | | | | | |
| No. of companies surveyed | 13 | 13 | 13 | 13 | 13 | 13 | 13 | 13 | 13 | 13 |
| Total investment | 8,364 | 6,210 | 7,009 | 9,815 | 9,000 | 7,314 | 9,241 | 11,831 | 15,753 | 15,678 |
| (% increase over previous year) | (−1.6) | (−25.7) | (12.9) | (40.0) | (−8.3) | (−18.7) | (26.3) | (28.0) | (33.2) | (−0.5) |
| **Car bodies** | | | | | | | | | | |
| No. of companies surveyed | 17 | 18 | 15 | 14 | 15 | 13 | 12 | 13 | 18 | 18 |
| Total investment | 482 | 530 | 550 | 643 | 536 | 515 | 715 | 970 | 1,327 | 1,437 |
| (% increase over previous year) | (32.9) | (10.0) | (3.8) | (16.9) | (−16.6) | (−3.9) | (38.8) | (35.7) | (36.8) | (8.3) |

*Source:* JAPIA

orders from an automaker and was therefore able to maintain a reliable and stable business relationship with the parent manufacturers, and an expansion of orders could be expected with the rising demand for automobiles. Another merit of the system was that parts manufacturers could strengthen their new social credibility and status, and, in particular, it became easier for them to obtain financial credit from other suppliers and banks. Thus, loan terms became favourable to the parts manufacturer and a credit guarantee could be given by automakers simply due to the company being a constituent part of the group system of a specific automaker. Payment conditions ascribed by automakers were also stabilized, and terms improved for the parts manufacturer within the group. A parts manufacturer of a group could also secure a cheap and stable supply of raw materials. The ratio of the cost of raw materials (such as glass, plastics, gilt and metal plates and steel) to the cost of the finished goods was high in the industry. A parts manufacturer in a group could place bulk orders for raw materials on an on-going basis and the automaker could guarantee a stable supply of raw materials through its financial power over the suppliers of raw materials.[7] Parts manufacturers would be well informed about automakers' current production schedules, new product developments and technological innovations. They could safely plan investment and personnel recruitment and could attend conferences on technical and managerial matters, as well as exchange personnel and engage in joint investment projects with the automaker.[8]

However, there were some disadvantages in the system, depending on the way it was worked. For example, any imbalance of technology and parts production between companies would become apparent, highlighting disparities in the production methods of the companies. Differences in standards of quality evaluation and product inspection might emerge.[9] It was also possible that agreements between parts manufacturers and automakers could encourage the parts manufacturers to sacrifice their own independence and originality in their approach towards self-management and the development of new products. Another possibility was that an automaker may put too much pressure on a parts manufacturer with regard to lowering unit prices instead of pursuing rationalization, technological guidance and personnel exchanges. In turn, parts manufacturers could end up adopting short-term policies, setting low wages and hiring part-time workers.

In spite of these potential disadvantages, parts manufacturers accepted a multi-tiered structure, based on a vertical division of labour. There was the need to organize a coherent group with a structure able to cope with the requirements of several production stages, ranging from primary parts manufacturers, using high technology and bulk production processes, to tertiary manufacturers, producing miscellaneous parts in small lots. Strong but flexible groups were formed, centering on the development of the most appropriate production scales and methods for each stage.

THE DEVELOPMENT OF TECHNOLOGICAL INNOVATION AND RATIONALIZATION

Japanese automakers started to rationalize management in the second half of the 1950s. This did not involve much investment in new technology, but it did change the system of production. Automakers began to operate final assembly lines, to synchronize production and to promote a vertical division of labour, placing orders with outside contractors, especially for the bulk supply of key components by primary parts manufacturers and labour-intensive products by secondary parts manufacturers.

The adoption of scientific managerial methods enabled manufacturers to introduce a standard pricing system for parts. They used a formula which multiplied the number of working processes and their hourly rates by a variable based on the prices of raw materials. The procedure then was for the automaker to provide the product specifications, for the parts manufacturer to submit price estimates and for negotiations to take place in order to arrive at agreed prices.[10]

During this period, primary parts manufacturers benefited from the rationalized management system without having to invest much in new technology. The 1960s, however, saw a vast amount of investment by automakers in the construction of modern, mass-production facilities and, consequently, the major parts manufacturers also started investing in new technology.

The Development Bank of Japan and the Small and Medium Companies Finance Corporation provided manufacturers with special low-interest loans for their investments in technological innovation under the Machinery Industry Promotion Act of 1956, which was later followed by the Machinery Electronics Act and the Machinery Information Act. Lending rates were 2 to 3 per cent lower than the market rates, although there were some seasonal fluctuations. The

**Table 18** Loans to Automobile Parts Manufacturers, 1956–80

i) Following the Machinery Promotion Act

| Source of loan | Japan Development Bank | | Small & Medium Companies Finance Corporation | | Total | | Interest Rates | | |
|---|---|---|---|---|---|---|---|---|---|
| Year | Amount (¥ million) | No. of companies | Amount (¥ million) | No. of companies | Amount (¥ million) | No. of companies | | JDB | Finance Corp. |
| 1956–1960 | 1,819 | 66 | – | – | 1,819 | 66 | 1956–60 | 6.5% | 6.4%–6.3% |
| 1961 | 1,416 | 32 | 208 | 11 | 1,624 | 43 | 1961–65 | 6.5% | 6.4%–6.3% |
| 1962 | 1,504 | 31 | 269 | 10 | 1,773 | 41 | 1966–70 | 7.5% | 7.4%–7.3% |
| 1963 | 2,193 | 35 | 818 | 32 | 3,011 | 67 | | | |
| 1964 | 3,445 | 38 | 687 | 28 | 4,132 | 66 | | | |
| 1965 | 2,945 | 27 | 344 | 11 | 3,289 | 38 | | | |
| 1966 | 2,640 | 29 | 185 | 6 | 2,825 | 35 | | | |
| 1967 | 4,165 | 34 | 514 | 18 | 4,697 | 52 | | | |
| 1968 | 3,925 | 33 | 462 | 19 | 4,387 | 52 | | | |
| 1969 | 3,405 | 21 | 371 | 15 | 3,776 | 36 | | | |
| 1970 | 3,185 | 22 | 289 | 11 | 3,474 | 33 | | | |

## ii) Following the Machinery Electronics Act

| Source of loan | Japan Development Bank | | Small & Medium Companies Finance Corporation | | Total | | Interest Rates | | |
|---|---|---|---|---|---|---|---|---|---|
| Year | Amount (¥million) | No. of companies | Amount (¥million) | No. of companies | Amount (¥million) | No. of companies | | JDB | Finance Corp. |
| 1971 | 2,770 | 23 | 275 | 6 | 3,045 | 29 | 4/71–10/73 | 7.5% | Almost the |
| 1972 | 2,265 | 20 | 74 | 3 | 2,339 | 23 | 11/73–1/73 | 7.7% | same as for |
| 1973 | 5,990 | 28 | 174 | 4 | 6,164 | 32 | 2/74–9/74 | 8.5% | the JDB |
| 1974 | 3,400 | 21 | 90 | 2 | 3,490 | 23 | 10/74–11/75 | 9.0% | |
| 1975 | 4,230 | 21 | 148 | 5 | 4,378 | 26 | 12/75–5/77 | 8.5% | |
| 1976 | 3,550 | 21 | 143 | 4 | 3,693 | 25 | 6/77–9/77 | 7.8% | |
| 1977 | 5,450 | 23 | 55 | 2 | 5,505 | 25 | 10/77–4/78 | 7.5% | |

## iii) Following the Machinery Information Act

| Source of loan | Japan Development Bank | | Small & Medium Companies Finance Corporation | | Total | | Interest Rates | | |
|---|---|---|---|---|---|---|---|---|---|
| Year | Amount (¥million) | No. of companies | Amount (¥million) | No. of companies | Amount (¥million) | No. of companies | | JDB | Finance Corp. |
| 1978 | 1,930 | 12 | 0 | 0 | 1,930 | 12 | 5/78–5/79 | 7.1% | Almost the |
| 1979 | 1,908 | 12 | 0 | 0 | 1,908 | 12 | 6/79–8/79 | 7.7% | same as for |
| 1980 | 2,207 | 8 | 0 | 0 | 2,207 | 8 | 9/79–4/80 | 8.2% | the JDB |
| | | | | | | | 5/80–10/80 | 9.5% | |
| | | | | | | | 11/80–3/81 | 8.8% | |
| | | | | | | | 4/81–10/81 | 8.4% | |
| | | | | | | | 11/81–12/81 | 8.8% | |

Source: JAPIA

number of machines invested in increased by four times, to over 48,000 units, during a ten-year period from 1955 to 1965. Over the same period, the number of up-to-date machines (less than five years old) increased from 30 to 55 per cent of all machines.[11] The special loans were made mainly to the larger parts manufacturers and played an important role in the development of the leading parts manufacturers. Some independent parts manufacturers were also assisted by these Acts.

At the same time, however, there were thought to be some benefits to a horizontal division of labour,[12] and this is said to have featured in the MITI's reorganization project for the three groups in the automobile industry, which had been included in the Special Industry Promotion Act in preparation for capital liberalization. The project was scrapped since the existing organizations within each automobile manufacturer were very much more in favour of the vertical division of labour.

During the period of assistance by the Machinery Industry Promotion Act, automakers reviewed and reorganized their traditional, group subcontracting system, (especially with primary parts manufacturers). There were inefficiencies in the production system in terms of duplication or fragmentation due to the numerous production processes, including small-lot production within one factory. This was an obstacle to the formation of a coherent production process and mass production lines. At the same time, following the rapid expansion of car production, both the number of production lines and the volume of parts increased. Some parts manufacturers were required to produce batches of one to two million units. Accordingly, improving the production technology of key components in order to lower unit costs and to raise quality standards became the next step to take. The less developed affiliated subcontractors had to be reorganized to permit the growth of the small and medium-sized machine manufacturers.[13] Some primary parts manufacturers began to use their own products to make larger parts and began to sell parts to manufacturers outside the group, while starting to adopt foreign technology. Primary parts manufacturers also strengthened their relationships with their parent automobile manufacturer by adapting their product lines, investment plans and new technology.[14]

The introduction of new technology proved profitable to the parts industry, especially the primary parts manufacturers. They introduced automatic pressing lines, large-scale pressing machines and synchronized processing lines. They also adapted their production lines to handle new raw materials. Press lines for sheet metal-cutting processes were developed in order to cut down on the number of assembly

**Table 19  Reorganization in Parts Manufacturers**

| Name of company | Year of reorganization | Form of reorganization | Participating companies | Objectives of reorganization & changes in products & production system |
|---|---|---|---|---|
| Sunbolt KK | 1963 | Established sales | Mikami Byo, Sannohashi Seisakusho, Kato Neje Seisakusho | Modify product lines and cut costs by expanding production in units following Nissan suggestion. |
| Yamakawa Kogyo | 1963 | Unification of sections to receive orders | Yakamawa Kogyo, Nagata Kogyo, Sugimoto Kinzoku, Suruga Koki | Take advantage of technological strengths of all 4 companies to specialize products. Jointly plan and set up pressing lines. |
| Kato Hatsujo | 1963 | Business tie-up | Ikegami Hatsujo | Undertake specialized production of wider range of products. |
| Aishin Seiki | 1965 | Amalgamation | Aichi Kogyo, Shinkawa Kogyo | Curtail duplicated investment, improve technology and personnel, standardize pedal parts, specialize products of both manufacturers aiming at 40% capital saving. |
| Oi Seisakusho | 1965 | Amalgamation | Kajiyama Kinzoku, Shinkawa Kogyo | Adjust product lines, cut costs by specialization and mass production. |
| Daido Metal | 1965 | Amalgamation | Nagato Metal | Failed to take advantage of technical tie-up. Nagato's management deteriorated under interest rate burden. |
| Saitama Kogyo | 1968 | Establishment of new company | Aishin Seiki, Shatai Kogyo | Aishin: improve parts distribution to Kanto district. Shatai: diversify from truck cabs |
| Koito Seisakusho | 1968 | Business tie-up | Imasen Denki | Curtail duplicated investment, modify competing product lines, undertake joint R&D. Proposals from Imasen. |
| Keeper | 1968 | Amalgamation | Asai Seisakusho | Curtail duplicated investment, modify competing product lines, undertake joint R&D. Prior to amalgamation 25% of Asai's shares were transferred to George Angus Ltd. (UK), Keeper's partner for tie-up. |
| Aishin Seiki | 1968 | Business tie-up | Nihon Clutch | Transfer production of clutches for heavy-duty vehicles to Nihon Clutch, affiliate to Isuzu, Aishin to undertake mass production of passenger vehicles. |
| Atsugi Jidosha Buhin | 1968 | Business tie-up | Tochigi Fuji Sangyo | Remodel drive shaft parts. Mass production to be undertaken by Atsugi, non-mass production items to be made by Tochigi Fuji. |
| Nagoya Rubber | 1968 | Business tie-up | Tokyo Rubber Seisakusho | Improve parts distribution for Toyota to Kanto district. Tokyo Rubber puts idle facilities to use due to stagnated Isuzu production. |
| Toppy Kogyo | 1969 | Business tie-up | Press Kogyo | Remodel production items such as wheels, metal mold and press parts; curtail duplicated investment. |
| Chu Seiki | 1969 | Business tie-up | Yuno Kogyo | Remodel production items, curtail duplicated investment by giving Chuo responsibility for mass production and Yuno responsibility for customized production. |
| Nihon Hatsujo | 1970 | Capital participation | Horikiri Bane, Shin-Dainippon Spring | Specialize in production of items such as sheet springs. Received requests from both Toyota and Hino. |

Source: Shoichiro Sei, *Structure of the Japanese Auto Parts Industry*, Kikai Keizai Kenkyu No. 9. Also articles in Nihon Keizai Shimbun, 1963–1970.

processes. Other new production lines included welding and painting, as well as metal moulding technology.[15] In the latter half of the 1960s, MITI planned to introduce a system utilizing a horizontal division of labour. The association between automakers and parts manufacturers was further strengthened when the two were faced with the need to synchronize production accompanied by the separation of sub-assembly lines. The parts factories took on the characteristics of a fully-integrated factory system.[16]

This technological innovation, which took place in the Japanese automobile industry in the latter half of the 1960s, did not simply involve the modernization of production lines, nor did it manifest itself solely with the automaker, but was part of an innovative wave which swept through the whole industry, affecting everything from the central manufacturers to the small parts manufacturers at the edge of the group. Group integration (see chapter 3) became crucial to the strength of the industry, which was reinforced by capital participation, co-operative organizations, associated business ties, technological exchanges and guidance, all initiated by the automakers.

This strength brought with it the capability to cope with a stream of engineering and management problems associated with the adoption of new technology and to move on to the further innovations in later years in regard to such matters as recall and safety problems, anti-pollution measures and energy-saving conservation measures. It was also the factor that brought about rapid improvements in productivity.

THE SPREAD OF THE JAPANESE STYLE OF RATIONALIZATION AND PROCESS INNOVATION

Group integration let to a series of process innovations in parts production and rationalization spread from primary to secondary and tertiary parts manufacturers. The 'just-in-time' system played a particularly important role in these developments.

The 'just-in-time' system had been introduced by some manufacturers in the 1950s but was not extensively adopted until the late 1960s.[17] The aims during the first half of the 1960s were to step up the speed of production and to create efficient synchronized mass production, based on large-scale investment. However, this was then supplemented to introduce more flexible management systems, particularly management by small groups. In other words, manufacturers began to appraise processes in terms of their efficient use of capital equipment and plant.

The quality in addition to the quantity of capital was taken into account and smaller management units were introduced as a recommendation by QC circles.[18] This type of management system could respond to proposals for improving productivity and quality on the production lines. The 'just-in-time' system, which requires the delivery of a specific number of parts at a specific time, was used extensively. This was often seen as a strategy by the automakers to transfer the problems and costs of storage to the parts manufacturers, in order to clear space in their warehouses by reducing inventory. However, pasts manufacturers were able to avoid storage problems by being flexible in their own organization of production – by varying product mix with low-volume production and using the same machine to produce various types of goods. By thus reducing the time required for re-tooling, shortening the time required for changing moulds, improving operation steps and changing the process layout, they did not need to bear the burden of storage.[19]

The 'just-in-time' system works in relation to the rate of operation made possible by the rationalization of the production lines. Efficiency improvements in the work rate require the maintenance of additional facilities and safety measures in order to prevent plant breakdowns and unforeseen accidents. These requirements can never be fulfilled unless there is positive co-operation and an exchange of ideas from workers on the job site. Workers on the job are encouraged to identify problems where rationalization is called for and to resolve these problems in a way which will spread to secondary and tertiary parts manufacturers.[20] This makes it possible for companies to respond easily to orders and at the same time highlights areas for rationalization. There is a flow of useful information through all levels in the organization. This acts as a voluntary check for defects such as the use of faulty products, wasteful use of time and raw materials and the operation of unsuitable machines in the production process. Accordingly, an improvement in product quality goes hand in hand with increased productivity.

The 'just-in-time' system was not adopted by parts manufacturers all at once. the system had to undergo various alterations, involving many steps, before manufacturers could expect parts makers to deliver specific quantities at specific times. Therefore, in order to adopt the rationalized system, automakers had first to set an example by seeing to their own rationalization, inspire employee participation in choosing the most efficient rate of operation, minimize defects and quantities of stock in transit.

Although there were differences in information and methods among automakers, much progress was made through the QC circle movement during the late 1960s. Primary parts manufacturers also adopted rationalization in the early 1970s, and secondary parts manufacturers in the late 1970s. For example, at Factory M of automaker C, the QC circle movement was active prior to the first oil crisis. The factory took up energy conservation measures in order to improve efficiency during hours of operation and kept stock in transit to a minimum after the oil crisis. The factory adopted the specific-time-delivery system and the frequent delivery system at the job site, which had centered around the primary parts manufacturers since 1978. All this reduced stocks among 36 companies to one-fifth over a period of three years.

Several common practices were found not only in this industrial grouping but in many other companies, in relation to the Japanese style of rationalization, as follows:

1 Process design and layout of production lines could be changed at any time, in accordance with the production pattern. In most cases, the alteration was carried out by workers on the job and not by specialists.
2 Production lines equipped with automatic stoppage devices and detector devices, alerting workers to defective operations, were extensively used. Devices indicating the state of an operation on the production line were also introduced by request. Workers on the job contributed greatly to the installation and improvement in the operation of these devices.
3 Machine tools were remodelled and relocated according to changes in the design of production lines. Alternative ways were explored to increase the number of machines per worker and to eliminate the superfluous movement of workers. Machinery compatible with the operation of small process lines was introduced, as suggested by workers.
4 Foremen did not need to make day-to-day checks on individual operations and instead could give instructions during inspections and follow-up procedures only when a defective operation or stoppage occured. They were therefore able to attend to fundamental policies in connection with process innovation.
5 In response to small-lot orders in a multi-product system, there were many ways to ensure flexibility in the production process (such as speeding up the die changes in pressing machines).

6 Machine tools, robots, dies were often designed by the workers themselves and produced in their own factories. Machines produced elsewhere were remodelled and parts obtained from outside were assembled within the factory. This was because ordinary machine manufacturers sometimes found it difficult to supply products which met the requirements of numerous and complicated automobile parts fully. As a result, the status of the engineering section was heightened within the factory.

7 In many factories the concept of Japanese-style rationalization had taken root and with advanced technological innovation in production lines many had a fully operational R & D section with testing machines. Companies which aimed at product innovation in production technology (including the use of new raw materials and energy conservation equipment) became much more prominent. They also filed several patents on technological innovations.

At this time, when automakers were concentrating on rationalization, some parts manufacturers adopted even higher levels of rationalization with even more advanced technological innovations than the automakers.

The application of new technology in the automobile industry in the late 1960s took place in the areas of system, safety measures, anti-pollution measures and energy conservation measures. The search for solutions to these problems drove superior parts manufacturers into researching into new technology. Examples of these were: air-cleaner manufacturer T's catalytic converters to meet pollution regulations; company S which set up a maintenance-free system in the form of the permanent joint STRUT method for shock absorbers on two box FF vehicles which had been developed by automaker T; manufacturer T was once severely attacked by public opinion for producing defective cars. Others are: company K, which developed the expertise for original gear manufacturing technology in response to a new market for agricultural machinery, at a time when orders from the parent automaker fell drastically as a result of the oil crisis; meanwhile company X created a unique new technology for lubricant products, and so successfully that it re-exported its patent and expertise to a foreign manufacturer which had previously exported the original technology to the company.

The examples of successful parts manufacturers illustrate that while process technology innovation is created under the Japanese way of rationalization, gateways to developments in product innovation seem to be opening up in the industry. The leading parts manufacturers play an important role in shaping the future of Japanese automobile technology.

CONCLUSION

The parts industry played a crucial role in the development of the Japanese automobile industry, as it formed a vertical division-of-labour structure, thereby establishing a mass production system that ensured flexibility in production and benefited automakers in production costs. Independent parts makers with specialized techniques also played a role in the growth of the parts industry. They had business relations with no particular manufacturers but were closely linked with automakers in the adoption of the 'just-in-time' system and technological developments.

This relationship ensured the response of parts makers to demands by automakers for the reduction of costs and improvements of technical standards. The relations with subcontractors changed after the late 1960s in favour of greater rationalization and more technological innovation. Factors, such as the progress of automobile and parts production technology, alterations in product design and the emergence of new problems, in regard to safety, pollution and saving energy, indicated the need for a reorganization and a review of traditional group affiliation and subcontract relations. The 'just-in-time' system emerged from the reorganization, on the basis of which Japanese-style process technology was born. The process innovation started with QC circle activities and the 'just-in-time' system and was most successful with medium-sized primary parts makers. This is because technological developments and process innovations often go hand in hand and primary parts makers can challenge technology in special or original fields. Automakers make use of their relations with these parts makers in order to prepare themselves for technological innovation. Progress in product innovation greatly affects the course of these relations which adapt as product innovation proceeds. Problems lie with the third-tier parts makers who are less adaptable to change. Small producers, making a part of an item of mass production or specializing in small-lot production can become vulnerable due to the lack of special techniques or skills for multi-kind/small-lot production.

The group relations between automakers and parts makers played a major role in solving new technological problems and promoting rationalization. The partnership between automakers and parts makers brought about high standards of quality and high productivity. This served to break down the rigidity of mass production systems – the tendency to keep too many products in storage and difficulties in altering facilities and process design – as well as to delay the onset of diseconomies of scale. It destroyed the myth of the trade-off between cost and quality in mass-production by making good use of comparatively small production facilities.

A problem lies in the future relations between automakers and parts makers in the light of automobile technological innovation. This depends on how well the relationship will cope with new trends such as material changes, a reduction in the number of parts and the use of robots and flexible robots. The following changes in the automaker–parts maker relationship are predicted with the progress of future technological innovations: firstly, changes in orders from automakers will include a reduction in the number of separate parts assembled by automakers, although this may be offset by an increase in the number of parts designed to deal with pollution and to make cars safer and easier to drive. Some materials producers will take up parts machining, working, for instance, with high-polymer plastics and ceramics. Automakers will shift from a conventional ordering system to one which promotes technical changes and a reduction in the number of parts, thereby weeding out the second and third single-item parts makers.

There are good prospects, however, for parts makers who can undertake multi-kind/small-lot production with a short lead time and utilize technology that can meet the product-planning needs of automakers. Whether or not automakers will be able to maintain affiliated relations with parts makers depends on the pace of technological product innovation. It also depends on whether or not Japanese-style rationalization, supporting affiliated relations, will be able to continue to respond in accordance to a new pattern of technological product innovation. Furthermore, it will depend on whether or not the economy-of-scale merit will decrease in the light of future technological product innovations, and whether or not changes will be caused in the form of process division in automobile production processes. Process innovation and the 'just-in-time' system were possible only due to the existence of a workforce that could make good use of production facilities as product innovation took place. Automation focused on hardware and this called for a skilled workforce that accepted rationalization. At present, innovation owes more to collective ability than individual genius. Any product innovation requires a flow of process innovations.

Automakers and parts makers have to monitor those in charge of process technology, and thereby make their relationship more fruitful. Mass production is no longer justifiable simply on the basis of the economics of scale and automobile parts makers, who are confronted with substantial changes and are at the mercy of the waves of radical technological innovation, obviously have the urgent task of innovating process technology through research and development. Parts makers will then be able to remain with the automakers, whether they are affiliated to a particular automaker group or not.

Parts makers helped to make the Japanese automobile industry competitive and responsive to technological innovation and have been confronted with new problems of rationalization accompanied by a rapid hike in the value of the yen to the dollar since 1985 and at a time of increasing internationalization. There is an important difference between parts makers with their own expertise, on the one hand, and, on the other, subcontractors who need detailed design drawings from automakers. Many subcontractors are single-item mass producers, using routine, large-lot machines; they show little technical originality. This is the reason such parts makers cannot meet the requirements of severe competition in technological development; they will suffer with a rise in labour costs, and will receive fewer orders due to the expansion of overseas production; both of these factors are caused by the rise in the value of the yen to the dollar. However, parts makers who can undertake and afford technological developments can maintain their competitiveness and take part in product planning by automakers from an early stage. At present, competition among automakers calls for more product planning and a shorter development cycle. Joint developments by automakers and parts makers are essential. In these circumstances, orders to parts makers have increased, even though the appreciation of the yen led to severe rationalization and more overseas production. Most parts makers have evolved in this way. Automakers do not need to supervise these parts makers as they can guarantee the quality of their products.

The appreciation of the yen after 1985 stimulated Japanese automakers to promote their overseas production in the USA, Europe and Asia, but parts makers also looked to operating abroad, especially in North America. By 1988 more than 180 small and medium-sized parts makers were operating abroad. Very few of them were asked to do this by automakers and many undertook joint ventures with local businesses or were given technical licences from local manufacturers. Once based in a foreign country, they can no longer depend on orders from a particular manufacturer and many of them have several customers, thus breaking looses from traditional affiliations. Japanese automakers are also increasing the import of parts, especially from the USA, thanks partly to the favourable dollar. In 1987, the value of imported parts from the USA was about US$5 billion. By 1992 this figure had risen to about US$9 billion. Pressure from the USA should boost this trade further. The need for increased Japanese imports of American parts was a major item on President Bush's agenda in his talks in Tokyo with Prime Minister Kiichi Miyazawa in January 1992.

It is worth noting that American and European automakers have set about affiliating and organizing parts makers since the 1980s. For instance, General Motors has set up a GM–Japan association, comprising 87 companies in Japan and plans to select highly-skilled parts makers and conclude long-term contracts with parts makers in Japan and America. Ford and Chrysler are also selecting parts suppliers, evaluating their technical standards and setting up associated organizations. European automakers are doing much the same thing. In short, along with the internationalization of the Japanese automobile parts makers, the parts procurement system in Japan is spreading to the USA and European countries.

**Table 20** Rationalization by Major Parts Manufacturers in the 1970s

| Name of company | Product | Period and Motive for Rationalization | Effects of Rationalization |
|---|---|---|---|
| Nihon Hatsujo (Independent) | Springs, seats | 1977: Separation of assembly from machining processes in the conveyor system and elimination of stock loss due to conveyor shift. | Removed 17 conveyor lines and installed workbenches of several-person groups to integrate machining and assembly processes. Saved time and man-power with the manual-feed method. Only 85% of total man-power required for the same output for 4 months, average stock days needed for production reduced from 8 to 3 and 34% of total plant space saved. |
| Masuda Seisakusho (Honda group) | Wheels, brackets | 1974: Overall review of welding and pressing processes. Implementation of Honda's 'Rationalization Project A'. | Raised press automation rate from 33% to 95% in 5 years by introducing press robots. Radically changed plant layout, manufactured automatic welders in-house and increased the use of low-cost coils instead of plates from 38% to 80%. Value added per employee increased from ¥270,000 per month in 1974 to ¥405,000 in 1977 and ¥550,000 in 1979. Break-even point reduced from 97% to 85% and to 80% in 1979. |
| Kanto Seiki (Nissan group) | Speedometers, fuel gauges, other meters | 1972–8: Review of the conventional conveyor-line production system. | Reduced the rate of defects to less than 1 in 10 by introducing: a 3-speed production method, automated machines for fitting complex parts of speed sensor, and 3-man modular assembly method for dial-mounting process. Used conveyor lines for fitting to dashboard in final process. Increased output by 1.7 times. |

| Name of company | Product | Period and Motive for Rationalization | Effects of Rationalization |
|---|---|---|---|
| Tokai Rika Denki (Toyota group) | Switches, locks, seat belts, ornaments | 1975: Radical improvement of management organization to eliminate delivery delays to users and inefficient job-site practices. Stock losses and inefficient management of facilities and personnel, which had gone unnoticed amidst elaborate production plans in the time of high economic growth, became apparent after the oil crisis. | Used conventional production plan secondarily and introduced kanban method with aid of Toyota staff to set up system for levelled production of items fed from previous process. Eliminated raw material, parts and product stocks. Minimized the amount of raw materials and parts on the production line. Had outside manufacturers supply parts just when needed. Reduced stock period of products and half-finished products form about 36 days in 1974 to 5.8 days in 1978. Reduced set-up time for 2,500 ton die-cast machine from 90 min in May to 1 min 15 seconds in Sep 1976. Increased suggestions from employees from 1,000 in 1975 to 15,000 in 1977. Reorganization of lines and reduction of stock increased usable space in plant by 40%. |
| Tsuda Kogyo (Toyota group) | Brakes, axle parts, electrical parts such as air-conditioners and heaters | 1973–4: Entry into the Toyota group in 1971 when a former Toyota executive assumed the presidency. Introduction of the self-education and improvement suggestion system to escape management slump. | Transferred 20 chiefs from their managerial posts to an 'improvement group' to study Toyota's production method. Restored them to former posts and put 20 group leaders in improvement group. Promoted QC circle activities in 1974 to encourage participation by employees. 35,000 suggestions were made in 1977 (37 per person, outnumbering Toyota's 10.3); this figure increased by 70% in 1978. Reduced costs by ¥139 million in 1977 and ¥200 million in 1978. |
| Toyo Radiator Nagoya Seisakusho (Toyota group) | Radiators | 1976: Reduction of cost, enhancement of response capability to customer needs, and promotion of effective use of limited plant area by introduction of kanban method to regulate each process instead of conventional large-lot production control. | Introduced kanban method into press process to subdivide the number of lots for pressed parts and reduce set-up time. Cut set-up time from 50 min to 10 min by standardizing die preparation and devising clamps for dies. Also brought kanban method into assembly line to reduce malfunction rate of machines from 600 to 40 hrs a month through intensive maintenance control. Delegated small-lot production to small groups of workers to establish responsibility system. Reduced finished product stock from a week to a day and a half; reduced half-finished product stock by 70%; reduced no. of processes by 20%. |

**Table 20**  continued

| Name of company | Product | Period and Motive for Rationalization | Effects of Rationalization |
|---|---|---|---|
| Daido Metal Kogyo (Independent) | Searing metal | 1978: Enhancement of the utility ratio of facilities requiring 40,00 to 50,00 set-ups to produce more than 30,000 items from 50% to 80% and reduction of administration division costs. | Set medium-range rationalization goals including a renewal of manufacturing facilities; replaced 50 production lines in 6 plants with up-to-date facilities. Introduced state-of-the-art lines and promoted reduction of set-up time and malfunction rate for high-speed, labour-saving performance to enhance production efficiency. Increased sales per employee from ¥750,000 to ¥1,000,000 per month in 1980 and raised the effective operation ratio of facilities to 80%. |
| Hiruta Kogyo (Mitsubishi group) | Press parts, including brakes, clutches and suspensions | 1975: Repeatedly rationalized since 1965 when it moved its base to Soja Industrial Park with 23 parts makers of the Mitsubishi Mizushima Seisakusho group. Intensified rationalization efforts following good results at Mizushima Seisakusho and introduced a multi-cycle delivery system (a kind of kanban method) after the oil crisis. | When introducing kanban method invited improvement suggestions from employees at each process of the production lines to reduce half-finished product stock and synchronize work processes. Shortened press-line conveyor and quickened press operation. New triple-speed pace revealed problems in press machine operation and personnel distribution. Provided automatic drilling machine and welder to enable one workman to operate several machines concurrently and to enable operation by female workers. The special machine development crew succeeded in in-house production of presses, lathes and other devices following improvement suggestions. Increased productivity by 5 times and reduced half-finished product stock from 20 days to 3 days in 13 years. |
| Akebono Brake Kogyo (Independent) | Brake parts | 1975: Adapting the management to a period of low economic growth after the oil crisis. Reduction of stock of 500 items to an average of 1.3 months' worth per sales branch office; alteration of production system; elimination of losses. | Reduced stock from 1.3 months to 0.2 months in one year by analysing market. Established a multi–kind small-lot production system to ship products weekly, and combined mixed line production with kanban method introduced in 1977 to reduce machine trouble time and press set-up time. Line-down time per month was cut down to 500 hours. Disk brake assembly lines were reduced from 20 to 9, and workers from 150 to 130, producing 300,000 to 350,000 pcs. per month. Net profit ratio increased from 0.9% to over 1 % in two years. |

| Name of company | Product | Period and Motive for Rationalization | Effects of Rationalization |
|---|---|---|---|
| Niles Parts (Nissan group) | Switches, car cigarette lighters, car clocks etc. | 1976: Replacement of the conventional conveyor assembly method by the rationalized NAP (Niles Action Plate) method to respond to rapidly changing, diversified orders classified by model from automakers. | Introduced a group production method to eliminate losses from arrangement of personnel and parts in the conveyor method, and to prevent worker morale from slumping due to imposed work processes. Then reduced number of workers at assembly processes from 9 to 4; then 4 to 2, and finally established one-man assembly. The one-man assembly system is suited to many of Niles' products such as illumination units and clocks, although not to those requiring a great number of parts and processes, or those which are mass-produced. Productivity in the case of illumination units improved by 94%. The small-lot/few workers production system, especially one-man assembly, is of great merit at Niles where between 300 and 400 different items are manufactured, though some of these, including combination switches, are still manufactured in the group production method. Reduced set-up times for resin moulds and press. Productivity at Itake plant improved by 40% in 1978. Increased the ordinary income ratio from 1% before rationalization to 3–4% in 1978. |
| Hongo Seisakusho (Honda group) | Pressed and welded parts | 1974: Rationalization by automating manufacturing facilities with in-house production of machines based on Honda's 'Project A'. | Made up for shortage of skilled workers with young workforce (average age: 26.7), and promoted in-house production of automatic machines (e.g. a table-top multi-spot welder). Received instruction for improving production control and material yield from Honda at the start of 'Project A' and became a good example. Monthly value-added output per person increased from ¥328,000 to ¥525,000; break-even point reduced from 88.1% to 83.9% in three years. |

*Source*: Nikkei Sangyo Newspaper (May 1978 – March 1979) and personal interviews.

# CHAPTER 5

# *The Sales and Distribution System*

INTRODUCTION

The distribution and sales systems for automobiles in Japan developed under a franchise system, with the manufacturer/dealer contract as the base. However, there is a sharp contrast between the USA and Japan in this field, especially with regard to the dealers' mode of selling. The distribution and sales methods in Japan are rather similar to those now in use in Europe, especially Germany. These contrasts can be attributed to differences in the historical backgrounds of the automobile markets, car users, distribution channels and sales environments. Because of both the differences in the distribution and selling systems of both countries, it is difficult to say which is the superior system.

The US type of franchise system is more efficient as a sales and distribution mechanism and more adaptable to market changes. However, there are weaknesses; for example, there is a lack of control over the manufacturers' marketing policies and customer services. In the Japanese system, manufacturers and dealers are much more closely related, leading to a speedier feedback of sales information and more extensive consumer control and services. However, there is a strong dependence on door-to-door sales and therefore higher salesmen expenses for the dealers, which push up their overhead costs.

The Japanese system worked well during the rapid expansion of the domestic car market. As the market matured, bringing about complicated changes in the demand for cars, the uniformity and rigidity of management caused a number of problems. Under the changing situation of a saturated market and the even more difficult changing demand structure, innovation on the part of dealers was called for in order to improve their business style and managerial practices. The information revolution, changes in design and development of automobiles and in methods of production have all had a big impact on the automobile distribution system.

What about the historical development of the distribution system in Japan, and what of its future? It is necessary to clarify how such differences between the automobile distribution and sales systems in

Japan and the USA evolved, and also to note the changes that have taken place in the system in Japan in response to the rapid expansion of the Japanese domestic automobile market, changes in manufacturing systems and the advent of the information age.

THE HISTORY OF THE SYSTEM

Automobile marketing in Japan came into its own after 1955, with the mass production of passenger cars. This was brought about by the manufacturers, though the sales and distribution arrangements of the prewar and immediate postwar periods did influence developments. The nature of automobile marketing in Japan, prior to the 1950s, was determined by the particular nature of the nation's automobile market and production system. Before World War II, American automakers dominated the Japanese market for passenger cars. Customers were the wealthy and the aristocracy, and also taxi-cab businesses. This foreign domination of the market was made possible because Japanese automobile manufacturers were not mass producers. Mass production calls for a wide range of production techniques, such as material and engine production, die casting, stamping and so on. There was no such consolidated technological development in Japan at that time, and since Japan's military government required and fostered the mass production only of trucks, this kind of development for passenger cars was not possible.[1]

Automobile marketing techniques, the franchise system and dealer support arrangements were introduced into Japan by General Motors and Ford when they began operating there in the 1920s. Once introduced they underwent certain modifications, in accordance with the nature of the market. After the 1936 Motor Vehicle Manufacture Law, which was designed to protect domestic manufacturers and shut out foreign competition, Toyota and Nissan adopted and modified these practices. Nissan led the way with the production of Datsun, the first mass-produced compact car, and set up a franchise system under the Nissan Motor Sales Company, in which one dealership was located in each prefecture. This was the beginning of the end of the dealer-led agent system.

The most notable marketing strategist in Japan at the time was Shotaro Kamiya. He had served as sales manager for Japan GM but resigned to take up the same position with Toyota Motors at the request of the company's founder, Kiichiro Toyoda.[2] Although he had a good grasp of GM's marketing techniques, he felt that the contractual nature of the relationship between manufacturer and dealer in the American franchise system was not appropriate to the Japanese market.[3] GM's franchise agreement required dealers to observe and comply with conditions relating to sales volume, method of sales, payment terms, and so on strictly. Failure to follow the terms of agreement led to the immediate cancellation of the franchise. This hardly made for good manufacturer-dealer relations and, in addition, failed to take in account the nature of traditional business practices in Japan.

It was Kamiya's task to build a sales network for Toyota trucks at a time when the firm was in its infancy and product quality was unstable. His years with GM had enabled him to become acquainted with Japanese Chevolet dealers; he was aware of their dissatisfaction and saw them as potential dealers for Japanese domestic cars. He persuaded them to become exclusive Toyota dealers and set up a dealer network.[4] He had planned to modify the GM franchise system by promoting much closer links between manufacturer and dealer and thus improving the relationship between the two.[5]

Wartime restrictions and the difficulties of the immediate postwar period made it impossible for Kamiya to realize his plans until after 1950, when Toyota Motor Sales (TMS) was separated from Toyota Motors; this was at a time of crisis brought on by recession and by a long strike in 1950. It was on the recommendation of a banking group that TMS was made into a sales finance company along US lines. From the start, however, Toyota viewed TMS not simply as a sales financing organization but as an instrument for the direction and development of its marketing system. In this way, the GM concept of market promotion was made to suit the Japanese context, just as Kamiya had planned before the war.[6]

Kamiya had given thought to the relationship between the manufacturer and regional sources of finance, emphasizing group coherence, but regional funds were not always adequate or forthcoming. TMS therefore supplied the money necessary to set up one dealer per prefecture.[7]

TMS adopted GM methods of financial management, credit management and inventory management and standardized accounting procedures for dealers. It later adopted GM's information system which required dealers to submit reports on the volume and terms of sales every ten days.[8] This resulted in TMS switching form a production-oriented policy (of selling as many cars as were produced) to a marketing-oriented policy (for the production of as many cars as could be sold).

Sales forecasting and planning were co-ordinated with production and project planning involving Toyota Motors, TMS and the dealers.[9] The introduction of these marketing techniques evolved as a result of the active leadership and initiative of TMS and reflected goals set by Toyota Motors. The system strengthened the corporate ties between manufacturer and dealer and provided a basis for the manufacturer's control over the dealer.

TMS also began to provide instalment credit facilities as part of its marketing strategy, partly due to inadequate facilities in Japan. The social prestige of distributors was traditionally rather low and banks were not inclined to lend them money. On the manufacturer's side, capital shortages meant that there was no alternative but to go to banks for financing. From the beginning banks played a prominent role in providing funds to manufacturers, who, in turn, made the direct sales financing of dealers possible.[10] TMS became active in both wholesale and retail financing, establishing an instalment sales system and, on the basis of its financial credibility, endorsing buyers' notes.[11]

Thus, TMS took on both distribution and sales finance. Marketing now meant dealer management, the operation of a franchise system and sales financing. The TMS scheme had considerable influence on the marketing plans of other manufacturers. Mitsubishi Motors and Daihatsu Motors, for example, fashioned their systems on the TMS model. Exceptions to this were Nissan Motors and later, Honda Motors, a relative newcomer, who set up a sales system quite different to those of other companies.

Nissan discontinued the operation of its Motor Sales Company after the war and began selling directly to dealers.[12] Before the war, Nissan dealers had been working for Ford so the franchise structure and stress on an exclusive franchise agreement of the Ford system were a considerable influence on Nissan's marketing. Another factor was the dissolution of Nissan's main holding company, as part of the occupation policy of breaking up 'Zaibatsu', which led to many changes in top management personnel. New executives saw direct manufacturer control over dealers as desirable, and the result was a system whereby Nissan exercised extensive control over the dealers, investing directly in them and overseeing their sales financing. Into the 1960s, Nissan was technology-oriented. Sales presented no serious problems as the market for passenger cars grew and new lines were introduced, and there was no need to set up a sales finance company. However, the acquisition of Prince Motors in 1966[13] and the rapid growth of car exports at about the same time caused Nissan to modify its marketing system, hence the Nissan Credit Company for consumers.

Japanese automobile manufacturers differed in regard to whether they distributed their products through motor sales companies or not. Most of them, however, sold cars directly to dealers, one per prefecture set up by each manufacturer. The stress was on group uniformity and close relations between manufacturer and dealer, bolstered by investment and sales financing on the part of the manufacturer. This, it should be said, was at the expense of the dealer's independence.

Honda Motors, on the other hand, set up regional offices and through them, special sales agents.[14] Honda began after the war as a manufacturer of motor cycles. It channelled its funds almost exclusively into equipment and technological development and did little to invest in a sales network. It organized a nationwide network of bicycle shops to sell its motor cycles and used them as bases for developing sales agents. These agents, such as they were, operated from the bicycle shops or, in some cases, farm equipment shops, There were many agents in each prefecture and no special territories or franchises. Agents operated freely; Honda imposed no sales quotas, although it held agents accountable for the payments of the cycles they had ordered. Honda also set up a nationwide network of service centres for the repair and maintenance of its motor cycles.[15] This relieved agents of the need to invest in such services and left them free to concentrate on sales. This system emphasized the agent's independence rather than financial obligation on Honda's part. It put stress on the ability of the individual agent and resembled American dealer policy. After Honda began automobile production, many agents became car dealers with the help of local funding. Honda's policy, however, did not change until the mid 1970s. Then, on account of their expanding passenger-car line, Honda changed their marketing arrangement and set up three marketing channels with large-scale dealers (similar to those of Toyota and Nissan).

In 1982, the Toyota Motor Sales Company combined with the Toyota Motor Company in order to benefit from concentration, as part of their worldwide strategy. It was not necessary to continue with the two organizations once the financial situation and market context had changed so much: the capital market in Japan had loosened up and a more mature market created high competition for new products. TMS had done its job and its functions and marketing philosophy were passed on to the new organization.[16] Following this, Mitsubishi and Daihatsu also consolidated their Motor Sales organizations.

Thus, marketing by Japanese automobile manufacturers differed in respect to organization and management, but they were characterized by a collective outlook based on a dealer network. They differed from systems where the manufacturer was dominant and where the exclusive, contractual nature of the relationship was stressed. In Japan, there is a reciprocal relationship between manufacturers and dealers and a marketing system which is based on co-operation and mutual trust.

SYSTEMS IN JAPAN AND THE USA

In the USA, Japan and even Europe the relationship between the automobile manufacturers and dealers is conducted through a franchise contract. The dealer is required to integrate with the manufacturer's marketing plan, but, at the same time, is expected to exercise managerial autonomy. Therefore, the dealer who has entered into a franchise contract is required to follow the manufacturer's marketing policy faithfully, in terms of functioning as a selling agent for the manufacturer, while also being required to act as an independent selling organization. Although the basic features of the franchise system itself are the same in both countries, there are certain differences between the USA and Japan. Although the franchise system was brought in from the USA, it was adapted to suit the individual conditions in Japan.

Thus, in Japan, the relationship between automobile manufacturers and dealers is stable and rarely does a dealer move from one group to another. This is not because the dealer is bound by an exclusive contract, but because the dealer values long-term profit and his common interest with a particular manufacturer.

In the USA, there is a king of dealers' metabolism and the dealer is free to change from one group to another. This, however, is because American dealers are in business for a short-term or quick profit. It is clear from NADA (the USA's National Automobile Dealers' Association) statistics that the number and frequency of changes among dealers is very high. In the USA, too, automobile manufacturers seek to encourage dealers to adopt their marketing policies, and to organize them, but it is taken for granted that the dealers may move from one group to another.

In Japan, the ties between an automobile manufacturer and its dealers are very close: the association is as much one of trust as of contract.

**Table 21**   Automobile Dealers in Japan and the USA in 1991

|  | Japan* | USA |
|---|---|---|
| Number of dealers | 1,844 | 24,000 |
| Number of sales bases | 17,100 | 24,000 |
| Average no. of employees per dealer** | 1677 | 37 |
| Average no. of new cars sold per dealer in 1991 | 4,350 | 520 |
| Total average sales per dealer in 1991 | ¥10.89 billion | $12,28 million*** |

*Source*: NADA and JADA statistics, 1992.
\*      Figures for Japan are for JADA-affiliated passenger car dealers only, mainly those selling cars over 1000 cc.
\*\*     Includes all employees: office staff, sales staff, mechanics etc.
\*\*\*    Equivalent to about ¥1.74 billion in 1991.

For example, dealers would agree to carry a larger stock of cars at a manufacturer's request during a sales promotion campaign. Also, if a dealer is not doing so well and is unable to move excess stock, manufacturers may offer loans or special payment terms to help the dealer. Support to dealers is sometimes in the form of incentives to promote sales, dealer investment by the manufacturer, and also the interchange of executives, or seconding sales personnel to dealers. As a result, in Japan it is rare for dealers to change from one group to another, except for mini-dealers, who account for about 20 per cent of total domestic sales volume.

There is very little difference between the USA and Japan with regard to franchise agreements on ordering, delivery, fixing price, the number of cars to be accepted, mark-up margin, terms of payment, warranty and cancelling contracts; but there is a difference between the USA and Japan in terms of the rigidity and flexibility of performance of the agreement. This difference is a reflection of whether the relationship is limited to a strictly business one or is in the nature of a partnership.[2]

Besides differences in the practical operating of the franchise system, there are differences in the business methods of the dealers and methods of selling. Firstly, there is a large difference in the business scale of a dealer, as well as the number of dealers. The business scale of dealers in Japan is several times larger than that of dealers in the USA, but the actual number of dealers is only about one in Japan to every thirteen in the USA. The number of dealers is exclusive of the 'mini-dealers' which, when taken into account, decrease the difference in the number of dealers belonging to each manufacturer. As shown in Table 21, in Japan in 1991 the number of employees per dealer was 1677 as compared with 37 in the USA and the number of new cars sold per dealer was 4,350 in Japan compared with 520 in the USA.

It is worth noting that the average Japanese dealer has 9 stores (selling bases), though the number of selling bases for the total market volume is roughly the same in Japan as in the USA. The number of new cars sold per year and the annual sales per selling base in Japan and the USA are very similar.

The number of personnel per dealer shows that the ratio of salesmen is still larger in Japan. Judging from the comparison of dealers by a simple average index, it can be assumed that a US dealer is roughly equivalent to one selling base of a Japanese dealer. Certainly, US dealers are far smaller in business scale than their Japanese counterparts. However, since the USA is so large, with a variety of market environments, the dealers there engage in various forms of business and vary in size from major dealers in the big cities to sub-dealers in the country. There is a considerable size difference between large dealers and medium to small dealers. Dealers with close to the average annual sales of 520 units are outnumbered by large dealers (several hundreds of whom sell up to 1,000 units) and by small dealers (with less than 300 units and sometime even only about 100 units).[17]

In sharp contrast, however, in order to benefit dealers, in Japan a one prefecture–one territory system is adopted and dealers vary less in scale and less in the range of products that are sold. Most dealer sales are close to the national average. In other words, dealers in Japan are mostly large enterprises and rather uniform in scale.[18]

There are some manufacturers using an 'occupational tie-up system' – sales that deal mainly in motor cycles and subcompact cars.

Japanese dealers generally operate on a large scale because they not only distribute cars but also service, act as insurance agents, sell car appliances and used cars and even engage in the car loan business. The large number of salesmen is due to a high dependence on door-to-door sales. In Japan, door-to-door sales account for a large proportion of sales, while in the USA, over-the-counter sales performed by fewer salesmen account for the bulk of sales. Personnel costs are high in the USA and door-to-door sales have been less popular because of the sparseness of the population and the ban on door-to-door sales in some states. The mode of selling has been to negotiate with customers who come to look at cars in the show room and/or are taken for a test drive. Customers visit the dealers of various manufacturers before deciding to buy.

In Japan, although customers visit the dealer's show room, most of them depend on a personal relationship with the salesman and it is taken for granted that various after-sale services and fixing the price of the trade-in will be taken care of by the salesman.

These days, in Japan, most dealers also undertake repair and servicing and are generally closely related to repair and/or maintenance shops. The insurance companies, for which the dealer is an agent, are selected and dealers are highly dependent upon the services rendered by such insurance companies. The salesman is highly trusted by the customer and takes care of car registration, automobile inspection, insurance, accident settlement, as well as repair and maintenance services, which are rather troublesome for the ordinary customer.

Thus, in Japan, the automobile is sold not just as an automobile but as a complete package, including all sorts of services for the car user.[19] However, dealers have realized that door-to-door sales are not efficient in large cities and are starting to place an emphasis on over-the-counter selling. After the purchase contract is concluded, the salesmen keep in touch with their customers, even contacting them privately to ask about their opinions or complaints.

Differences between the American and Japanese sales systems extend as far as the pay system. While in the USA a salesman receives a commission per car sold, the Japanese salesman receives a basic fixed salary (subject to length of service) and a percentage of commission on every car sold. Thus, while there are salesmen in the USA who may earn more than the president of a dealership, that is seldom the case in Japan. In Japan, salesmen work in teams; able senior salesmen support and give advice to junior salesmen. The fact that the proportion of the fixed salary to the total is high is perhaps questionable when salesmen have different abilities in selling cars, but this point is resolved by promoting able salesmen within the enterprise. The range of tasks the salesman has to do points to the importance of team work. In Japan, the image of salesmen is still rather low and the dismissal rate higher than that of employees in manufacturing trades. Most o those who quit change to some other trade; rarely do they move to a dealer of a different automobile manufacturer. This is because customer trust is lost if salesmen change to another dealer.

It is recognised that in order to treat salesmen as professionals, rates of commission should be increased. But when the number of jobs of a salesman is taken into account, importance is inevitably attached to the basic salary. Until the mid-1960s (when the car sales system had not yet been established) salesmen worked on a commission system, but this has given way to the present personal sales approach in which great importance is attached to the various customer services which have become part of the job of selling cars.

CUSTOMER SERVICES

The Japanese automobile distribution and sales system has developed in terms of a 'trustee' context. Its problems emerged as the market changed from one of high-growth to one of saturation. Since the late 1970s, more emphasis has been placed on consumer services from both manufacturers and dealers, including an extensive quality warranty. Japanese dealers have always worked under the guidance of automobile manufacturers not only for the sale of new cars but also for after-sale service, the determination of trade-in prices for used cars, the registration of new cars, the procedures for compulsory periodical car inspections, arrangements for car inspections, settlement of car accidents and troubles; even repair and maintenance are all offered as a package service. Accordingly, the contact between salesmen and their clients is very close and the salesman, even after reselling a car, engages in extensive follow-up procedures with the owners, being alert to the user's needs and complaints. The car owner, on the other hand, entrusts a worthy salesman with almost everything concerning his car. A car salesman in Japan is a sort of consultant.

User services are the responsibility of the dealer, aided by the manufacturer's service manual. Manufacturers make every effort to provide a quick supply of repair parts and maintenance servicing.

This powerful guidance and support rendered by the automobile manufacturer is closely linked to a positive approach to quality warranty. In Japan, car recall was a controversial matter when in 1967 the Highway Safety Act was passed in the USA. The administration's response to the issue was very quick and prompted an immediate response from the automobile manufacturers, which led to a marked improvement in car quality as well as maintenance. This is largely due to the insight of Japanese automobile manufacturers: improvement of car quality and maintenance service was the strongest weapon for establishing a good reputation for Japanese cars in other countries. As the Japanese automobile industry was quite competitive, importance was also given to after-service functions at the dealer stage.[20]

Since the 1980s, the majority of dealers have had their own comprehensive servicing plants and have established a system for providing a quick and complete response to all kinds of demands in every field of car servicing. Although the total share of repair and service work undertaken by dealers is only a little over 15 per cent of the total, the establishment of a service network, through ties with designated repair shops, has made it possible to give all-round and speedy service to the customer. Another notable point is the effort being made to train more car mechanics and to qualify them to comply with the car inspection system, which is very severe.[21] The establishment of an integrated maintenance and after-sale servicing system has come about through the well-organized tie-ups between manufacturers and dealers. Dealers also attach importance to maintenance and after-sale servicing of imported cars. Sales of imported cars, especially those from Germany, have been increasing steadily. BMW (with an incorporated distributor in Japan) and Yanase (the sole agency for Mercedes Benz and GM cars) have attached particular importance to maintenance and after-sale servicing with good results. This has contributed much to raising the brand image of imported cars. In the same fashion as Japanese car dealers, they are offering a package of services for their customers.

Things are somewhat different in the USA, where customer services are rarely offered by dealers as a package: in fact the dealer or salesman usually has nothing to do with servicing. As for insurance, the normal practice in the USA is for buyers to find an insurance company independently.

There are differences in the car manufacturer's guarantee and dealer service system because of the differences between the USA and Japan in terms of the car qualification system. In the USA, there are some dealers with their own repair shops and such dealers are increasing. Most of these repair shops are for replacing damaged or worn-out parts, but they remain independent of salesmen.[22]

Most repair shops in the USA specialize in body repair, transmissions or steering and braking systems, but some offer all-round repair services, as in Japan. Also, there are regulations in some states against overcommitment by dealers concerning repair services. Each automobile manufacturer is keen to increase its market share and wants its dealers to concentrate on the sale of new cars, and not bother with servicing. Therefore, dealers have been rather indifferent to investment in this field, at least until the 1970s. Even in the early 1990s, dealers' service is limited to the manufacturer's period. As for repair services in contrast to Japan, there is no standard service price list and there is intense competition among insurance companies.[23]

There is no national standard for car inspection in the USA. In some states there is no system at all and in others car inspection amounts to nothing more than a simple check.[24] Hence, in the USA, it is up to the user to choose a repair shop, and the dealer seldom has anything to do with such services.

Thus, in the USA, dealers are engaged solely in the sale of new cars and, unlike in Japan, they seldom offer a package of user services, resulting in incomplete maintenance and/or after-sale service by dealers. Sometimes there is even no manufacturer's warranty.

The Japanese automobile manufacturers have had this in mind while setting up distribution channels for Japanese cars in the USA and have emphasized their relationship of trust with dealers, and – following the example of Volkswagen's success in the USA – emphasized the importance of maintenance and after-sale servicing. Japanese manufacturers have also encouraged US dealers to accept a system of 'kind-to-the-buyer' services and this is one factor accounting for the success of Japanese cars in the US market.[25] In other words, Japanese manufacturers succeeded in transplanting their extensive user services into the USA and thereby improved the reputation of Japanese cars. During the car recession of 1980–2, the US automobile manufacturers began to follow suit by offering repair services. With the development of electronics in automobiles, it has become imperative to offer quality assurance and dealer service.

MARKETING AND DISTRIBUTION STRATEGIES

There have been substantial structural changes in the Japanese automobile market accompanied by an expansion of demand. Total domestic automobile sales amounted to 7,525,000 units in 1991, a decrease of 3.2 per cent from 1990's peak figure of 7,775,000 which came at the end of a decade of non-stop growth. Along with this growth came changes in the type of demand – bigger cars grew in popularity as did small cars with luxury options and imported cars. As shown in Figure 8, the average price of a new car (excluding minicars) went up from 1.7 million yen in 1985 to 1.95 million in 1987 and to 2.14 million in 1991. Expensive cars (priced at over 2 million yen) increased in the market from 24 per

**Figure 8**   Percentage Distribution of New Passenger Cars by Price, 1985–91

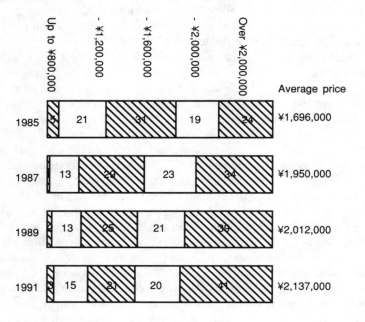

*Source*: JADA
*Note*: Minicars excluded

cent in 1985 to 34 per cent in 1987 and to 41 per cent in 1991.

Classified by price, passenger cars of 1.2 million yen or more increased their share from 74 per cent in 1985 to 85 per cent in 1989, falling back slightly to 82 per cent in 1991 (see Figures 8 and 9).

The demand for cars with automatic transmission, high-performance engines, and/or four-wheel drive has also increased (see Table 22 and Figure 10).

The import of foreign cars fell to 35,000 in the slump of 1983, but increased by 36 per cent in 1986 and then in 1987 rose amazingly to 100,000. It then peaked at 220,000 in 1990, falling back to just below 200,000 in 1991. Table 23 gives a detailed breakdown of car imports to Japan by maker. Some US and European automobile manufacturers are looking to new markets in Japan, setting up their own distributors or using the sales networks of Japanese car makers.

Other trends include a rise in the number of female drivers, the

**Figure 9**   Percentage Distribution of Used Passenger Cars by Price, 1985–91

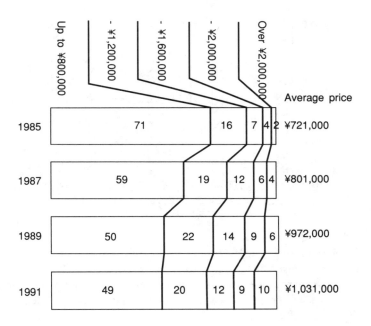

*Source*: JADA
*Note*: Minicars excluded

**Table 22**   Sales of Four-Wheel Drive Vehicles, 1984–91

| Year | No. of vehicles sold* | No. of 4WD vehicles sold | 4WD share (%) |
|------|----------------------|--------------------------|---------------|
| 1984 | 3,837,039 | 122,861 | 3.2 |
| 1985 | 3,888,550 | 156,717 | 4.0 |
| 1986 | 3,962,686 | 215,318 | 5.4 |
| 1987 | 4,190,151 | 269,591 | 6.4 |
| 1988 | 4,778,529 | 387,018 | 8.1 |
| 1989 | 5,351,428 | 498,047 | 9.3 |
| 1990 | 5,756,389 | 658,712 | 11.4 |
| 1991 | 5,533,918 | 810,433 | 14.6 |

*Source*: JADA
* Passenger cars (excluding minicars) plus small trucks.

**Figure 10**    Sales of Passenger Cars with Automatic Transmission, 1983–91

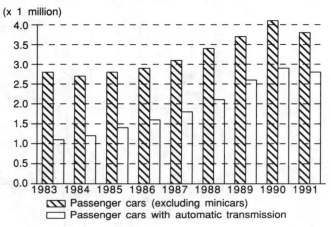

Source: JADA

number of older, high-income users, the number of two and even three-car households and an expanding youth market.[26]

These changes are a result of the aggressive promotion and marketing strategies of the manufacturers. Though most Japanese demand was originally for compact cars, the market has become much more complex and diverse. The nine passenger-car makers in Japan (extending from full-line production to compact-car production) compete vigorously with each other. The fact that an oligopolistic structure was not formed and that tough competition has existed throughout the history of automobile production in Japan have worked to reduce economies of scale that have not been all that beneficial, allowing small-scale manufacturers, with an annual output of 500,000 cars, to survive. However, even the small-scale manufacturers have been creative and original in their product concepts, giving their competitors a hard time. Their production systems have been flexible enough to respond to varying market needs, as well as to manufacture various models in small quantities. This has resulted in a diverse market structure, competition in product development, a substantial reduction in lead time and speedy design changes.[27]

This flexibility in changing product concepts to meet user needs (even in the market of compact cars) arises out of the Japanese automobile sales system, through which dealers' information about customers is fed back quickly. Automobile sales have been promoted by dealers who have an exclusive franchise with manufacturers. Five

**Table 23**   Car Imports to Japan by Maker, 1975–91

| Country of origin | Maker | 1975 | 1980 | 1985 | 1989 | 1990 | 1991 |
|---|---|---|---|---|---|---|---|
| USA | GM | 7,102 | 5,979 | 1,265 | 7,231 | 8,513 | 9,261 |
| | Ford | 8,140 | 4,446 | 452 | 5,967 | 6,030 | 2,959 |
| | Chrysler | 1,040 | 619 | 51 | 973 | 1,432 | 1,491 |
| | Honda USA | – | – | – | 4,697 | 7,534 | 14,302 |
| | Nissan USA | – | – | – | 31 | 69 | 52 |
| | Toyota USA | – | – | – | 146 | 2,109 | 862 |
| | DSM (Mitsubishi) | – | – | – | 23 | 2,886 | 1,112 |
| | Others | 88 | 14 | 48 | 16 | 29 | 89 |
| | Total | 16,370 | 11,058 | 1,816 | 19,084 | 28,602 | 30,128 |
| UK | Rover Group* | 1,286 | 3,132 | 1,655 | 10,655 | 14,431 | 12,491 |
| | Jaguar | – | – | 426 | 2,703 | 3,547 | 2,951 |
| | Rolls Royce | 61 | 39 | 74 | 610 | 1,035 | 609 |
| | Others | 241 | 207 | 358 | 551 | 640 | 1,079 |
| | Total | 1,946 | 3,673 | 2,513 | 14,519 | 19,653 | 17,130 |
| Germany | VW | 14,085 | 14,002 | 12,987 | 34,674 | 36,770 | 30,195 |
| | Audi | 2,613 | 3,803 | 5,391 | 14,306 | 16,691 | 14,367 |
| | Opel | – | – | 111 | 2,643 | 4,021 | 2,725 |
| | Ford Germany | 233 | 275 | 89 | 2 | – | – |
| | Benz | 2,725 | 3,887 | 9,194 | 31,511 | 38,844 | 34,187 |
| | BMW | 1,631 | 3,187 | 11,766 | 33,076 | 36,527 | 33,798 |
| | Porsche | 311 | 855 | 619 | 4,053 | 4,589 | 3,776 |
| | Others | 520 | 29 | – | 28 | – | – |
| | Total | 22,108 | 26,038 | 40,157 | 120,293 | 137,442 | 119,048 |
| France | Renault | 10 | 253 | 311 | 1,992 | 2,481 | 2,448 |
| | Peugeot | 1 | 126 | 59 | 4,586 | 5,414 | 4,651 |
| | Citroen | 497 | 693 | 635 | 3,908 | 6,117 | 3,749 |
| | Others | 2 | – | 4 | 1 | 6 | 6 |
| | Total | 510 | 1,072 | 1,009 | 10,487 | 14,018 | 10,854 |
| Italy | Fiat** | 585 | 813 | 2,219 | 3,106 | 4,208 | 3,804 |
| | Alfa Romeo | 645 | 294 | 77 | 1,103 | 1,260 | 1,600 |
| | Others | 48 | 577 | 196 | 355 | 465 | 350 |
| | Total | 1,278 | 1,684 | 2,492 | 4,564 | 5,933 | 5,754 |
| Sweden | Volvo | 700 | 1,244 | 1,489 | 7,122 | 10,915 | 10,127 |
| | Saab | 38 | 102 | 544 | 2,631 | 2,798 | 2,236 |
| | Total | 738 | 1,346 | 2,033 | 9,753 | 13,704 | 12,363 |
| Others | | 140 | – | 152 | 1,724 | 2,354 | 1,907 |
| TOTAL | | 43,090 | 44,871 | 50,172 | 180,424 | 221,706 | 197,184 |

*Source*: Japan Automobile Importers' Association (JAIA), quoted in Nissan Motor Co., Ltd.'s *Jidosha Sangyo Handbook 1992/1993*.
* Figures for Rover Group and Jaguar are combined for 1975 and 1980.
** Ferrari, Lancia, and Autobianchi are included in Fiat.

major manufacturers, with an annual output of more than one million, have several sales channels for each of their main models. The dealers have well-trained and well-educated sales personnel to offer customers various services, as well as visiting and in-store sales of cars, thus competing with each other to ensure customer trust and satisfaction.

Consumers' behaviour in buying cars has changed significantly in recent years; they visit show rooms and study the features and performance of cars, and it is important that manufacturers should learn about the consumers' likes and dislikes from their dealers. The order-entry system (backed up by an on-line computer network) is designed to keep the dealer's stock to a minimum and to process information on orders for greater production efficiency in line with the flow of orders.[28] This system can only be effective, however, when teamed with dynamic sales bases and salespersons' relationships with customers.

Changes have taken place in the sales strategy and policies of automobile manufacturers. The way car dealers have developed their business activities under unstable circumstances, featuring structural changes due to high-oriented demand and changes in the purchasing behaviour of customers in the recent domestic automobile market, is incredible. The major manufacturers, for example, have taken steps to achieve the product mix that best helps dealers' profits and provides for the different needs of customers; they have also set up regional sales headquarters for a distribution system free from conventional restrictions and therefore more responsive to changing demand charac-teristics in particular districts. Medium-sized manufacturers have chosen a clearer definition and image for their products, the relocation of their dealers' bases and the reorganization of their regional sales network. Dealers with exclusive franchises (especially the very large dealers) are doing well in the main cities: in one instance, dealers exclusively franchised by one particular manufacturer have been integrated into one large group. In another instance, dealers have held joint exhibitions and promotional events to complement in-store sales promotions. In some districts, dealers frequently share display space with other businesses, such as restaurants and supermarket chains. Taking advantage of the popularity of foreign cars, some department stores and supermarkets have started commercial links with trading companies to enter the automobile market. This trend will encourage existing dealers to build or acquire stores and devise new business forms that suit the peculiarities of regional markets.[30]

**Table 24**   Number of Vehicles for Lease by Type, 1966–92

| | *Passenger cars* | *Buses* | *Trucks and vans* | *Others* | *Total* | *Percentage increase over previous year* |
|---|---|---|---|---|---|---|
| 1966 | 813 | 19 | 657 | – | 1,489 | – |
| 1967 | 1,463 | 50 | 3,173 | – | 4,686 | 315 |
| 1968 | 2,490 | 121 | 7,307 | – | 9,918 | 217 |
| 1969 | 3,840 | 174 | 11,706 | – | 15,730 | 59 |
| 1970 | 6,635 | 364 | 18,522 | – | 25,571 | 63 |
| 1971 | 10,177 | 529 | 24,637 | – | 35,393 | 38 |
| 1972 | 13,106 | 681 | 29,265 | – | 43,052 | 22 |
| 1973 | 16,506 | 760 | 40,153 | – | 57,419 | 33 |
| 1974 | 22,124 | 1,421 | 45,494 | – | 70,039 | 22 |
| 1975 | 23,227 | 1,103 | 60,624 | 303 | 85,257 | 22 |
| 1976 | 26,800 | 1,254 | 69,096 | 388 | 97,538 | 14 |
| 1977 | 29,694 | 1,332 | 31,131 | 532 | 112,689 | 16 |
| 1978 | 36,470 | 1,454 | 89,602 | 542 | 128,068 | 14 |
| 1979 | 42,644 | 1,550 | 108,592 | 1,050 | 153,836 | 20 |
| 1980 | 49,633 | 1,900 | 131,192 | 913 | 183,638 | 19 |
| 1981 | 57,068 | 2,433 | 167,223 | 1,310 | 228,034 | 24 |
| 1982 | 62,980 | 2,866 | 185,227 | 2,247 | 253,320 | 11 |
| 1983 | 73,607 | 3,078 | 209,215 | 3,167 | 289,067 | 14 |
| 1984 | 93,755 | 3,914 | 252,483 | 3,840 | 353,992 | 23 |
| 1985 | 115,150 | 4,834 | 308,180 | 7,202 | 435,366 | 23 |
| 1986 | 147,322 | 5,394 | 368,410 | 11,152 | 532,278 | 22 |
| 1987 | 191,856 | 6,446 | 438,820 | 12,239 | 649,451 | 22 |
| 1988 | 245,494 | 7,629 | 539,573 | 16,059 | 808,755 | 25 |
| 1989 | 307,453 | 5,225 | 611,159 | 15,936 | 942,774 | 17 |
| 1990 | 422,142 | 10,847 | 684,258 | 72,122 | 1,189,369 | 26 |
| 1991 | 455,801 | 12,153 | 701,919 | 87,892 | 1,257,765 | 6 |
| 1992 | 607,626 | 18,991 | 896,032 | 144,466 | 1,667,115 | 33 |

*Source*: Ministry of Transport

Another change in the Japanese automobile market is the rapid expansion of vehicle leasing, particularly of passenger cars, trucks and vans. As shown in Table 24, this business has been increasing at around 20 per cent a year since the early 1970s, the number of vehicles for lease rising from 85,000 in 1975 to 435,000 in 1985 and to 1.19 million in 1990. The total number of cars, buses and trucks available for lease in 1992 came to almost 1.67 million.

This expansion reflects the growing significance of software and services in the Japanese economy. Most car leases are for companies using commercial vehicles nation-wide. Car leasing by individuals seems to be just beginning to increase. Maintenance leases account for the overwhelming share of total car leases in Japan. Companies recognize the convenience of leasing – a saving on management and maintenance costs – and regard lease charges as an annual expense.

The lease market was pioneered by specialist car-lease companies and general lease companies which possessed the know-how of the business. The general lease companies succeeded in this line of business for several reasons: they could promote the type of service that consumers required; they had a nationwide organization, including maintenance service facilities; they could charge lease fees lower than purchase instalment payments; and they could offer a full range of models.

Automobile manufacturers and dealers have come to appreciate the great value of leasing as a channel for automobile distribution and have begun tackling it aggressively. As the car-lease market made distinct progress, lease companies affiliated to car makers and finance companies (in addition to the general and specialized car-lease companies) and began devoting their energy to this field of commerce. One car dealer after another entered the business, utilizing their own servicing capacity. What with servicing and distribution companies and also some gas stations entering into this business, the number of leasing establishments has increased threefold in the past ten years.[31]

The expansion of the Japanese automobile market (including leasing) has been helped along by the expansion of financial facilities for consumers. The instalment sales legislation was amended in 1983, allowing the easy extension of instalment terms. There was also the expansion of low-interest consumer loans from finance agents and an increase in the use of credit cards by younger customers. Although the extent of automobile instalment finance can be estimated from the records of car dealers, finance companies and independent consumer finance companies, the true figures are difficult to obtain since low-interest personal loans are sometimes used to buy cars. The standard instalment term of up to 24 months has been stretched to 36 months, and the initial payment amount seems generally to be decreasing. The tendency of the Japanese automobile market toward high-grade orientation is closely related to the trend of the instalment finance market. The increasing levels of financial information and services being offered to the consumer are a key factor when forecasting future market trends in Japan.[32]

CONCLUSION

The franchise system for automobile distribution and sales originated in the USA some seventy years ago and it is over forty years since it was adopted by Japan. The system has undergone many changes in the USA, and likewise in Japan, but there are significant differences in practice between the two countries. In Japan, the managerial unit is quite large and much weight is attached to door-to-door sales. The system has survived because of an extensive provision of consumer services. In the USA, the level of consumer services was low, dealers having merely been retailers. In both countries, the system has adapted to the information revolution and is also being given a higher status.

In Japan, automobile manufacturers have been developing new selling systems and new forms of business. For example, Nissan Motor, which had a national sales organization, set up a regional organization to meet the needs of local markets and established a production system to allocate particular types and models of car to each region. Mazda Motors developed Autorama, which is currently marketing the Ford brand. Entirely different from the conventional dealer system, Autorama has also set up a chain of family restaurants and supermarkets selling car accessories and sports goods. In the case of Toyota, a new over-the-counter sales system was established in the 1980s with its chain of Vista stores. Honda Motors has many small dealers who have been encouraged to think more of profits than market share and to seek out customers who may be attracted to the uniqueness of its products. Thus, many Japanese automobile manufacturers have not been satisfied simply to continue to aim for the benefits of scale and a franchise system that is dependent on door-to-door sales; they now wish to highlight the special features of their products, and this calls for new styles and systems of salesmanship.

Customer-needs-oriented product development is under way in the Japanese market, stimulated by structural changes. So also is the development of new business forms and the flexible application of the policy of channelling distribution in accordance with the market environment of specific regions. This approach is also found in the USA and European countries, which have been influenced in recent years by changes in the market structure and/or the appearance of new niches in the market. From an international point of view, a versatile and flexible distribution and sales system designed for various classifications of regions, countries, products and customers will be needed as markets become more sophisticated. A manufacturer may classify its products

**Table 25**   Number of Dealers and Salespersons per Maker

| | Date | Dealers | Sales bases | Salespersons | Cars sold in 1992 |
|---|---|---|---|---|---|
| Toyota | Sep 92 | 310 | 4,887 | 40,000 | 2,228,941 |
| Duo* | Dec 92 | 34 | 34 | 160 | N.A. |
| Nissan | Sep 92 | 212 | 3,200 | 27,400 | 1,199,439 |
| Mazda | Dec 92 | 1,128 | 2,573 | 12,000 | 424,348 |
| Autorama** | Dec 92 | 113 | 318 | 1,600 | 58,563 |
| Mitsubishi | Dec 92 | 311 | 1,343 | 11,700 | 744,192 |
| Isuzu | Dec 92 | 102 | 559 | 4,500 | 164,129 |
| Honda | March 92 | 1,362 | 2,500 | 10,300 | 596,042 |
| Daihatsu | Dec 92 | 79 | 719 | 5,000 | 433,621 |
| Fuji-juko | Dec 92 | 63 | 536 | 3,800 | 307,521 |
| Suzuki | July 92 | 132 | 800 | 6,000 | 536,448 |

*Source*: Jidosha Journal, January 1993.
* Affiliated to Toyota. Set up in April 1992 for the supply of VW cars.
** Affiliated to Mazda. Supplies Ford cars.

into two categories – those products for particular oversea destinations and those for general overseas use. This kind of shift towards an international view of the industry and its products is bound to have an affect on the distribution side of the business.

The information revolution enables car manufacturers to have reliable and up-to-date financial data on inventory, turnover and sales, thereby promoting the integration of the manufacturers and their dealers. This will help to ensure the efficient control of stock and a supply system that can respond quickly to customer needs. It is even argued by some that the information revolution may, in future, make for a no-store system of sales through networking sales and service information for customers. However, the role of a dealer, as a source of information about consumers, will not easily disappear. Although investment in information processing equipment will become greater, the human element will continue to be a decisive factor in automobile sales. Only a salesperson can properly understand and take account of a customer's needs. Indeed, the more information-oriented the automobile industry becomes, the more important competent salespersons will become. Their expertise will be the 'software' of the system.

While megadealers will dominate in the big cities, manoeuverable 'mini dealers' linked by network will develop in other areas. New distributors in the system will keep existing dealers on their toes.

Generally, changes in product strategy, product characteristics and the production system precede changes in the distribution system, but inevitably lead to changes in the distribution system itself, in terms of services offered, including financing and maintenance. One thing which is unlikely to change, however, is the human factor. The personality of the salesperson will continue to be at the heart of the Japanese automobile sales system.

# CHAPTER 6

# *Japanese Automobile Companies*

## TOYOTA MOTORS

Toyota Motors is well known as a financially sound enterprise. For the year to June 1992 its total sales came to almost nine trillion yen, although net profits dropped sharply from previous years, down to about 200 billion yen (compared with 360 billion in 1990). The company has so much spate capital that it has been nicknamed 'The Toyota Bank'. In 1989 its financial earnings totalled 139 billion yen, more than the trading profits of the Tokai Bank which, in that year, was ranked ninth among the metropolitan banks of the world. The appreciation of the yen reduced Toyota's profits but the company soon recovered to become Japan's most profitable automaker.

For the year to June 1992, Toyota's output was about 3.04 million vehicles, equal to about 31 per cent of the total domestic output (including minicars) and placing Toyota far above second-ranking Nissan Motors. In the same year, Toyota exported 1.7 million vehicles – 42 per cent of its total output and equal to 29 per cent of the Japanese automobile export market, compared with Nissan's 16.5 per-cent share. Toyota once set itself a 'Global 10' goal of securing a 10 per-cent share of the world automobile output, and the above production figure for 1991/2 shows it is now near achieving this goal (world output for 1991 being roughly 44 million vehicles). Toyota ranks third to GM and Ford in global output and Toyota's sales revenue was only about 60 per cent of GM's in 1991 and less than Ford's, but it consistently makes more absolute profit than either.

Toyota Motors was founded in 1937 by Kiichiro Toyoda, carrying out the wishes of his father, Sakichi Toyoda, who had been world-famous for his role in the development of the automatic loom. Until the foundation of the company, Kiichiro Toyoda belonged to the Automobile Manufacturing Division of Toyoda Automatic Loom Works, working on the production of a prototype passenger car in one small part of the plant. At that time the Japanese government decided to exclude foreign-made cars which dominated the Japanese market, especially those of the three major American automakers who were engaged in 'knock-down' production in Japan. The Automobile Manufacture Enterprise Act was intended to promote the production of automobiles within Japan and Toyota, Nissan and Isuzu were authorized for this task.

In spite of the founder's plan to aim for the mass production of cars, the government compelled Toyota to mass produce military trucks. However, even during wartime, Toyota continued secretly to develop and improve cars, which resulted in the production of the Toyopet Crown. While other manufacturers linked up with foreign concerns, especially in Europe, to produce cars by licence, Toyota rejected Ford's offer, being convinced of its own independent ability to produce cars.

Toyota nearly went bankrupt in 1950 when the economy went into a depression. There was a severe fall in truck sales. The Nagoya branch of the Nippon Bank urged the metropolitan banks to organize a syndicate in order to assist Toyota, but the syndicate called for a substantial reduction in the workforce as a condition for assistance. This caused a labour dispute and Kiichiro Toyoda resigned from the presidency.

The bank syndicate advised Toyota to form two separate companies out of its production and sales divisions, the Toyota Motor Company and the Toyota Motor Sales company. Taizo Ishida, acting as the president of Toyoda Automatic Loom Works and head of the Toyoda family, succeeded Kiichiro Toyoda as president of Toyota Automobile Industries. Shotaro Kamiya, the sales manager of General Motors in Japan during prewar days, took on the presidency of the Toyota Motor Sales company.

Toyota survived the management crisis and the labour dispute and, thanks to an increased demand during the Korean War, made a come back. It seemed as if the founder, Kiichiro Toyoda, would resume office, but he died in 1953 and President Ishida kept his post. Later, Ishida was succeeded as president by Eiji Toyoda (nephew of Sakichi and cousin of Kiichiro). Working together with Kamiya, he led Toyota, while assisting the new president through his position as chairman of the board.

How did Toyota, which was on the verge of bankruptcy with a history of ups and downs during wartime and postwar times, become such a superb company in just thirty-five years? One reason stems from the unity of all the companies in the Toyota group, with Toyota Motors at the core of a 'centripetal circle'. There are many other company groups such as Mitsubishi and Sumitomo that are unified but none as tightly as the Toyota group. It formed one quality parts maker after another. Among these manufacturers are Nippondenso, Aisin Seiki, Toyoda Gosei, Toyoda Koki, each of which are major parts makers with stable management. Toyota had a big geographical advantage, as all its parts makers were located within fifty kilometres of the main Toyota plants.

Immediately after the first oil-price shock, when the companies in the group had to reduce output, they united under a slogan which could be translated as, 'Break even at 70 per cent!' Under these austere conditions, corporate activities, such as the 'Kanban' system and Total Quality Control (TQC), were especially beneficial. The 'Kanban' system was based on Toyota's philosophy of improving productivity along with quality, and is known as the 'just-in-time' system, (keeping stocks to a minimum at each process).

Toyota's sales and marketing systems were also key elements in the success of the company. The Toyota Motor Sales company was created exclusively for selling and marketing, while the Toyota Motor Company had responsibility for development and production, receiving marketing information and ideas for product planning from the sales companies. This gave Toyota a marketing advantage over its competitors. Kamiya adopted the GM-dealer franchise system and set up a nationwide network of local dealers on the principle of one dealer in each prefecture. Car marketing by a network of franchised automobile dealers in Japan resulted from Toyota's method. The establishment of a nationwide network of efficient dealers with local capital boosted Toyota far above the domestic competition, giving it a decisive advantage in the domestic market.

The Toyota Motor Sales company did not merely promote a well-organized network of dealers throughout the country, it also assisted them by financing sales and stocks, and quickly fed back marketing information through intensive control and analysis of the sales data from the dealers for efficient product planning.

The Toyota Motor Sales company played an important role during this period of growth, and ended this thirty-two years of independence in 1982 when the two divisions were amalgamated. The dual system had led to some discord and Toyota needed greater group unity in order to deal with new circumstances, such as lower economic growth, market maturation, internationalization and technological innovation. At first, it was feared that the merger would lead to greater conflicts in the corporate organization, but the new arrangement bore fruit in terms of sales.

Toyota continues to enjoy a well-organized system of supply and component production, fully utilizing technological innovations and high standards of production technology. Another influential factor is the management system that gives development staff full authority to develop products freely and flexibly, according to the basic strategy of product planning. Thus, Toyota's advantages consist of unity of quality parts makers with higher technological standards, sales and marketing capacities and product planning efficiency.

Labour/management relations in the company have been good since 1962 when labour and management agreed to a new contract. Labour relations were seen as important enough for directors and the Chariman of the Board to take part in collective wage bargaining.

Toyota's marketing strategy is based on securing a stable share of the domestic market and exploring overseas markets. Toyota's 'Global 10' strategy required an increase in exports and in output overseas. Since a rapid increase in exports was not expected, Toyota has been endeavouring to strengthen marketing and domestic sales and is aiming for more 'knock-down' exports.

Toyota in 1991 had about 41 per cent of the domestic automobile market (excluding the minicar market) with sales of about 2.34 million vehicles and plans to raise this to 50 per cent, as this would ensure a stable replacement demand arising out of high brand loyalty. Success would give Toyota the chance to promote production overseas. Toyota's strategy in regard to new models includes promoting the existing basic models that sell well (and individualizing some of them) as well as strengthening its domestic sales channels. Also, despite the fact that up to the mid-1980s it concentrated on a production line of at least 10,000 units a month, Toyota is now promoting the development of more specialized vehicles that have a demand of up to only 2,000 units a month. Toyota's product planning in the past tended to be rather conservative, favouring cars that could be guaranteed to have a general appeal and to sell steadily. Recently, however, Toyota has been more adventurous, aiming to come up with some unique, exciting models to add to its range.

Toyota has a vigorous technological strategy and, until 1990, was making yearly investments in plant and equipment of around 300 billion yen, updating its manufacturing facilities through the introduction of industrial robots and the various computer-related components of the so-called Flexible Manufacturing System (FMS) such as LAN (local Area Network), the in-company information network, CAD (Computer Aided Design) and CAM (Computer Aided Manufacturing). The Flexible Manufacturing System is designed to deal with a wide variety of products in relatively small product lots.

Toyota also devotes a substantial amount of money to research and development, some of which is in areas at the cutting edge of science and so may deserve to be called fundamental. Despite the economic downturn of the early 1990s, Toyota continues to invest around 250 billion yen annually in R & D. Even though it has an affiliated electronics maker, Nippondenso, Toyota created an electronics research department in 1989 for the development of electronics technology (including semiconductors). It has also put considerable effort in to research in the field of electronic model design.

Looking ahead, Toyota needs to branch out if it is to maintain its rate of growth. As things are, Toyota seems to have no plans to undertake any new enterprises even though it has spare funds in the region of one trillion yen. The company started a housing enterprise in 1975, but sales have been very low and housing specialists from Misawa Home and other housing companies have been taken on in order to promote the business. Other new businesses include an affiliation with Daini Denden and participation in international communications activities.

What are Toyota's weak points? They are its excessive attachment to production efficiency and an inward-looking, centrist tendency. Since 1990, however, Toyota has set out to overcome its shortcomings by simplifying its decision-making process and dropping hierarchical executive titles, amongst other measures, in order to spread responsibility more widely. As for its inward-looking tendency, this came to be reflected in its cautious approach to overseas strategy. Now Toyota needs to establish itself as a global enterprise. Indeed, it has already begun to exert itself in this direction. Although Toyota lagged behind its competitors in terms of internationalization, but 1989 it managed 31 overseas production plants in 21 countries. Most of these plants, however, were small and in developing countries.

To help boost its overseas efforts, in February 1984 Toyota established a joint venture with GM, called NUMMI (New United Motor Manufacturing, Inc.). Production at the Fremont plant in California, which has an annual output capacity of 300,000 vehicles, began in December 1984.

In 1986, Toyota set up a plant in Georgetown, Kentucky as Toyota Manufacturing USA, Inc. (TMMU) where production started in 1988 at the rate of 200,000 a year of the Camry passenger car aimed at the US market. The Georgetown plant also produces engines and axles. In September 1989, Toyota launched its 4.0 litre luxury-class car the Lexus (known as the Celsior in Japan) in the USA. In Canada, Toyota built a car plant in Ontario with an annual capacity of 65,000 units which began production in 1988 and, in British Columbia, a wheel-making plant with an annual capacity of 480,000 wheels which started up in 1985.

As for Europe, Toyota started the joint production of cars with VW in Hanover in 1989 and is due to open two plants (one for cars, one for engines only) in the UK in late 1992.

Now that the high value of the yen has become firmly established there are problems not only in terms of shrinking profit margins on exports but also of growing trade friction. In this climate, the challenge for Toyota is how to get more young managers for a stronger international policy.

Toyota, as a leading manufacturer of contemporary Japan, has given highest priority to social contribution as its corporate goal.

NISSAN MOTORS

Nissan Motors is the second largest automaker in Japan and ranks fourth in the world. It turns out a wide range of popular cars and leads the industry in terms of technological developments. It accomplishments are symbolized by the fully-automated Kyushu plant, a robot-automated manufacturing system. Nissan is the only automaker to come close to Toyota's full-line production.

It has been vigorously promoting development overseas. However, a fall in its share of the domestic market, rising sales costs and heavy overseas investment are taking their toll. Nissan is now far behind Toyota in terms of financial achievements.

Nissan's sales for the year to March 1992 amounted to 4.27 trillion yen. Net profits for the same year were 54 billion yen, down sharply from a highpoint two years earlier of 85 billion yen. It produced 2,324,000 automobiles, roughly 5 per cent of world production, of which 965,000 were exported. As well as cars, it produces forklifts, textile machinery, aircraft machinery, marine engines and rockets, small trucks and buses. In 1992, cars and commercial vehicles accounted for 81 per cent of total sales. Parts accounted for 16.5 per cent while the rest, aviation and textile machinery and suchlike, accounted for 2.5 per cent. Cars are turned out on the full-line manufacturing system and range form the sub-compact 1.0 litre March model to the 4.5 litre President. In Japan, as of 1992, Nissan had twelve manufacturing plants and five assembly plants. It also commissions production from its affiliated companies such as Nissan Shatai, Aichi Kikai and Nissan Diesel. Nissan has 23 overseas production bases including 9 capital-affiliated companies, in 20 countries. Its domestic sales network comprises 213 companies and 3,170 bases belonging to five groups – Nissan, Motor, Sunny, Cherry and Prince. Overseas, Nissan sells its products in 155 countries through about 175 distributors and 7,200 dealers.

It was in 1933 that Nippon Sangyo and Tobata Imono (holding companies of the Nissan 'zaibatsu') created the Automobile Manufacturing Company as a joint investment venture. The name was changed in 1934 to the Nissan Motor Company. Nissan was licensed to manufacture automobiles along with Toyota and Isuzu. The founder was Yoshisuke Ayukawa, head of the Nissan 'zaibatsu'. When Nissan was about to tie up with GM in 1940, the military government forced the company to give up the idea. In prewar days, Nissan mass produced the compact Datsun passenger car, leading the Japanese automobile industry in terms of the mass production of passenger cars.

Nissan suffered during and after the war because its plants were located in districts convenient for the production of military suppliers and materials, and therefore could not take advantage of a centralized production and supply system like that of Toyota. The Nissan 'zaibatsu' was dissolved after the war. Management executives were not easily replaced and the company fell behind in postwar sales promotion. In this respect, Nissan made a poor start during the postwar days. While Toyota had fostered locally-capitalized dealers earlier on, Nissan made such a late start that it had no locally-based dealers; even in 1990, most of its dealers were directly managed by the manufacturer. Katsuji Kawamata of the Industrial Bank of Japan took on the management of Nissan in the early 1950s but there was a major labour dispute in 1953.

From 1952 until 1960, Nissan was tied up with Austin of the UK for the licensed production of cars. Meanwhile, Nissan also proceeded with the development of its own models in the Yoshiwara plant. This resulted in the production of the Bluebird, which swept the country in 1959. This model was in severe competition with Toyota's Corona. Nissan launched the Sunny to counter Toyota's Corolla and then joined up with the Prince Motor Company in 1966, adding two new models, the Skyline and Gloria, to create a full product line-up.

Nissan had excellent designers and engineers and rivalled Toyota in product planning. It has turned out a number of well-known cars and trucks including the Bluebird, Skyline, Datsun pick-up truck, Fairlady and, in foreign markets, the 280Z.

Despite proficient product planning, Nissan has not been able to take advantage of this in terms of marketing concepts and has fallen behind Toyota in total product strategy. Nevertheless, Nissan has led its competitors in introducing mechanical innovations in automobiles. Notable accomplishments include the use of the turbocharger and the development of car electronics.

Nissan has also made innovations in production processes, such as the synchronizing system (similar to Toyota's 'Kanban' system) featuring a delivery system and computerized parts stock management. To compensate for the handicap of not having plants and parts suppliers close at hand, Nissan was the first to introduce industrial robots into the final assemble process. Its factory automation rate is high. Like Toyota, Nissan has major parts makers in its group, such as Atsugi Automobile Parts (now Atsugi Unisia), Calsonic, Kanto Seiki (now Kantus) and Tsuchiya Seisakusho.

Nissan Motors is characterized as being urban and sophisticated. As soon as management decisions are made, the whole company carries them out through to its overseas branches. Nissan is one of the major members of the Fuyo Group, and its management is closely connected with the political and business worlds, in contrast to Toyota, which concentrates on producing automobiles. Though Toyota is said to be related to the Mitsui Group, it draws a clear line against any close association with corporate organizations that are affiliated to big 'keiretsu'. The Nissan group is made up of Fuji Heavy Industries, Nissan Diesel and major parts makers, while Nissan Motor is linked to the major companies of the Fuyo group. Nissan teamed up with Hitachi Seisakusho in the development of electronic devices and equipment.

Aggressive overseas operations are a part of Nissan's strategy and it has been more active than other automakers in locally-based production abroad since it began production in Mexico in 1966, and especially during the eight years of Chairman Ishihara's presidency. In January 1980, Nissan shared in the capitalization of Motor Iberica of Spain, taking up 36 per cent of the stock and starting on the production of commercial vehicles. Nissan has now completely affiliated with the Spanish automaker and has been expanding its output. Nissan established the Nissan Motor Manufacturing Company in Smyrna, Tennessee in July and a joint venture with Alfa Romeo of Italy in December, (starting the production of Nissan's sub-compact cars in March 1983). Nissan also tied up with VW for the commissioned production of the Santana in the Zama plant. In February 1984, it decided to produce in the UK, starting in Newcastle in 1986 with the production of the Bluebird car. In April 1989, Nissan unified its European operation with the establishment of Nissan Europe in Holland. In January 1990, Nissan North America, Inc. was founded.

The biggest project in Nissan's overseas operations was a plant in the USA. Nissan made an investment of US$745 million in the construction of the plant with fully-automated manufacturing facilities. It began production of small trucks in the Tennessee plant in 1983 and in 1985 began production of the Sunny car (locally called the Sentra). The plant moved to full production early in 1987, with an annual output of 240,000 small trucks and cars. Later on, the plant was expanded to produce engines. This plant features a unique management system in which all employees participate under the direction of the president. So far, this localized management system has been impressive. Its local parts procurement rate is now a little over 70 per cent. Calsonic and major parts makers of the Nissan Group are now based in the USA, and a supply system of Mexican-produced engines has been organized. Nissan's first overseas link was with Mexico, and now, since the construction of a large, modern factory in Aguascalientes with a yearly output of 200,000 vehicles, Nissan (the only Japanese car maker to have production facilities in Mexico) can claim a leading position in the Mexican automobile industry. By April 1989 it had turned out a total on one million cars there. In July 1992, sales started in the USA and Canada of the Quest multi-purpose car, the fruit of a joint project between Nissan and Ford, in which Nissan is responsible for development and Ford for production.

Another big project has been a plant in the United Kingdom. The buildings were completed in 1985, and the plant started with an annual output of 24,000 of the Auster model from the summer of 1986. By 1992 it had a production capacity of 300,000 cars a year and was turning out the Primera, with the new Micra (known in Japan as the March) going into full production in the autumn of 1992.

Nissan has also been promoting joint ventures with local capital in Taiwan and Thailand.

Taking a long-term view of overseas strategies, Japanese automakers will be up against more in the way of a slump in export due to trade friction and the rising value of the yen. It is considered that increasing the export of finished automobiles and even basing plants in foreign countries may be a hard task. Possible undesirable situations in the future include a rise in the home-parts production rate through Local Content Acts and other regulations in developed countries, though they have had to be home-produced mainly in Southeast Asia and other developing countries. However, production bases abroad will allow for a system with a greater international division of labour through the mutual use of complementary parts, and re-exporting parts and automobiles will contribute to the economy, positively affecting the trade balance of those countries.

Former President Ishihara's endeavours to promote overseas operations has resulted in a well-organized network of overseas ventures based in North America, Latin America, Europe, Oceania and Southeast Asia. The policy of President Kume and of his successor, President Tsuju has been to strengthen and expand this organization. In other words, one of Nissan's objectives is to become an international parts maker as well as an automaker, through the completion of an international division-of-labour system.

Since this strategy calls for high standards of design and the development of components production, Nissan will seek to co-ordinate the work of the group's parts makers: Nissan will also manage product planning to take account of each country's market and thereby the design and specifications of the products manufactured in Japan.

Nissan's overseas strategy might make for an investment burden on the company and perhaps it should not proceed any further in this direction. For the future, Nissan has to complete the establishment and consolidation of its position.

Nissan's future corporate strategy should also be viewed in the light of its technological policies. Nissan has created a well-organized product planning system, emphasizing both fundamental and applied research. Research is being carried out on new materials such as ceramics, electronics and gas turbines at its central research laboratory in Yokosuka. Nissan sees the gas turbine as a totally new, energy-saving, high-output engine for the next century, and would like to undertake more joint research with other makers on a national basis along with the Industry and Technology Agency of MITI.

Just as the Integrated Circuit research association did in the development of semi-conductors, Nissan will play a leading role in the research work on engine power. Nissan is also very active in the fields of electronics and ceramics undertaking both in-house and joint research and development (especially for engine combustion control) and working closely with Hitachi Seisakusho in electronics. As for ceramics, Nissan is close to putting the combustion chamber exhaust system and engine power-driven valve system to practical use.

In addition to the central research laboratory, Nissan has set up a new technical centre in Isehara, close to its plants in Zama and Atsugi. It also integrated the Nissan group and the former Prince group into one research and development system for general product planning concerned with production technology and the environment.

Nissan has advanced the research and development of new types of high-performance robots (such as the multiple-jointed robot and sensor robot) at its Machine Tool Division in the Zama and Oppama plants. Nissan was the first among Japanese automakers to introduce industrial robots, and now has a high robot content in its major plants. Nissan manufactures most of the robots for itself and sends them to overseas plants.

Another important aspect of Nissan's technological strategy is its astronautical concerns which the company intends to develop. Nissan's astronautical sales amounted to 38 billion yen in fiscal 1991. It is the biggest enterprise in the field of solid-fuel rockets. Nissan signed a comprehensive technical assistance contract in space development with Martin Marietta of the USA in 1982, and has continued to strengthen this connection. Space technology covers a wide range of fields, such as precision technology, solid fuel and communications. New media, like information technology, are also closely related to space development. In short, Nissan will exploit space technology for uses besides automobiles. In this connection, Nissan plans to develop a technical tie-up with Fuji Heavy Industries in order to link Nissan's rocket technology with Fuji's aircraft technology, and thereby explore the promising field of artificial satellites and space stations.

In the short run, Nissan faces the difficult task of improving domestic sales while also strengthening its overseas strategy. Nissan will continue to make efforts to help dealers with their sales promotion and organizational improvements. By switching to more local capital and introducing a sales and distribution information system, Nissan's regional sales headquarters are getting dealers to respond more to local circumstances. Apart from supporting dealers, Nissan has set itself the task of developing technology and products which really cater to users' needs. In 1988, Nissan had success with 'first-in-the-field' products such as the large Cima luxury car, the Cefiro specialty car, the Silvia, a new model of the Primera and so on. Nissan also developed the large

4.5 litre Infiniti model which began to sell in the USA from the end of 1989.

HONDA MOTORS

When considering the Japanese enterprises which have contributed to the growth of Japan's postwar economy, Sony and Honda must come to mind. This is because both producers started out as small businesses, each with an engineer/founder, and became world-famous major companies in just twenty years.

Honda has provided the Japanese automobile industry with some unique technological innovations and types of corporate activity. These include the manufacture of motor cycles, the creation of the Honda motor-cycle brand (with a win in the Isle of Man TT race) entry into the mini-compact car market with the N–360 and entry into the sub-compact market with the Civic utility model, the development of the CVCC engine (the first to comply with the standards set in the Muskie Act on car exhausts) and a variety of technological developments by Honda Technological Research Laboratory and the Honda Engineering Institute.

Honda's sales for the year to March 1992 came to 2.9 trillion yen and net profits to 32.6 billion yen. With about 31,000 employees it produced a total of 1.33 million four-wheel vehicles. Honda's major products are of three types – automobiles, two-wheelers and general products such as engines power generators and tillers. Of its total sales, four-wheelers make up 78 per cent, two-wheelers 10 per cent, general products 3 per cent, and components for local production (of cars and two-wheelers) 9 per cent. Honda supplies more than one third of the global market for two-wheelers, exporting 65 per cent of its output, and it exports 94 per cent of its general products. This high export ratio accounts for Honda's image as an international enterprise.

In Japan, Honda has seven manufacturing facilities of which four are automobile assembly plants. It has sixty-nine overseas production bases, including two-wheeler and parts plants, in forty countries: ten of the bases in ten countries produce and assemble automobiles. Honda has a national sales network with three channels – Honda Verno, Honda Clio and Honda Primo, with 1,570 dealers and 2,433 bases in all (1992 figures).

Honda is the latest of the car makers. It was founded in 1948 in Hamamatsu (Shizuoka Prefecture) with capital of just one million yen

and with twenty employees. It launched into the automobile manufacturing business in the mid-1960s. How did it become a world-famous
automaker in only thirty years?

Honda's success was due to its founder, Soichiro Honda – an engineer
and entrepreneur – and Takeo Fujisawa, the sales and financial manager.
The two were responsible for the development of Honda's corporate
character and its organizational culture (which has been maintained
by the whole company under their successors, ex-Pressidents Kiyoshi
Kawashima and Tadashi Kume and incumbent President Nobuhiko
Kawamoto).

What was Soichiro's thinking and philosophy? Soichiro developed his
own technical ideas on the basis of his many years of experience as a
creative engineer. He saw the necessity of linking the creative urge to
make something new with the practical research of fundamental matters.
Creation calls for courage in order to break away from existing ideas
and practices and to explore new possibilities. 'Schumpeter's creative
destruction' is not possible without efforts to create something new.
Soichiro's ideas were based on the view that the purposeful acquisition
of as much technique and knowledge as possible is essential for the
development of new products, and that single-skill jobs and excessive
specialization do not lead to creative activities.

Soichiro stressed that success cannot be won without failures but
failure is not to be feared; something must be learned from the failure.
On the other hand, however, he insisted that even 1 per cent of failure
must not be permitted for 'creative destruction' in regard to research
items with definite job purposes and patterns.

Honda provided labour and personnel management which eliminated
the requirements of educational background and seniority, and successfully applied the principle of 'ability first' for motivation on the job.
Fujisawa promoted the above two managing principles so that more
employees can incorporate Soichiro's technical thought. He provided
a specialist staff system which employed a qualification system for
personnel evaluation to give all employees a chance to be promoted
to specialist posts, ranking as high as managerial functions, with a
view to abolishing the discrimination of educational background in
regard to the type of jobs (technical or clerical) and the type of
personnel functions (clerical or manufacturing) This specialist staff
system offers all engineers and workers who do not graduate from
college or university a chance to obtain an equal voice and position
with managerial functions.

Honda's 'ability' principle is embodied in successive streams of managerial executives, giving scope to young engineers for the development of new products and giving employees more room to have their say.

The future strategy of Honda includes an overseas policy of expanding locally-based production in such countries as the USA and Canada, and a technological development policy to match its product planning.

Honda's enthusiasm for overseas development stems from its initial policy of promoting all its products in foreign as well as home markets. While some European manufacturers had started to produce small two-wheelers, Japanese manufacturers – including the pioneering Honda – succeeded in developing dependable two-wheel products.

Honda has actively promoted locally-based production and parts procurement and employment since it started exporting two-wheelers in the early 1950s. In the early 1960s, in Belgium and other parts of the world, Honda began knock-down production and licensed production. In recent years, Honda has been exporting more motor cycles as knock-down sets than as finished products. Global fame as a motor-cycle manufacturer has brought outstanding growth and success to the company. Above all, success as a two-wheeler manufacturer in the USA paved Honda's way for the Civic car in 1970. In just a few years, Honda came to rank as third in the number of cars exported to the USA.

All Japanese automakers have found the USA to be their biggest foreign market but Honda has relied much more heavily on this market because of its difficulties in expanding in the domestic market. Also, because Honda's product concepts for the Civic and Accord along with its brand recognition as a two-wheeler manufacturer were also in line with what US consumers seemed to want to buy.

A much as 70 per cent of Honda's exports went to the USA: the USA was Honda's lifeline, and in order to minimize US–Japan trade friction, Honda decided on the radical strategy of US-based production. In 1977, Honda informed the Ohio State government of its plans to build a plant in Marysville. Honda started with the production of large two-wheelers (which had not been manufactured in Japan), constructed an assembly plant for cars and began producing the Accord car in 1982. The plant had 3,000 local employees, turning out 60,000 motor cycles and 220,000 Accords a year.

Honda decided to undertake locally-based production before any other Japanese automaker. The decision was epoch-making since other manufacturers began such policies later on only after trade frictions had emerged and voluntary curbs on exporting cars to the USA had started. Honda's locally-based plants carried little risk, employing well-trained workmen with experience of working routines and production system know-how, most of whom had been mere beginners from local agricultural districts, and started with the manufacture of two-wheelers.

By 1988, Honda was producing Accords and Civics in the Ohio plant, meeting its target of 360,000 cars a year. Starting in 1988, 8,000 a year of the Accords manufactured there have been exported back to Japan. It started producing engines for two-wheelers in 1985 and engines for the Civic in autumn 1986 at a plant in a neighbouring region, and a second plant there soon afterwards. Honda has also completed a put into operation an assembly plant in Ontario, Canada, with an annual capacity of 100,000 cars and this is linked to the Ohio plant. The Ohio plant supplies the Canadian plant with engines and other components, and the Canadian plant will expand its capacity to supply finished products to America. With all these operations underway, Honda is already producing around 600,000 vehicles a year in North America alone.

Honda concluded a contract in 1979 with the British Leyland Corporation (now the Rover Group) for the licensed production and joint development of cars, and in 1981 BL began producing the Triumph Acclaim, a model based on Honda's Ballade. The Legend model was developed in co-operation with the Rover Group and was first marketed in Japan in 1985, and in the USA and Europe a year later. A similar project developing a new model is in progress in the early 1990s. Honda has a network of locally-based production of two-wheelers in Europe, Asia, the Middle East and Latin America. It produces two-wheelers in a technical tie-up in China, and has recently begun producing two-wheelers and cars in India.

Honda's technological progress calls for a brief account of the organization and function of the Honda Technological Research Laboratory and Honda Engineering Institute. The Research Laboratory has its general research centre in Tochigi and is divided into three organizations – two-wheelers in Asaka, four-wheelers in Wako and general-use products in Asaka-Higashi (where development research on new products and new models is carried out along with fundamental research). This laboratory was established independently of Honda with a view to generating original ideas of innovative technology since a company-bound research and development division tends to think of more immediate profit. It can charge Honda for each design and product-planning project and in 1992 received between 6 and 7 per cent of all Honda's sales revenue. The laboratory has made some findings in original research, such as the low-pollution CVCC engine. The laboratory is now more active than ever, covering several new fields such as car electronics, ceramics, new materials and information engineering.

Honda Engineering, the other research and development institution, is engaged in the development of industrial robots, FMS and NC (numerically controlled) machine tools and metal sinters. There is also Honda Research of America, an institute for research and development in the USA and Honda R & D Europe in Germany.

Honda has traditionally promoted in-house production, according to the requirements of job sites in the plant, but its production system has been made more flexible. Starting with the manufacture of compact cars, Honda has carried out its unique product planning with successes such as the Civic, Accord, Integra and Legend. The range of product planning has expanded to large cars, sports cars and specialty cars. Honda is keen to boost domestic sales with its outstanding product planning capacity and improved sales network.

MAZDA MOTORS

Mazda, the only major automaker in western Japan, recovered from its financial crisis in 1974 through the assistance of the Sumitomo Bank Group, the co-operation of labour and management, and tie-ups with Ford. The company had been an industrial leader in the Hiroshima district under the name of Toyo Kogyo until it was renamed Mazda in May 1984. It was founded by Jujiro Matsuda as a cork stopper manufacturer in 1920 and renamed Toyo Kogyo in 1927 when it launched out n to the machine-tool industry. It began to produce three-wheel vehicles in 1931. Although the company manufactured automobiles on an experimental basis during the war, it was then engaged exclusively in the production of weapons.

Mazda resumed the production of three-wheel trucks in December 1945. It appointed an agent in each prefecture and completed a national sales network by 1949. It enjoyed a good reputation as a manufacturer of three-wheel trucks. Mazda launched the small Lombar truck in 1958 and the mini R-360 Coupe four-wheeler car in 1960.

With the production of automobiles, Tsuneji Matsuda – successor to the founder and engineer manager – turned his attention to the potential of the rotary engine; this was initially researched by Dr F. Wankel

(Germany), and the patent belonged to the NSU Corporation, which also adapted it for commercialization in 1961.

Mazda had a hard time putting the rotary engine to practical use and many in the company were sceptical of its prospects. Tsuneji Matsuda set up an independent, in-house research division and invested in brain power and product-planning expenses for design, development and research. The person who was then supervising the development of the rotary engine was Kenichi Yamamoto, who later became chairman. Matsuda's decision determined the fate of the company, because he favourably evaluated promising potentialities of the principle of the rotary engine through long years of experience in the field of mechanical engineering. The rotary engine is designed so that the piston can transmit a rotary motion through a triangular rotor, thus offering the following advantages: greater driving power efficiency, less vibration and noise, less cost with a smaller number of parts, and compact and light-weight design for smooth high-speed performance. Although it was advantageous in principle, there were many technical problems to solve in the application of the idea, of the rotary engine, and none of the US and European automakers had managed to find the solutions. Yamamoto's development crew, led by Yamamoto himself, struggled to solve one technical point after another. The biggest problem of all was to eliminate wavelike wear in the contact metal of the engine housing, caused by the vibration of the rotor. This was resolved by altering the shape of the apex seal inside the housing and by using a special carbon for the seal. This was towards the end of 1964, nearly five years since the start of the project.

Mazda launched the first car with a rotary engine, the Cosmo Sports, in 1967, and thereby made its name. This allowed Mazda to grant a production licence to NSU and also to several other automakers, including GM. Mazda's success in the development of the rotary engine was the fruit of its revolutionary product-planning policy which featured fundamental research instead of mere applied research; Mazda's brand image enabled it to launch the popular Familia car and the Luce, creating a boom in cars with rotary engines.

Mazda then had a stroke of bad luck. The first oil-price shock happened just after Mazda had increased the output of rotary-engine cars and promoted their export, especially to the USA. Sales of the rotary-engine car fell drastically since the rotary engine was not as fuel-efficient as the conventional engine (even though rotary-engine cars offered superior high-speed performance). GM had begun work on the production of rotary-engine cars, but withdrew from the project, affecting Mazda enormously. Even though GM produced more large-size engine cars when they decided to give up the project, it damaged Mazda considerably. The fuel-efficiency of the rotary engine has been improved and is now equal to that of the reciprocating engine. Mzada's slump in the USA in 1974 hindered sales of rotary-engine cars in Japan, resulting in a management crisis.

Mazda survived the crisis with financial help from a syndicate including the Sumitomo Bank, which sent manpower including executives, by selling assets and temporarily transferring surplus employees to dealers, also by a reduction in output, labour–management co-operation and by receiving aid from Hiroshima's entire political and commercial world. Mazda came out of the red in 1976 and started to recover from its bad fortune. The company – a family affair – entered a new era of management as Yoshiki Yamazaki, with a technical background, assumed the presidency after the third president, Kohei Matsuda.

Yamazaki initiated a new production system and the promotion of QC-circle activities, reorganizing the company by reducing costs and developing new models with a team led by Yamamoto and another former chairman Moriyuki Watanabe. This allowed Mazda to rationalize production and produce several successful cars such as the RX-7, a budget-priced high-performance sports car, the Cosmo, the New Familia in 1980 and the New Capella in 1983. Mazda thereby began to regain business and substantially reduce its debt-ratio, formerly the highest among Japanese automakers.

Sumitomo, apart from helping it out of its crisis, also acted as an agent for Mazda in its financial links with Ford, a business partner for the licensed production of small trucks in 1979. Ford became a stockholder with a 24 per-cent share. Mazda's partnership with Ford has matured and now Mazda supplies Ford with engines and transaxles and markets Ford's products in Asia and Oceania. The tie-up with Ford played a crucial role in Mazda's policy of internationalization.

Mazda has domestic production bases in three districts – Hiroshima, Miyoshi and Hofu. Miyoshi has a test course and a diesel-engine plant. The Hofu plant has advanced production lines incorporating industrial robots. Mazda produces three kinds of engine – rotary, reciprocating and diesel – and a wide range of vehicles from passenger cars to small trucks and buses.

Mazda's domestic sales system as of 1992 is made up of five dealerships – Mazda, Infifni (known as Auto until November 1991),

Autorama, Autosam and Eunos – comprising about 1,170 companies with 2,760 sales bases. Autorama was launched in 1982 as a channel for Ford cars. Eunos and Autosam were set up in 1989 and sell Mazda models as well as imported foreign cars. (Autosam accounts for about 800 of the companies and 900 of the sales bases mentioned above, but only for 1,700 employees out of the total 33,000 employed by the five dealers.)

Mazda has set up overseas production bases in 23 countries and has about 135 distributors and 5,600 dealers who market Mazdas through overseas trading companies. In the USA, its major overseas market, US Mazda is the general distributor, with a national sales network of about 750 dealers.

For the year to March 1992 Mazda's total sales came to 2.3 trillion yen and its net profits to 9.3 billion yen. In the same year, Mazda produced a total of 1.38 million passenger and commercial vehicles. The company had about 30,000 employees with an average age of around 40. Mazda is planning to employ more young people.

The key to Mazda's future strategy is to promote overseas business backed up by its links with Ford. This has been expanding year after year, starting with the commissioned production of engines and transaxles and continuing through participation in Ford's strategy on the international division of labour. Mazda produces small cars, parts and components. Its production technology and Ford's product-planning are integrated in order for both automakers to strengthen their co-operative system toward the promotion of an international division of labour, linking Ford's head office with Europe and Ford–Mazda.

As soon as Chairman Watanabe and President Yamamoto took office in 1984, Mazda announced that it would start locally-based production in the USA. Mazda has since invested US$550 million in a modern manufacturing facility on the site of one of Ford's former plants in Flat Rock, Michigan. This is one of Mazda's major overseas projects based on a close partnership with Ford. The plant has been in full operation since 1987 with an annual capacity of 240,000 vehicles producing the MX–6, the 626 (known as the Chronos in Japan) and the Probe, which has been exported to Japan since 1988. Mazda met the full cost of the plant, and the cars have been supplied to both Ford and Mazda distributors. Mazda employed union members of the UAW for the new plant and signed a new union contract, simplifying the managerial structure. Its promotion of locally-based production was noted as an experimental case of the Japanese-style system adapted to the American cultural and spiritual climate.

Mazda has also been promoting production through an international division of labour with Ford and Kia, the second largest automaker in the Republic of Korea. Mazda was already associated with Kia Motors, having an 8 per-cent stake in the capital. Kia Motors produces the Festiva – a fuel-efficient, economy car developed by Mazda in Kia's new plant – and supplies the models to Ford (with some gong to Japan as well through the Autorama marketing channel). This arrangement allows the three-company alliance to develop the automobile industry in developing countries and to compete well with other automakers such as GM, Toyota and Nissan. Thus, Mazda has found a way of using the excellent and cost-effective workforce in the NIES countries and Mexico for the manufacture of highly cost-competitive economy cars, while devoting the remaining corporate energy to the development of new technology and the enhancement of product-planning capacities, thereby also helping Ford in its global strategies. The partnership between Ford and Mazda has changed from simple complementary work to strategic integration.

Mazda has also put great effort into enhancing its technological development capacity. To this end Mazda has a laboratory in Yokohama, where research and development is carried out in fields such as car electronics, new materials, production technology and manufacturing systems, including industrial robots.

Since 1986, Mazda has launched a succession of new models as well as a variety of engines ranging from the compact to the heavy-duty.

MITSUBISHI MOTORS

This company started in 1970 as a joint venture between Mitsubishi Heavy Industries, owning 85 per cent of the stock, and Chrysler with 15 per cent. In 1985, President Tate of Mitsubihi Motors and Chairman Iaccoca of Chrysler agreed on the cancellation of a basic contract of their joint venture. Following this, Mitsubishi Heavy Industries had a 50 per-cent share in Mitsubishi Motors, Chrysler 10 per cent and other companies 40 per cent. In the autumn of 1988, shares were listed on the stock exchange, and by the end of September 1989 the shareholding ratio had shifted greatly to: Mitsubishi Heavy Industries 28 per cent, Chrysler 13 per cent and other companies 59 per cent. By 1992 the position was: Mitsubishi Heavy Industries 26 per cent and Chrysler 6 per cent.

Although Mitsubishi Motors was established in 1970, its automobile enterprises date back to 1917, when Mitsubishi Zosen, a shipbuilding company, turned out the Model A car, the first Japanese mass-produced car. This car business was suspended in 1921, but vehicle production was resumed in 1932 with the large Fuso bus. The company was renamed Mitsubishi Heavy Industries in 1934, and merged with Mitsubishi Aircraft to produce large trucks and military vehicles.

After the war, Mitsubishi Heavy Industries resumed the production of trucks and buses, and in 1950 was divided into three parts to produce trucks, buses, Jeeps and three-wheel trucks. In 1964, the three were again incorporated into Mitsubishi Heavy Industries. With the liberalization of capital, President Makita entered into a contract with Chrysler in 1969, and separated the automobile manufacturing division from Mitsubishi Heavy Industries. The automobile division was then incorporated as Mitsubishi Motors. At first, Chrysler held 15 per cent of the capital and planned to increase it to 30 per cent but failed to do so due to a management crisis. After the Chrysler crisis, both companies enjoyed a partnership based on equal terms.

The line of business included a production of cars from the minicar Minca model to the large Devonair, in addition to commercial cars ranging from the Minicab to trucks, buses and industrial engines. Mitsubishi has manufacturing facilities in eight plants in Nagoya, Mizushima, Kyoto and Tokyo, and operates knock-down production in thirty-two countries.

Although Mitsubishi Automobile Sales Company used to supervise domestic sales as a distributor, Mitsubishi Motors and the Sales Company were combined in April 1984 to provide three sales channels – Galant and Car Plaza for cars and Fuso for trucks and buses – made up in 1992 of 310 companies with 1,320 sales bases. Mitsubishi markets its products in North America through the Chrysler sales network and distributors affiliated to Mitsubishi Motors.

Mitsubishi has invested in overseas operations in 19 countries and has substantial holdings in about thirty companies abroad. Of these, about half are involved in automobile production and are based predominantly in Southeast Asia (Thailand, Indonesia, the Philippines and Malaysia). Other manufacturing operations are located in Korea, Taiwan, Australia, New Zealand, India, the Netherlands and the USA.

For the year to the end of March 1992, Mitsubishi's sales came to 2.55 trillion yen and net profits to 27 billion yen. Mitsubishi had 26,500 employees and turned out 1.4 million units, of which 640,000 were exported. Mitsubishi also supplies components and production licences to Chrysler, Hyundei Motors (Korea) and Proton of Malaysia. Mitsubishi excels in design and development and, since the early 1980s, has improved its production technology considerably.

Perhaps it can be said that Mitsubishi's weak point is in marketing products and this is a possible reason for a certain inability of Mitsubishi's cars to 'hit it off' despite the outstanding product-planning capacity demonstrated by the Mirage and the Galant series. Mitsubishi's line of production ranges widely from large-size trucks and buses to mini passenger cars. Such a wide range of products makes it difficult for Mitsubishi to demonstrate its strength in efficient product planning. Mitsubishi Motors Corporation is quite adept at utilizing aid from other companies, developing close unity with the Mitsubishi Group as one of its member companies. Back-up and co-operation from group companies include electronics from the Mitsubishi Electric Corporation, computerization of production facilities from Mitsubishi Heavy Industries and overseas marketing from the Mitsubishi Shoji (Trading) Company. This would be much more effective if Mitsubishi Motors itself could develop a more active overseas strategy.

The key to the future is how to develop the tie-up with Chrysler. A most significant factor in its overseas operations is the locally-based production at Diamond–Star Motors (DSM) in the USA, a joint venture with Chrysler announced in 1985 and put into operation in the autumn of 1988. The construction of a plant with an annual capacity of 240,000 units in Bloomington-Normal (Illinois) was quite a risk judging from the financial state of Mitsubishi Motors but it was significant in developing the partnership with Chrysler. The plant has up-to-date facilities with a highly-automated assembly process, and produces stylish small cars which are distributed through Chrysler's and Mitsubishi's (USA) marketing channels. In 1991m Mitsubishi purchased Chrysler's stock ownership of DSM, but the business partnership of both companies still continues.

The success in locally-based production has deepened the partnership from that of mere production by commission to co-operative ventures and product planning. Another point of note is the way in which Hyundei Motors (Korea) – which is technically and financially tied up with Mitsubishi – has been brought into the Chrysler–Mitsubishi alliance. Mitsubishi Motors Corporation exports annually more than 250,000 engines as well as small-size passenger cars to Chrysler.

The extent to which Chrysler and Mitsubishi can consolidate their international efforts depends on mutual understanding and appreciation of each others' merits. Other overseas projects include participation in the production of cars in Malaysia and investment in Chinese Motor of China – Taiwan for the joint production of trucks and commercial-use cars. Malaysia has a high car ownership ratio and good traffic conditions. Since Malaysia is a promising market and a sound production base, the Malaysian project offers Mitsubishi substantial profit, acting as an entry to the whole of Southeast Asia. Mitsubishi also has production bases in Thailand and the Philippines, further strengthening the construction of an international division-of-labour network after the yen's revaluation.

Through partnerships and tie-ups, Mitsubishi has sought to supply various parts of the world with components and development technology as well as finished products. At the same time, the company has taken measures to revive distribution channels, reorganizing and reviewing sales, in its sluggish domestic market. It is crucial for Mitsubishi to stay ahead of its competitors in product-planning capacity and not rely entirely on its brand image and colour to make its products more impressive.

FUJI HEAVY INDUSTRIES

Fuji Heavy Industries is well known for its product planning of four-wheel-drive vehicles. In prewar days and during the war, Fuji was renowned for the manufacture of fighter planes, known as Nakajima Airplane (founded by Chikkuhei Nakajima). After the war, Fuji was divided into fifteen companies, one of which was renamed Prince Motors which later merged with Nissan. Five of the remaining companies merged to become Fuji Heavy Industries.

In 1958, Fuji marketed a minicar, the Subaru 360, with the intention of producing a people's car. The Subaru 360 was a monocoque construction and favourably received. In 1966, Fuji marketed a small, front-wheel-drive car, the Subaru 1000, which was also highly praised. Although the major banks advised Isuzu, Mitsubishi and Fuji to link up in 1968, Fuji chose to link up with Nissan, promoting its independent strategy.

Fuji had been closely connected with personnel administration at Nissan and the Industrial Bank of Japan: its President Isamu Kawai was from Nissan and its Chairman Toshihiro Tajima from the Industrial Bank of Japan. In the autumn of 1972, Fuji launched the four-wheel-drive Subaru Leone van, which became famous for its powerful driving performance in cold districts and mountainous regions. Subaru is now very well known as a maker of '4WD vehicles' both at home and abroad. Although other automakers now have 4WD models, Fuji continues to lead this market due to its pioneering technology and expertise.

In 1992, Fuji had about 15,000 employees and was made up of five divisions – automobiles, machinery (general-use engines, freezing units, pumps, power generators), other vehicles (railway vehicles, rail motor vehicles, rail buses), buses and aircraft. The automobile division makes up about 82 per cent of total sales, the other division sharing between four and eight per cent each. Fuji has its domestic manufacturing facilities in four places – Ohmiya, Utsunumiya, Gunma (cars), and Isezaki (buses). Fuji also operates knock-down produciton in Taiwan, Thailand, New Zealand and Malaysia, marketing in about 100 countries, including the USA. Fuji's domestic sales network falls into three channels – Subaru (affiliated dealers made up of 63 companies with about 500 bases), Scope (special-contract dealers with about 360 stores), and about 22,000 other stores. The line-up of products as of 1992 included the Subaru Bighorn Wagon, the Legacy, the small Leone model, the Justy two-box economy car, the Domingo one-box car, the 3.3 litre Alcione specialty car and the 660 cc Vivio and Sambar light cars and trucks.

For the year to March 1992, Fuji's total sales came to 824 billion yen, and net profits to just 1.3 billion yen, a significant improvement on the previous year, however, which saw a net loss of about 66 billion yen. Total output amounted to 516,000 units (plus those produced by commission from Nissan). The Alcione and Leone, which have a high rate of added value, are exported. Since 1988 however, production of the Leone has been reduced in favour of the Legacy with its newly-developed horizontally-opposed engine. The four-wheel drive production ratio is 65 per cent of small-size cars. Fuji needs to continue to promote its unique and original merchandising in order to survive the competition of other mass producers and to strengthen its partnership with Nissan to a higher level than the present tie-up for licensee production.

Fuji's basic policy is to hold on to original product planning, and it is attempting to equal the strategy of automobile manufacturers such as Audi and BMW. Fuji worked with VDT of the Netherlands in developing the world's first continuously-variable transmission, and also with parts makers in developing new mechanisms such as the Electro-Pneumatic Suspension and the Automatic 4WD Shift. Fuji's specialty car, the Alcione, was well received by the young and has sold well since its launch.

One of Fuji's strong points is its procurement skills and expertise, developed through many years of experience in aircraft and industrial-use vehicles. Another strong point is its high standard of engine technology. The Alcione Project PART II achieved domestic sales of 30,000 cars a month. Leone 4WD is selling well in parts of the USA and Canada. Fuji has also ensured the financial stability of its affiliated dealers in Japan.

Fuji is to enhance its merchandising capacity and promote a balanced strategy for both domestic and overseas markets. It has to clarify its relationship with Nissan in terms of commissioned production and technological development. Former President Tajima declared that Fuji would co-operate with Nissan's rocket technology team (for the joint development of the Patriot).

Abroad, Fuji's biggest operation is a production facility which it set up in co-operation with Isuzu in the USA at Lafayette, Indiana in 1987. Fuji has a 51 per-cent stake in this operation, which began production in 1989 of the Legacy and Isuzu's Rodeo van. As of 1992, the joint production capacity of the plant was 160,000 units a year, but it is planned to raise this to 240,000.

DAIHATSU MOTORS

Daihatsu, the only automaker in the Kansai region, is a long-established company which started out making internal-combustion engines. It was so well-received as a manufacturer of marine engines that army landing boats used to be called 'Daihatsu', and to this day the company excels in diesel-engine technology. Daihatsu is the longest-established company organization of all the existing automakers in Japan. It marketed three-wheel cars in 1930 and small four-wheel trucks in 1937, but it failed to get into mass production. Daihatsu began operations in the Ikeda plant near Osaka (also the present head office) in 1939. Daihatsu produced marine engines and weapons during the war, and manufactured mainly marine engines after the war. Daihatsu marketed the three-wheel Bee car in 1951, and was then renamed the Daihatsu Motor Corporation at the end of that year. It entered the four-wheel automobile industry with the production of the small four-wheel Vesta truck in 1958 and the compact four-wheel Hijet truck in 1960. Its car production started in 1963 with the small Compano Wagon car, which was followed by the Berlina 800 in 1964.

With the liberalization of capital and reorganization of the automobile industry, Daihatsu tied up with Toyota. It joined the Toyota group in 1967. Toyota subscribed capital funds of 15 per cent, felled some executive posts, commissioned Daihatsu to produce some of its models, and helped in the rationalization of plants and the improvement of production technology.

The Daihatsu Automobile Sales Company was set up in 1968, but this was merged with the parent company in 1981 in order to improve management efficiency.

In 1977 Daihatsu launched the popular Charade car, an economy model which won the 'Japanese Car of The Year' award. In 1981 Daihatsu made a contract with the Innocenti Corporation of Italy to supply it with the Charade 1000 cc three-cylinder engines and transmissions that are incorporated in the Charade and, in 1985, supplied 15,700 engines including diesel engines.

As of 1992, the line-up of Daihatsu products included three 660 cc minicars – the Mira, the Lisa and the Opti – the popular Applause car, the Charade, the 2.8 litre diesel 4WD Rugger, the 1.6 litre 4WD Rocky, the Delta truck and the 660 cc commercial use Hijet van. It also produces the Corolla van, the Blizzard and Townace under commission from Toyota.

Daihatsu has four production facilities – Ikeda, Kyoto, Shiga–Ryuo and Tada. Daihatsu Diesel, its affiliated company, produces diesel engines. Daihatsu has assembly plants in Ikeda, Kyoto and Shiga–Ryuo. The Kyoto plant, where Charades are assembled, has the highest output/manufacturing space ratio in Japan. Daihatsu is known for its production efficiency and flexibility in mixed -model manufacturing lines, from remodelling older facilities to computerizing production systems by introducing industrial robots and also Toyota's 'Kanban' system.

Daihatsu has overseas production facilities at eleven sites in 9 countries. Now, in the early 1990s, it is putting particular emphasis on strengthening sales to other Asian countries, following disappointing domestic sales in fiscal 1991 and its withdrawal from the US market in February 1992.

The domestic sales network is made up of about seventy-five affili-ated dealers (with about 700 sales bases) and 36,000 other stores. Total sales for the year to March 1992 amounted to 783 billion yen and net profits to 3.6 billion yen. Total output by the 12,000 employees was about 660,000 units in addition to the units produced under licence for Toyota. Daihatsu has the lowest export ratio of all Japanese car makers, exporting just under 190,000 vehicles in fiscal 1991.

Daihatsu has had an active overseas promotion policy. It signed a technology transfer contract with the Chinese government in 1984 and began producing the light Hijet commercial-use van in Tienchin. It also started producing the Charade in Taiwan, and in 1985 put an engine-assembly plant into operation in Indonesia. Daihatsu started exporting to the USA in 1987 and was planning to introduce a 1500 cc model there in order to strengthen its product line-up. In 1992, however, the company announced its retreat from the US market. From now on, Daihatsu's strategy will be to focus more on the Asian and European markets, including eastern Europe.

ISUZU MOTORS

Isuzu Motors is the oldest Japanese automaker, producing large and medium-sized trucks, buses and passenger cars. Under a technical tie-up with GM, Isuzu has played a part in GM's global strategy.

Tokyo Ishikawajima Zosen was, in 1918, a shipbuilding company which started in the automobile business along with Wolseley of the United Kingdom. Its automobile manufacturing division was incorporated into the Ishikawajima Automobile Manufacturing Company. This then merged with Dat Automobile Manufacturing and the Tokyo Gas–Electric Industries and was licensed by the Automobile Manufacturing Enterprise Act, (along with Toyota and Nissan). During the war and postwar years, the three automakers came to be called 'The Big Three'. Ishikawajima was renamed the Diesel Automobile Industries in 1941, and manufactured trucks and military vehicles. It changed its name to Isuzu Motors in 1949. It was then producing trucks and buses. In 1953, it arranged technical transfers with Rootes of the United Kingdom to produce cars, the first being the Hillman Minx.

Isuzu's Fujisawa plant was built in 1962 and designed to mass produce 150,000 small cars a year: this is still one of their major plants. In 1961, Isuzu launched the Bellel car, the first in Japan with a diesel engine. With a growing trend toward the liberalization of capital and reorganization of the industry in the late 1960s, Isuzu planned to link up with some of the smaller domestic automakers, namely Mitsubishi and

Fuji, but this was aborted due to Fuji's membership of the Nissan group and the association of Mitsubishi with Chrysler.

In 1971, on the advice of the Daiichi–Kangyo Bank and Itoh Chu-Shoji (Trading Company), Isuzu formed a link with GM through GM's investment in Isuzu in order to strengthen their management base. (GM is still the largest stockholder with a capital holding in 1992 of 37.5 per cent.) The marketing of Isuzu's small trucks was then done through GM's sales network. Isuzu also took part in the joint development and production of small cars with Opel of Germany, a GM subsidiary. Isuzu marketed the Gemini in 1974 and the Florian Aska in 1983, and also supplied GM with one million transaxles for J–cars until 1983. In 1981, Isuzu formed a marketing link with Yanase, the largest distributor of foreign cars. When GM tied up with Suzuki Motors, Suzuki took on some of Isuzu's stock and Isuzu some of Suzuki's stock.

Isuzu produces small cars, and a full line-up of trucks and buses, small and large. In 1992, trucks and buses made up about 55 per cent of its total sales, cars about 13 per cent, components (especially diesel engines), motor boats and other products the remaining 32 per cent. In early 1993 Isuzu announced their retreat from passenger car production.

Isuzu operates knock-down production in 45 countries, and has recently started to export to some Asian countries including China. The Thai production base tops other overseas bases in terms of its output of trucks and commercial cars.

Isuzu's domestic sales network consists of three channels – Isuzu, Motor and Auto (plus a subdealer of Gemini) making a total of about 260 companies. Isuzu also markets specialty cars through Yanase.

For the year to October 1991, Isuzu's total sales came to 1.15 trillion yen, on which it made a net loss of 47 billion yen. This was the second time that Isuzu had dipped into the red in the last ten years, the other time being in 1986 due to the sudden rise in the value of the yen.

In June 1987, Isuzu announced its intention to start production in the USA in partnership with Fuji Heavy Industries. Production began at Lafayette, Indiana in September 1989. Also, in 1989, Isuzu began production of commercial vehicles in a joint venture with GM at Luton, England (GM 60 per cent, Isuzu 40 per cent). Isuzu's overseas activities also included technical co-operation in the production of commercial cars with Hindostan Motors of India in 1983, and technical assistance to China Motor Industries for the production of 40,000 small trucks as part of a product-and-technical trade contract in 1985.

Isuzu has been a forerunner in developing electronic car components. It brought out the first electronically-controlled ceramic engine and developed an electronically-controlled automatic five-shift transmission, featuring the advantages of a manual transmission (with low fuel consumption, low noise and ease of operation).

Isuzu intends to strengthen overseas exports and bases and to play a crucial role in GM's small-truck strategy. One of Isuzu's corporate themes is to improve the product-planning capacity of finished products and components so that it can be at the centre of the small-vehicle group and diesel engine technology. It also intends to strengthen its sales network in America and improve its domestic sales system.

SUZUKI MOTORS

Michio Suzuki founded Suzuki Loom Manufacturing in 1909 and was engaged in the manufacture of weapons and machines during the war. In 1952 it marketed bicycles with an auxiliary engine and thus made a start as a manufacturer of two-wheelers. In 1954, it was renamed Suzuki Motors and marketed the mini, four-wheel Suzulite car in 1955. It entered the outboard-motor industry in 1965, and the housing industry in 1974. It marketed the mini Fronte 360 car in 1967, the mini four-wheel-drive Jimny car in 1970, and the low-priced mini Alto car in 1979. The Alto was so inexpensive – priced at only ¥479,000 – that Mr Hanai, former Chairman of Toyota, said, 'I have no idea how the cost has been kept that low.' The Alto was a great success and managed to turn round a declining market.

Suzuki has had a positive overseas strategy. Firstly, it tied up with GM and Isuzu in 1981. Suzuki then signed a contract with the Pakistan National Automobile Corporation for the locally-based production of four-wheelers, concluded a similar contract with Multi Corporation of India and another technical contract with Santana Corporation of Spain in 1982. Other overseas projects included a partnerhsip with the China Airline Technical Company for the production of small trucks (this was in 1984), a tie-up with Aberio Corporation of Spain for knock-down production of two-wheelers and a joint venture with Indian Motorcycles Private, Ltd. of India for the production of two-wheelers.

Suzuki leads the mini automobile industry with a one-third share of the total number of minicars sold in Japan. The minicar line-up as of 1992 comprised the following 660 cc models: the Alto, the Cervo, the Cappucino, the 4WD Jimny and, aimed at the commercial market, the Alto Van, the Carry and the Every. Apart from these minicars, Suzuki produces the 1.6 litre Escudo Wagon and the Cultus economy car which comes in engine sizes between 1.0 and 1.5 litres. Of Suzuki's total sales in 1992, four-wheelers made up 72 per cent, two-wheelers about 16 per cent and others 12 per cent.

GM holds 3.5 per cent of Suzuki's capital and Isuzu about 2.7 per cent; Suzuki, in turn, holds 1.2 per cent of Isuzu's capital.

Suzuki has manufacturing facilities at five sites – at its head office at Hamanagun in Shizuoka Prefecture, Toyokawa, Kosei, Iwata and Osuga. Four-wheelers are produced at the Kosei and Iwata plants and abroad in 19 countries.

Suzuki's domestic sales network for four-wheelers comprises the Cultus and Suzuki stores (which also deal in two-wheelers). Together, they are organized into about 130 companies and 800 bases. Apart from these, Suzuki products sell through about 40 thousand sales outlets in Japan. Overseas, four-wheelers are sold through about 150 sales agencies in 100 countries.

For the year to March 1992, Suzuki's total sales came to 1.05 trillion yen and net profits to 8.9 billion yen. With a little under 13,000 employees Suzuki turned out 863,000 four-wheelers.

In the technological field, Suzuki developed an oil-cooled engine for two-wheelers. It has automatic transmission and four-wheel drive in its mini commercial-use cars and seating specially designed for female drivers, responding to the needs of women, who tend to be the purchasers of small, second cars.

Suzuki was faced with two major difficulties in the 1980s. One of these was the slump in demand for two-wheelers due to competition from Honda and Yamaha. The other was a reduction from 80,000 to 60,000 in 1984 of the number of Cultus cars exported in association with GM. In response to this export slump Suzuki embarked upon a joint venture with GM for locally-based production of the Cultus in Canada in autumn 1986. Production began in spring 1989 and although in 1992 Suzuki only exported 10,000 Cultus cars to North America it managed to supply GM with 100,000 units of this model produced at the Canada plant.

It has also started a joint business with Deiu to produce minicars and has signed a contract to manufacture the Cultus in Hungary with production due to begin in October 1992. The plan is to target the Hungarian domestic market at first, but then to expand production so as to be able to export to other European countries.

HINO MOTORS

Japanese major truck manufacturers include Mitsubishi, Isuzu, Hino and Nissan Diesel. Hino Motors is the only specialized producer of large and medium-sized trucks and buses belonging to the Toyota group. Hino Motors was formerly Hino Heavy Industries, which was separated from Diesel Automobile Industries (now Isuzu Motors) in 1942. It Produced special army vehicles up until the end of the war.

It was renamed Hino Industries in 1946 and started to market trailer trucks in 1947. After that, Hino produced trailer buses, trolley buses and buses with underfloor engines (the first of their kind in Japan). In 1948, Hino set up a separate sales company, now the Hino Automobile Sales Company. Hino entered into a technical tie-up with Renault of France in 1953 and produced Renautl cars up until 1963. Hino then began to market their own cars – the Contessa 900, the Contessa 1300 and a small truck, the Briska. Hino joined the Toyota group in 1966, which enabled Hino to reduce its own car division and to deal exclusively in large trucks and buses, and also to make full use of its capacity to produce cars commissioned by Toyota. Toyota held 11.2 per cent of Hino's capital in 1992.

Hino produces for itself various kinds of trucks and buses, tractors and diesel engines, and in the 1980s began the production of double-decker buses. It has manufacturing facilities in Hino, Hamura and Nitta, and operates knock-down production in 30 countries abroad. Its domestic distributor (Hino Automobile Sales) is made up of 56 dealers with 235 bases; overseas, it has about 100 distributors.

For the year to March 1992, Hino's total sales came to 637.5 billion yen and net profits to 7.35 billion yen. It had just over 8,000 employees and turned out 86,000 vehicles, of which 26,000 were exported.

Hino sought to diversify its products in response to changes in market circumstances after the oil crisis. The need to improve transport efficiency and the reorganization of the expressway system increased the demand for long-distance and urban delivery vehicles. Hino Motors immediately responded to this market trend with the entry of new products such as the medium-sized Hino Ranger trucks, the Super Dolphin – a large truck with a powerful and efficient diesel engine ranging in size from 8.8 to 19.7 litres and capable of carrying a load of up to 11,750 kg – and a small bus, the Hino Rainbow.

In the mid-1980s Hino suffered from a slump in the domestic market for standard trucks. Hino's membership of the Toyota group meant that its output of small trucks and the Tercel and Corsa compact cars commissioned by Toyota was fixed. The company rationalized some of its methods (in accordance with Toyota) and succeeded with its own product planning for trucks and buses and exports of large trucks. It was particularly successful with its large trucks in the late 1980s and early 1990s, profits reaching a peak in fiscal 1990, thanks both to the growth in domestic consumer demand as the 'bubble economy' expanded ever further and to its development of highly-acclaimed, innovative models.

Hino has anticipated market trends and conditions in many countries and is promoting a global export strategy which includes the improvement of cars destined for export, the establishment of a local sales and servicing system and the promotion of locally-based production. Notably, in 1985, Hino concluded an export contract with China (its export partner of 22 years) for 16,000 medium-sized trucks on a product/technology trading basis. Hino has been involved in a joint venture in Thailand since 1964, and this now has a local content ratio of 45 per cent. In Burma, Hino operated the assembly of large trucks and buses with a local content ratio of 70 per cent. In 1985, Hino signed a contract on diesel engine technology with Ashoka Rayland Corporation of India and, in 1986, founded a joint company in Pakistan. In addition, Hino has, since the 1980s, been planning joint ventures, technical co-operation and locally-based production in Malaysia, Indonesia, Australia, South Africa and China.

Hino started a joint venture with the Mitsui trading company in order to export large trucks to the USA in 1985. In 1992, Hino exported 1,580 large trucks to the USA.

In May 1992, marking its 50th anniversary, Hino launched its 'Vision for the 21st Century'. By the year 2001 it plans to raise annual sales to one trillion yen. Also in May 1992 it reached agreement with Mitsubishi, Isuzu and Nissan Diesel to supply these companies with engine technology for a new generation of buses.

NISSAN DIESEL MOTORS

This company is a specialized producer of large trucks and buses in the Nissan group. Nissan Diesel was once famed for the production of a two-cycle engine, the Uni-Flow Scavenging Diesel Engine, with the trademark of 'UD'. Its history dates back to 1935 when Japan Diesel Industries was established for the manufacture and marketing of diesel engines. It obtained the patent of a two-cycle diesel engine from German Krupp Junkers in 1936. The company was renamed Kanegafuchi Diesel Industries in 1942 and Minsei Industries in 1946 when it began the production of large trucks and buses. A separate sales division was set up in 1955, the Nissan–Minsei Diesel Sales Company, with a 50 per-cent share of the capital. It was renamed Nissan Diesel Motors in 1960. Its vehicle and engine assembly facilities were moved from Kawaguchi to a new plant in Ageo in 1962, where it established a mass production system. In 1981, it began operations in the Gunma plant, specializing in 4-ton trucks.

In 1992, large and medium-sized trucks accounted for 58 per cent of total sales, buses 14 per cent, engines 13 per cent and small trucks (produced on commission from Nissan Motor) 15 per cent. Since 1950, Nissan has had a share in the company's capital (39.8 per cent as of March 1992). It now has domestic production facilities in Ageo and Gunma (having closed down its Kawaguchi plant in 1987 in order to concentrate its activities), and operates knock-down production overseas in 20 countries. Nissan Diesel markets domestically through Nissan Diesel Sales Company, using 47 companies with about 220 bases, and 70 distributors in about 100 countries. Total exports over the years amount to something in the region of 200,000 units.

For the year to March 1992, Nissan Diesel's total sales came to 377 billion yen, and net profits to 1.4 billion yen. With 5,600 employees it turned out about 57,000 vehicles plus the small trucks it manufactured under commission from Nissan Motor. It exported 16,500 trucks and buses. Its export markets are worldwide: Southeast Asia accounts for about 50 per cent and Oceania 10 per cent.

Like Hino, however, Nissan Diesel has experienced some difficulty in the US market. It set up an affiliated sales company, Nissan Diesel America Inc. in the USA in 1984 and started exporting large trucks there in 1985. In the same year, it concluded a contract with Navistar International (the top-ranking American truck producer) for the supply of medium-sized trucks. Through these two channels it sold 1,586 vehicles in 1988. The contract with Navistar came to an end in

1990. In 1992 Nissan Diesel managed to export about 3,000 trucks to the USA.

In 1985, Nissan Diesel concluded a contract with China Second Motor Manufacturing (one of China's largest truck production bases, located in Hupei Province) for technology transfers and consultation about constructing new plants. This venture was regarded as one of the national projects in China's seventh five-year plan. Nissan Diesel sent a number of engineers and technicians to China and the co-operation bore fruit in 1990 when the first trucks started coming off the production lines. The contract with China Second Motor Manufacturing came to an end in September 1991, but a memorandum on co-operation signed at that time maintains the links between the two companies.

As of 1992, Nissan Diesel has been in negotiation with the Vietnamese government regarding technical transfer for the production of mid-size trucks and buses. Co-operation with Korea's Deiu was also under negotiation in 1992. Nissan Diesel's future prosperity depends largely on business with other Asian countries rather than with the USA.

Nissan Diesel has future strategic objectives to promote technological development for casting and for large diesel engines such as turbo and direct-injection types; it also plans to improve product-planning capacity and production technology standards to meet the nees of a diversified market.

**Table 26** Vital Statistics of Japanese Automobile Manufacturers 1971–92

| Maker | Year (accounting month) | No. of automobiles produced (passenger cars in brackets) | No. of finished vehicles exported (KD sets in brackets) | Sales (¥ million) | Net Profit (¥ million) | No. of employees |
|---|---|---|---|---|---|---|
| Toyota* | 1970(5) | 1,516,969 (978,345) | 415,352 | 784,471 | 21,403 | 38,200 |
| | 75(6)** | 2,421,305 (1,768,736) | 901,430 | 1,809,871 | 48,211 | 44,600 |
| | 80(6) | 3,320,498 (2,258,621) | 1,611,646 (79,900) | 3,310,181 | 143,568 | 47,100 |
| | 85(6) | 3,540,646 (2,458,671) | 1,901,802 (159,197) | 6,064.420 | 308,309 | 61,700 |
| | 90(6) | 4,028,149 (3,181,919) | 1,608,497 | 7,998,050 | 360,803 | 70,800 |
| | 92(6) | 4,033,357 (3,179,080) | 1,694,732 | 8,940,898 | 200,862 | 71,700 |
| Nissan* | 1971(3) | 1,421,142 (949,349) | 461,027 | 799,316 | 28,487 | 48,600 |
| | 76(3) | 2,111,957 (1,532,858) | 975,294 | 1,770,198 | 52,214 | 51,500 |
| | 81(3) | 2,648,674 (1,933,700) | 1,475,453 (189,687) | 3,016,190 | 85,911 | 56,300 |
| | 86(3) | 2,438,520 (1,836,182) | 1,408,024 (206,731) | 3,754,172 | 64,752 | 56,700 |
| | 91(3) | 2,379,634 (1,990,068) | 959,054 | 4,175,013 | 78,159 | 56,900 |
| | 92(3) | 2,323,720 (1,936,566) | 964,139 | 4,270,523 | 54,191 | 55,600 |
| Honda | 1971(2) | 387,552 (280,315) | 23,094 | 316,331 | 16,432 | 12,200 |
| | 76(2) | 430,260 (351,289) | 214,582 | 563,805 | 11,954 | 18,500 |
| | 81(2) | 978,475 (859,717) | 690,176 (7,400) | 1,344,892 | 30,137 | 22,900 |
| | 86(2) | 1,160,821 (986,708) | 677,195 (241,980) | 2,245,743 | 45,232 | 28,100 |
| | 91(3) | 1,375,236 (1,199,888) | 678,574 | 2,800,199 | 46,667 | 31,600 |
| | 92(3) | 1,330,648 (1,195,623) | 664,875 | 2,911,044 | 32,566 | 31,500 |
| Mazda* | 1970(10) | 423,097 (211,790) | 71,858 | 221,706 | 14,474 | 25,900 |
| | 75(10) | 640,418 (370,070) | 315,356 | 496,488 | -1,671 | 33,300 |
| | 80(10) | 1,102,749 (721,211) | 684,307 (78,320) | 1,031,066 | 15,740 | 27,300 |
| | 85(10) | 1,160,929 (785,707) | 807,966 (170,180) | 1,569,553 | 31,173 | 27,600 |
| | 91(3) | 1,434,787 (1,128,465) | 856,798 | 2,225,714 | 27,011 | 29,600 |
| | 92(3) | 1,381,431 (1,091,403) | 859,155 | 2,304,110 | 9,273 | 29,800 |

| Maker | Year (accounting month) | No. of automobiles produced (passenger cars in brackets) | No. of finished vehicles exported (KD sets in brackets) | Sales (¥million) | Net Profit (¥million) | No. of employees |
|---|---|---|---|---|---|---|
| Mitsubishi* | 1971(3) | 468,607 (248,776) | 31,588 | – | – | – |
| | 76(3) | 533,041 (307,459) | 187,240 | – | – | – |
| | 81(3) | 1,124,213 (669,459) | 598,389 (83,658) | 1,107,946 | 8,355 | 23,800 |
| | 86(3) | 1,188,636 (594,996) | 664,900 (85,740) | 1,578,823 | 25,332 | 23,000 |
| | 91(3) | 1,366,508 (857,206) | 617,019 | 2,313,636 | 25,208 | 25,500 |
| | 92(3) | 1,407,801 (916,929) | 640,385 | 2,554,055 | 27,023 | 26,500 |
| Fuji Jyuko* | 1971(3) | 231,377 (154,318) | 19,700 | 116,845 | 2,080 | 13,500 |
| | 76(3) | 190,921 (118,464) | 57,977 | 200,370 | 1,322 | 13,600 |
| | 81(3) | 440,329 (203,394) | 241,992 (8,500) | 464,846 | 11,333 | 13,800 |
| | 86(3) | 611,575 (280,180) | 297,840 (3,000) | 768,424 | 12,921 | 14,100 |
| | 91(3) | 545,606 (334,374) | 186,300 | 755,803 | -66,461 | 15,200 |
| | 92(3) | 515,653 (325,994) | 190,404 | 823,917 | 1,288 | 14,800 |
| Daihatsu | 1970(4) | 259,850 (100,720) | 24,636 | 95,606 | 4,330 | 7,100 |
| | 75(6)*** | 292,470 (108,656) | 18,552 | 165,064 | 2,226 | 8,000 |
| | 80(6) | 403,543 (147,313) | 109,318 | 331,357 | 4,563 | 9,100 |
| | 85(6) | 577,476 (158,657) | 146,902 (29,106) | 515,911 | 6,642 | 10,800 |
| | 91(3) | 691,208 (421,300) | 147,699 | 787,502 | 6,934 | 11,900 |
| | 92(3) | 664,271 (421,853) | 189,304 | 783,393 | 3,616 | 11,800 |
| Isuzu* | 1970(10) | 149,773 (23,482) | 17,513 | 198,675 | 1,445 | 11,700 |
| | 75(10) | 245,077 (65,913) | 112,752 | 356,302 | -8,721 | 13,300 |
| | 80(10) | 479,971 (106,096) | 261,478 | 687,713 | 4,954 | 15,500 |
| | 85(10) | 570,135 (194,131) | 393,934 (41,500) | 1,016,500 | 13,384 | 16,000 |
| | 90(10) | 572,326 (214,476) | 373,573 | 1,195,873 | 7,640 | 13,400 |
| | 92(10) | 489,762 (140,144) | 299,56 | 1,145,629 | -47,281 | 13,600 |

**Table 26** continued

| Maker | Year (accounting month) | No. of automobiles produced (passenger cars in brackets) | | No. of finished vehicles exported (KD sets in brackets) | | Sales (¥ million) | Net Profit (¥ million) | No. of employees |
|---|---|---|---|---|---|---|---|---|
| Suzuki | 1971(3) | 284,210 | (156,772) | 2,980 | | 136,657 | 7,932 | 10,000 |
| | 76(3) | 180,242 | (42,009) | 21,738 | | 166,966 | 1,468 | 8,800 |
| | 81(3) | 503,390 | (94,491) | 115,143 | | 457,779 | 4,793 | 9,100 |
| | 86(3) | 824,664 | (250,436) | 328,145 | (60,954) | 722,336 | 6,120 | 12,200 |
| | 91(3) | 861,359 | (524,703) | 268,455 | | 1,011,428 | 9,412 | 12,600 |
| | 92(3) | 863,249 | (541,208) | 285,949 | | 1,046,791 | 8,887 | 12,800 |
| Hino | 1971(3) | 55,165 | | 7,043 | | 122,354 | 5,692 | 6,400 |
| | 76(3) | 60,472 | | 17,633 | | 236,415 | 2,985 | 7,700 |
| | 81(3) | 74,611 | | 25,479 | | 389,394 | 4,676 | 8,300 |
| | 86(3) | 71,283 | | 31,388 | (1,510) | 470,590 | 4,423 | 8,300 |
| | 91(3) | 101,125 | | 37,122 | | 657,057 | 12,544 | 8,200 |
| | 92(3) | 86,344 | | 25,659 | | 637,479 | 7,348 | 8,300 |
| Nissan Diesel* | 1971(3) | 22,511 | | 2,226 | | 74,632 | 3,661 | 3,900 |
| | 76(3) | 26,450 | | 10,110 | | 124,983 | 2,150 | 5,300 |
| | 81(3) | 47,210 | | 21,434 | (280) | 271,000 | 2,865 | 6,400 |
| | 86(3) | 36,339 | | 15,418 | (56) | 261,550 | 1,214 | 6,100 |
| | 91(3) | 63,506 | | 22,503 | | 393,762 | 3,021 | 5,200 |
| | 92(3) | 57,346 | | 16,550 | | 377,219 | 1,395 | 5,600 |

*Source:* JAMA, *Jidosha tokei geppo* (Monthly automobile statistics report); and *Yuka shoken hokohusho* (annual report on company stock values); both quoted in Nissan Motor Co., Ltd.'s *Jidosha Sangyo Handbook 1990* and Jidosha Sangyo Handbook 1992/1993.
*Note:* * Knock-down (KD) sets are included in the production and export export figures 1970 and 1975/1971 and 1976.
** Figures for 13-month period.
*** Figures for 14-month period.

# CHAPTER 7

# *Conclusion*

TECHNOLOGICAL INNOVATION

The late Professor Abernathy pointed out in his last work, *The Industrial Renaissance*, that the automobile industry has become not merely a matured industry but is stepping a path towards becoming a de-matured industry. He says in the book that every industry has its own life cycle in relation to technological development and change: from its infancy an industry grows to maturity and then follows a decline.

Technological innovation is of two types – one is innovation of product technology, which revolutionizes the characteristics of manufacturing methods of products; the other is innovation of process technology, continually being added, under a fixed technological system, e.g. mass production technology through standardization, for the further improvement of production efficiency and quality. Needless to say, it is the innovation of product technology that alters the life cycle of a particular industry. Examples include the replacement of vacuum tubes by transistors, the appearance of semiconductors and large-scale integrated circuits, the recent appearance of ceramics, optical fibres and genetic engineering. It is difficult to predict the form of such technological innovations and they often appear quite suddenly. On the other hand, innovation of process technology is cumulative and helps the industry to survive. If process innovation contributes only to reducing costs, without any great change in product design or concept, it may only serve to lengthen the period of the industry's maturity. However, if the innovation is such as to effect the product concept, it will bring the industry into a new life cycle. Even if such radical product technology as can revolutionize the manufacturing methods of products is not initiated, the innovation of process technology can also de-mature the industry by stages.

In this context, automobiles with a new type of driving power (other than those with gasoline engines, including gas turbine cars, electrically-powered cars and hydrogen-powered cars) cannot completely replace gasoline engine cars, though they have been successful at an experimental stage. The future of the drive mechanism, the heart of automobiles, is uncertain. On the other hand, process technology has been advancing step by step ever since Henry Ford established a mass-production system which was designed to improve efficiency by synchronizing production lines and speeding up operations. While process technology continued to alter, changes to the model were also made at regular intervals, the engine mechanism and the transmission and suspension improved. All of these developments were made possible by process technology innovations which have combined to help the continued expansion of automobile technology and demand, playing a role in prolonging the maturity of the automobile industry.

Regulations on fuel efficiency (in order to reduce environmental pollution) and problems of energy saving triggered changes in car design and production technology, as did a more rapid promotion of electronics and new materials technology. The innovation of the drive mechanism and engine designs (such as the front-wheel-drive/front-engine cars) the advancement of design technology backed up by the CAD and CAM systems for reducing weight and improving performance, the adoption of extensive computerization of production processes through the introduction of industrial robots – all of these played a part in lengthening the period of maturity. The innovation of process technology has gone beyond technological developments and assumed new aspects such as parts procurement and the 'just-in-time' production systems.

The trend towards de-maturation in the automobile industry is global. The design and styling of cars, the development of the engine, driving unit and suspension, and the automation of production processes have gone through massive changes. Although large cars have been reduced in size and medium-sized and compact cars have increased their market share, the 1980s saw a marked trend in favour of a greater range of models, for new models to be introduced at shorter intervals, for a shorter lead time in developing new models and the appearance of one new-concept car after another. It is worthy of note that the innovation of process technology has shifted from the aim of reducing costs through scale economies to achieving earlier scale economies and more flexibility in multi-kind/small-lot production. The so-called FMS (flexible manufacturing system) was also a factor in the acceleration of this trend. This freed the automobile industry from conventional and rigid production systems and made it more adaptable to changes in the market environment and ups and downs of both quantity and kind.

THE JAPANESE CHALLENGE

The de-maturation of the automobile industry is taking place in other countries besides Japan. But the Japanese automobile industry, which may be seen as setting the trend and pace, ignited the de-maturation, causing quite an impact on the automobile industries of the world. What is now going on in the industry internationally appears to be that enormous waves of competitiveness, generated by technological innovation and the improvement of labour/management relations, are transforming the automobile industry, a so-called matured industry, into a dynamic de-matured industry. The industry is being regenerated by the challenge from the Japanese, who have, for a time, altered the map of the world's automobile industry.

The term, 'Japanese Challenge', can apply to other areas besides the automobile industry. In comparison with international competition in the automobile industry, the remarkable accomplishments of the 'Japanese Challenge' are regarded as the improvements in labour/management relations, the production-parts procurement system, technological inno-vation, the widespread introduction of new materials, electronics and industrial robots; all of this was achieved by close co-operation with related industries such as the materials, electronic and mechanical industries.

The two oil crises caused upheavals in the world automobile industry, and not just for a short time. For instance, Detroit lost its ranking in the world industry. It would be a mistake to analyse events exclusively in terms of large US cars versus Japanese compact cars, as a result of the second oil crisis, since this overlooks the nature of the 'Japanese Challenge' and its impact, especially on OECD countries. Although trends became more pronounced after the oil shock, a shift in demand from large-size cars to compact cars prevailed swiftly in the US automobile market, the underlying trends were already there but without being noticed. Since the 1960s there had been the emergence of certain phenomena, such as the retention or deterioration in productivity, the lowering of quality standards and stagnation in technical standards of US-made cars behind high values added per unit, ensuring high profitability from large-size US cars. On the other hand, the productivity and quality of Japanese cars were improving and technical standards were also rising to further distinguish their products from those of their competitors by the early 1970s. Judged in terms of profitability, large-size cars were supposed to have more than four times the profitability of compact cars. The true difference in competitiveness between Japan and the USA seems to have been too small to perceive.

Since for many years large-size cars made in Detroit had secured more profit per unit than Japanese and European cars, Detroit rested in peace on its high profitability without endeavouring to improve productivity and quality. After all, the market for large cars was not threatened by foreign automakers. Therefore, the 'Big Three' of Detroit managed to have their own way in business, in spite of the fat that excessive stockpiles flooded manufacturing processes, a deep distrust prevailed between labour and management and inefficient and irrational labour practices and poor communication with parts makers prevailed. Holding a large stock of parts was thought to ensure the speed-up of the line and the continuance of stability in production, and therefore productivity. Labour/management problems were superficially solved merely by improving working conditions, wages and social insurance benefits. No attempt was made to get to the heart of labour problems. Parts makers were made to reduce prices without trying to raise the technical standards; manufacturers were faced with thinking of ways to ensure a stable supply of parts from parts makers who were in severe competition with one another. Some minor factories went in for their own production of parts.

In spite of their high profits, they did not commit themselves to much research and development, and did not invest in facilities and equipment. Their product planning was directed towards variations in types and models of cars and the development of optional features in equipment and design. Little innovational effort was made with regard to the fundamentals of automobile – the engine, suspension, steering, and so on. Major technological developments by US automakers, since World War II, are only the overhead-valve (OHV) 8-cylinder engine and automatic transmission. They accepted innovative components such as the fuel injector and disk brake that had been developed and put into use by European producers. They remained with old-fashioned, worn-out manufacturing facilities for a long time, and were slow to introduce up-to-date machines and equipment. They invested almost exclusively in jigs and tools to meet the requirements for model changes.

Why did Detroit have no intention of making strategic investments into research and development or facilities and equipment during an age of prosperity? Detroit's managers try to gain as much superficial profit as possible during their limited terms of office; this is because they are usually evaluated in terms of how much they can distribute as dividends to the stockholders. The US automobile industry declined, not because it produced only large-size cars and failed to adapt itself to changes in the market environment, but because the way it did so accumulated an increasing number of problems. Detroit became swollen in constitution, which was veiled by the large amount of superficial profit created by large-size cars. Therefore, in spite of its sales, Detroit needed to produce at least 10 million cars a year in order to make a profit. It became less and less competitive in terms of productivity and quality, and less responsive and adaptable to environmental requirements with regard to safety, pollution and fuel efficiency.

Though not as bad as their US counterparts, European automakers had problems with their production systems that did not help productivity, quality or labour/management relations. The European industry was also boosted by the high economic growth of the European Economic Community (EEC). In Europe, too, there were high-class automobile manufacturers like Mercedes Benz and Volvo, which promoted research and development and never aimed to make profits simply through mass production. However, even they had problems – especially in their labour/management relationship – in spite of their fine creative engineers. They had expanded their production capacity during the 1960s but they were becoming less competitive and failed to rationalize after the first oil crisis.

In short, both US and European automakers kept to their old-fashioned manufacturing facilities and production systems until they ran into the second oil crisis. They were faced with rapid changes in the social environment and many unsolved problems that led them into decline. Thus it was that the later-starting Japanese automobile industry began to dominate the world industry, especially after the second oil crisis. Not that global changes in the automobile industry are to be described simply in terms of a market-sharing competition between a 'backward' USA and Europe and a 'forward' Japan. De-maturation-promoting technological innovation, the renewal of manufacturing facilities, and new trials in the whole system have come about in the industry throughout the world since the mid-1980s, and it is the Japanese who have taken up the 'Challenge'. In effect, Japan has offered the global industry a new lease of life.

NEW ISSUES
How did the 'Japanese Challenge' affect the world automobile industry and what problems did it pose? The challenge was significant in

breaking through conventional customs and practices in a mature automobile industry. The prevailing view was that the industry must be tailored to mass production and structured as an oligopoly; priority must be given to the pursuit of the economy of scale. A simple, uniform and inflexible production system prevailed, allowing minimal changes in technique and processes. Large-scale facilities had to be integrated, production speeded up, and full-line capacity used.

Under these conditions, markets would inevitable be flooded and the quality of products would suffer. Processes could not respond quickly to changes in the market, technology and the general social environment. The automobile industry could not respond to qualitative changes, diversification and individualization in the users' needs with full-line production and variation of models alone. The lead time needed to be reduced by individually-targeted product planning, in combination with a multi-kind/small-lot production system. Such a system can handle, for instance, the technical modifications required in response to government policies on safety, pollution and fuel efficiency. This can be clarified by noting that the American automobile industry had serious difficulties in responding to such regulations and consequently became much less competitive. In a conventional, rigid production system, mechanical and engineering innovations cannot be readily implemented, and problems quickly appear when trying to introduce new technology in new industrial fields in order to enhance fuel efficiency and improve performance.

In Japan, as we have seen, there are as many as eleven automakers in a dynamic and competitive structure (though there are tie-ups between some of them). Along with the major automakers with an annual output of two to three million cars, there are also several small-scale automakers producing up to 500,000 units a year. The 'Japanese Challenge' relates to the dynamic nd flexible structure of the industry and the systems of production of each of the major producers, the Japanese-style management system, labour/management relations, production and parts procurement. Not all these elements of the Japanese automobile industry were deliberate creations of industrialists or government, rather, they tend to reflect a Japanese way of doing things.

Of all the OECD countries, Japan was the last to start producing automobiles and since it had to start off with little capital and rather low technical standards, it had little choice but to call on the good sense and diligence of its workforce. Priority was given to the most effective utilization of the manufacturing facilities along with minimum manpower for tailoring product planning to market needs. Collective co-operation in the social and corporate systems in Japan was very effective, in all aspects of economic and corporate activities. Co-operation, co-ordinating social systems and corporate organizations based on the strong consciousness of belonging and the group identity of social and corporate members, worked to heighten various forms of collective efficiency such that given goals were attainable. This applied at the micro level of each company, at the level of groups and related industries, and also at the macro level of the industry as a whole and of the economy's commercial and financial systems along with the national government.

Although collective co-operation of this type is not limited to the automobile industry, it stands out in this case, especially in terms of labour/management reconciliation, QC activities, and close co-operative relations with materials and parts suppliers. Technological innovations in production processes go hand in hand with technological development and product-planning capacity is backed up by a co-operative workforce. The automakers linked up with materials and parts makers and distribution, sales and service on the output side. These features cannot be expressed or measured in numerical terms but, taken together, they do account for the competitiveness of the Japanese automobile industry and its ability to adapt to all manner of changes in conditions and circumstances.

The main points that the 'Japanese Challenge' has thrown up are as follows:

1 The Japanese system has revealed the limits of productivity gains from large-scale mass production of a standardized product since this overlooks the significance of qualitative changes in development and process technologies of the automobile production system.
2 In the production of automobiles, it is important to build up process technology on the job site, even when facilities are automated. It is also important to build up 'software' in process control, quality control and purchase control.
3 It has pointed out the demerits of the pursuit of excessive standardization and mass production of single-lot items, and clarified that there are conditions in which the demerits can be overcome by devising mass-production processes that can be readapted into multi-kind/small-lot processes. This is largely due to the fact that

the Japanese automobile industry originally had to serve a diversified market with limited manufacturing facilities.

4  It is necessary to make production much more responsive to business fluctuations, changes in the market environment and technical alterations. Process designing needs to be altered and facilities made flexible enough to cope with design alterations from the manufacture of parts to the final assemble.

5  It is important to learn about process technology on the job site. All workers should be part of QC circles; dependence on specialists should be minimized.

6  The product-planning system calls for the participation of parts makers from an early stage. It is also important for well-organized teamwork between the design department and other departments, such as production, sales and market research etc., to work effectively in order to reduce lead times and costs. Japanese automakers pioneered corporate innovations, including the utilization of the teamwork concept for product planning and simultaneous engineering, which since the late 1980s have been noted globally.

7  It is important to maintain collective corporate power (including materials and parts makers) and dynamism in related industries of the economy, even though their connections with the automobile industry are not direct.

INTERNATIONALIZATION OF THE INDUSTRY

With the emergence of the 'Japanese Challenge', the Japanese automobile industry became internationally competitive and began expanding exports rapidly. This was the start of the internationalization of the Japanese automobile industry. The industry had a strong international flavour from the beginning. International exchanges and transfers of technology were common, ranging from planning technology to design technology. The international nature of the automobile industry is borne out by the fact that more than one third of the world's output of about 45 million cars is exported. The high intensity of internationality in the automobile industry is manifested in multinational management with locally-based production through European and US automakers for their overseas operations. However, the automobile industry could not promote the internationalization of business operations so readily. Examples of European and US automakers show that they first established a position as international merchandisers before multinationalization. The

Japanese automobile industry simultaneously developed its value as an international merchandiser and multinationalized its management.

The first step in the internationalization of the Japanese automobile industry was to make its cars internationally competitive. Locally-based production and joint production in various parts of the world are the new forms of internationalization. Japanese automakers took large risks in locally-based production overseas, since it meant the acceptance of different types of labour practices and labour/management relations, production systems, management systems, parts procurement systems and material supply logistics. The appreciation of the yen, however, made overseas-based production more attractive.

Today the new possibilities of the division of labour and co-operation between manufacturers call for global strategies with longer-term perspectives instead of regarding locally-based production as a means of reducing trade friction. This standpoint is being recognized, especially in the USA.

Toyota, Nissan and Honda each have their own methods of overseas operations, especially in the USA. Toyota tied up with GM for locally-based production with joint management (NUMMI – New United Motor Manufacturing Inc.) in Fremont, California, while the other two made a sole entry to establish a 100 per-cent affiliated concern. On the basis of its experiences in NUMMI, Toyota also made a sole entry in Kentucky and started full-scale operations in 1988. Mazda made a sole entry (using a Ford plant) and started production in Michigan in 1987. Mitsubishi began on the basis of joint management with Chrysler in Illinois in 1988. Mazda and Mitsubishi produce cars for their partners and for their own distributors separately. Toyota chose to use GM's manufacturing facilities and to employ UAW members while Nissan, Honda and Toyota (in Kentucky) trained new workers and had little to do with the UAW. Mazda and Mitsubishi employed UAW members to start production. Comparing Nissan in Tennessee with Honda in Ohio, each had different ideas about the size and layout of their plants, production systems and parts-supply systems. Nissan built a large robot-operated plant. Honda started with two-wheelers and then switched to four-wheelers. Honda was the first to have a base in the USA with quite small investments, and has expanded in stages. Honda started operations in Ohio with an engine-assembly plant, and also an assembly plant in Canada in 1986. Both automakers associated with each other for business development, and aimed at producing 500,000 units a year at their second plant in Ohio. Both the Isuzu–Fuji Juko plant in Indiana

Table 27  Manufacturing Operations of Japanese Automobile Makers in Developed Countries

| | Honda (First Plant) | Honda (Second Plant) | Honda (Engine Plant) | Nissan | Mazda | Mitsubishi | Toyota | Toyota (Camry) | Toyota (Engines & Axles) | Fuji, Isuzu |
|---|---|---|---|---|---|---|---|---|---|---|
| Country | USA | | | | | | | | | |
| Japanese Maker | Honda | | | Nissan | Mazda | Mitsubishi | Toyota | Toyota | | Fuji, Isuzu |
| Type of Entry | Sole Entry | | | Sole Entry | *Sole Entry | **Joint Venture with Chrysler | Joint Venture with GM | Sole Entry | | Joint Venture |
| Name of Company | Honda of America Mfg, Inc. | | | Nissan Motor Manufacturing Corporation USA | *AutoAlliance International, Inc. (AAI) | Diamond-Star Motors Corporation | New United Motor Manufacturing Inc. (NUMMI) | Toyota Motor Manufacturing USA, Inc. | | Subaru-Isuzu Automotive Inc. |
| Established | February 1978 | | | July 1980 | January 1985 | October 1985 | February 1984 | January 1986 | | March 1987 |
| Current Share in Equity | Honda of America 97.58% Honda 2.42% | | | Nissan (USA) 100% | *Mazda 50% Ford 50% | **Mitsubishi 85% Others 15% | Toyota 50% GM 50% | Toyota 20% Toyota (U.S.A.) 80% | | Fuji 51% Isuzu 49% |
| Location | Marysville, Ohio | | | Smyrna, Tennessee | Flat Rock, Michigan | Bloomington-Normal, Illinois | Fremont, California | Georgetown, Kentucky | | Lafayette, Indiana |
| Vehicles/Parts Produced | Accord | Accord, Civic | Engines, Steering Components | Nissan truck (1-ton pay load), Sentra, Engines & Axles | MX-6, 626, Ford Probe | Mitsubishi Eclipse&Mirage, Eagle Talon & Summit, Plymouth Laser | Prizm, Corolla, Small Truck | Camry | Engines & Axles | Legacy (Fuji), Small Truck (Isuzu) |
| Start-Up | Nov 1982 | Dec 1989 | Sep 1986 | June 1983 | Sep 1987 | Sep 1988 | Dec 1984 | May 1968 | Nov 1988 | Sep 1989 |
| Annual Production Capacity | 360,000 units | 150,000 units | 500,000 engines | 250,000 units (450,000 in '92) | 240,000 units | 240,000 units | 300,000 units | 240,000 units | 300,000 units | 160,000 units |
| Employees | 6,300 | 500 | 1,600 | 4,800 | 3,500 | 2,900 | 3,600 | 3,500 | 500 | 1,900 |
| Total investment | US$883 million | US$380 million | US$670 million | US$1.2 billion | US$550 million | US$600 million | US$1.15 billion | US$800 million | US$300 million | US$500 million |
| Affiliated Technical/Design Centres | Honda R&D North America, Inc. Honda Engineering North America | | | Nissan Research & Development Inc. Nissan Design International, Inc. | Mazda R&D North America, Inc. | Mitsubishi Motors America, Inc. | Toyota Technical Center USA, Inc. Calty Design Research, Inc. | | | Isuzu Technical Center of America, Inc. Subaru Research & Design, Inc. |

| | Canada | | | | UK | | | |
|---|---|---|---|---|---|---|---|---|
| Japanese Maker | Honda | Toyota | Toyota | Suzuki | Nissan | Honda | Isuzu | Toyota |
| Type of Entry | Sole Entry | Sole Entry | Sole Entry | Joint Venture with GM Canada | Sole Entry | Sole Entry | Joint Venture with GM | Sole Entry |
| Name of Company | Honda of Canada Mfg., Inc. | Toyota Motor Manufacturing Canada Inc. | Canadian Autoparts Toyota Inc. | CAMI Automotive Inc. | Nissan Motor Manufacturing (UK) Limited | Honda of the U.K. Mfg., Ltd | IBC Vehicles Limited | Toyota Motor Manufacturing (UK) Ltd. |
| Established | June 1984 | January 1986 | March 1983 | October 1986 | April 1984 | February 1985 | September 1987 | December 1989 |
| Current Share in Equity | Honda 50.14% HAM 49.86% | Toyota 100% | Toyota 100% | Suzuki 50% GM Canada 50% | Nissan 100% | Honda 4.1% Honda Motor Europe 75.91% Rover Group 20% | GM 60% Isuzu 40% | Toyota 100% |
| Location | Alliston, Ontario | Cambridge Ontario | Delta, British Columbia | Ingersoll, Ontario | Tyne and Wear, England | Swindon, England | Luton, England | Burnaston, England; Deeside, Wales |
| Vehicles/Parts Produced | Civic | 1.6-liter Corolla sedan | Aluminum wheels | Cultus, Escudo | Primera | Mid-size Car, Engines | Fargo, Carry, RV | Carina; Engines |
| Start-up | Nov 1986 | Nov 1988 | Feb 1985 | April 1989 | July 1986 | Oct 1989 | Sep 1989 | Late 1992; Mid 1992 |
| Annual Production Capacity | 100,000 units | 65,000 units | 480,000 wheels | 200,000 units | 300,000 units | 100,000 cars 70,000 engines | 60,000–70,000 units | 200,000 units (100,000 units in first phase); 200,000 units (100,000 units in first phase) |
| Employees | 1,900 | 1,100 | 120 | 2,400 | 3,500 | 2,000 (planned) | 2,100 | 3,000 (1,700 in first phase); 300 (200 in first phase) |
| Total Investment | C$280 million | C$400 million | C$43 million | C$615 million | £900 million | ¥70 billion | £34 million | £700 million; £140 million |
| Affiliated Technical/Design Centres | – | – | | – | Nissan European Technology Centre Ltd; Nissan European Technology Centre (Brussels) N.V. | Honda R&D Europe GmbH | – | Toyota Technical Center of Europe; Toyota Europe Office of Creation |

| Country | Germany | Spain | Portugal |
|---|---|---|---|
| Japanese Maker | Toyota | Nissan | Toyota |
| Type of Entry | Joint Production | Capital Participation | Joint Venture with Salvador Caetano |
| Name of Company | Volkswagen AG | Nissan Motor Ibérica, S.A. | Salvador Caetano I.M.V.T., S.A. |
| Established | – | January 1980 | – |
| Current Share in Equity | – | Nissan 67.6% Local 32.4% | Toyota 27% Local 73% |
| Location | Hanover | Barcelona | Ovar |
| Vehicles/Parts Produced | Toyota Hilux, VW Taro | Safari, Vannette, Trade, Trucks, Parts, Engines & Transmissions | Dyna, Hiace, Hilux, Land Cruiser, Coaster |
| Start-Up | Jan 1989 | Jan 1983 | Oct 1968 |
| Annual Production Capacity | 15,000 units | 80,000 units | 12,000 units |
| Employees | – | 6,890 | 2,225 |
| Total Investment | N.A. | N.A. | N.A. |
| Affiliated Technical/ Design Centres | – | Nissan Motor Ibérica, S.A. | – |

*Source:* JAMA, *The Motor Industry of Japan,* 1992. (Table based on JAMA member firms' official announcements as of June 1992.)

*Note:* 1) * Ford became an equity partner in AAI in June 1992, increasing capitalization to US£760 million, and the company name was changed from Mazda Motor Manufacturing (USA) Corporation to AutoAlliance International, Inc.

2) ** Chrysler sold its stake in Diamond-Star to Mitsubishi in October 1991. The plant continues to produce Chrysler vehicles. "Other" sharing in equity are Mitsubishi affiliates.

and the Suzuki–GM plant in Ontario (Canada) started operations in 1989. Thus, eight of the eleven Japanese automakers have locally-based production in North America. The annual output capacity per plant averages about 250,000 units, a total of about 2 million cars a year. With an increasing number of Japanese automakers in the USA, Japanese parts makers have also found new markets there. Already well over one hundred parts makers are based in the USA, and many others in Asian countries, such as Korea, Taiwan, Thailand, Malaysia and the Philippines. A few of them went independently but the majority expanded through technical tie-ups or joint management with local manufacturers. With the approach of the single European market in 1992, more Japanese automakers and parts makers began to locate in Europe. Nissan started production in the UK in 1986 and has since been followed there by Honda, Isuzu and Toyota. The UK has so far been the main base for large-scale passenger-car production by Japanese automakers in Europe, but as of 1992 they were also involved in manufacturing operations (some for cars, some for trucks and buses) in Germany (Toyota), Italy (Daihatsu), the Netherlands (Mitsubishi, production due to start in 1995), Belgium (Mitsubishi), Ireland (Nissan Diesel, Hino, Mitsubishi, Isuzu), Greece (Nissan, Hino), Spain (Nissan, Suzuki), Portugal (Nissan, Toyota, Mazda, Mitsubishi, Isuzu) and Hungary (Suzuki). Some parts makers have also been seeking markets in Europe through technical tie-ups and joint ventures.

A variety of methods are adopted by automakers for locally-based production, although the stabilization of labour/management relations and the transfer of Japanese-style management systems in some form or other is a constantly recurring theme. Generally speaking, while labour/management relations can be greatly improved to ensure stability of employment, Japanese production technology and systems may not be so easy to accept. Local circumstances call for flexibility. Local plant superintendents and workers may run into problems themselves in the Japanese-style production system, and therefore may not be able to adopt everything that is done in Japan. The transference of Japanese-style management and production systems is part of the internationalization process which also contains a powerful cultural ingredient.

The aim of Japanese enterprises is not merely 'localization', but also the furtherance of corporate links and an international division of labour. Today, when technology is changing so much and so often, Japan cannot expect to excel in product planning, design, component and other innovative technologies just because it has the advantages of its own production technologies and systems. The same goes for the European and US automakers. Thus, greater attention will be paid to various forms of international tie-up, e.g. strategic alliances.

Internationalization is now part and parcel of the global scenery. The economies of the world are closer than ever before, more and more poorer countries are being industrialized and trade barriers keep coming down. Internationalization has always been seen in Japan as a way of catching up and overtaking Europe and the USA, just as in the days of international trading. The whole ethos of the Japanese automobile industry enabled it to accept the need for internationalization and make a success of it.

Global strategies are necessary not as a theoretical matter but as a positive and practical imperative. Goals need to be defined and redefined from time to time and their internationalization made part of their attainment.

The Japanese automobile industry has faced up to de-maturity by promoting more co-operation with home production and the transfer of technology to developing countries with a potential market and not only to the mature OECD countries.

FUTURE PERSPECTIVES

The global de-maturation of the automobile industry has just begun and technological innovations will surely continue to emerge, but radical innovations in product technology (of the drive mechanism, for example) remain uncertain. There are prospects for new types of batteries and hydrogen engines but their practical introduction cannot be foretold. All that can be said is that de-maturation in the automobile industry will be fully-fledged when radical innovation in product technology is achieved. Of course, innovations may well require technological developments in other industries beside the automobile industry.

However, if the automobile industry waits for other industries, it may not be able to keep up with the rapid changes when innovations appear. Product technology innovation does not appear by chance but is the result of efforts in promoting higher standards of process technology, including electronics, new-materials technology and information technology, fundamental research and development and design technology. In this high-tech age, automakers need to adopt high standards in their process technology in order to survive de-maturation and prepare for innovation in product technology. Japan's position at the cutting edge of the semiconductor and electronics industries, as well as of basic technology, illustrates what is needed. Product technology includes not only radical changes in automobile mechanisms but also innovations in software and information systems.

What are the conditions and the key elements of 'a new lease of life' for the industry? In essence, there is the need to continue attending to labour/management relations and outstanding process technology. But not simply in terms of a co-operative policy or QC activities, but much higher standards of process technology that can meet the needs of the high-tech age. Process technology needs to cover the technique and the skills of workers as well as the special knowledge and the expertise of specialists and engineers. Also, it needs to respond efficiently to rapid situational changes, including the high-tech development of related industries such as the parts and peripheral technology industries, advancements in the computerization of manufacturing facilities with the aid of industrial robots and the introduction of flexibly-systematized manufacturing facilities with industrial robots. Special engineers will play an increasingly important role in the fields of development, design, styling and production technology. They should never forget the significance of developing the technique and the skills of workers. In this sense, technical training and the multi-skill worker system are essential.

Although a degree of reliance needs to be maintained between labour and management, the relationship will require a base for promoting spontaneity and creativity on the job site rather than a co-operative policy for too much collectiveness in groups. The goal for labour and management, in close co-operation with each other, is to create a situation where working hours can be reduced to the international standard without sacrificing levels of quality and productivity and spare time used for technical training and creative studies.

The conditions for tailoring the 'Japanese Challenge' to this high-tech and information-oriented age, or the key points in evaluating the competitiveness of the Japanese automobile industry in the future, are stable labour/management relations, a workforce which is well educated and high standards of process technology. Detroit and all European automakers are promoting radical updating and the automation of facilities, the improvement of labour/management relations, and introducing the Japanese-style parts procurement system and QC-circle activities. The promotion of cost-efficient management, updating of facilities and build-up in R & D investments in Detroit is remarkable, as is the European automakers' policy of updating facilities and improving the automation rate. It is true that Europe and the USA have begun a counter-challenge to Japan, but it will take them several years to tailor a workforce with a high educational background and to improve labour/management relations. This has compelled them to devise methods of automation and to increase investment in facilities and equipment.

Detroit cannot yet match Japan in up-to-date facilities or investment in facilities and equipment. High standards of process technology will continue to be the source of Japan's competitive strength. The Japanese automobile industry has the advantage of being served by efficient materials and parts industries and benefits from the dynamism of the whole of the Japanese high-technology industry. Problems could arise, therefore, if there were a decline in this dynamism or a deterioration of the industrial structure.

The Japanese automobile industry, which set about de-maturing the world automobile industry with the 'Japanese Challenge', does not necessarily have a promising future. It is certain that automobile industries of the world will compete harder and harder, and trade friction will linger for a long time. The industrial society of Japan and Japanese-style management form an extremely close co-operative system which might jar, affecting the competitiveness of the Japanese automobile industry. The Japanese automobile industry itself might jar, depending on the conditions of labour/management relations, the automation of manufacturing facilities and the improvement of working conditions, and in its partnerships with parts makers. Furthermore, Japanese automakers have been competing very hard with one another, both at home and abroad.

As long as trade friction lingers due to a trade imbalance between Japan and the USA, much pressure will be placed on the automobile industry as a result of increasing competitiveness in all Japanese industries. This prevents a complete removal of the self-restriction on trading with the USA. Japanese automakers, who were not so enthusiastic about seeking markets in the USA in the early 1980s, eventually decided to base there for local production due to the indirect incentive of avoiding friction and the fall in exports as a result of the rise in the value of the yen to the dollar.

The expansion of locally-based production raises the question of whether cost efficiency can be ensured along with quality standards.

In short, locally-based production cannot be undertaken exclusively as a way of avoiding trade friction or counteracting an appreciating yen. Locally-based production should have a strategic logic, suited to the internationalization of the automobile industry. It will need to offer opportunities, such as technical tie-ups, a mutual supply of components with producers in other countries, joint production, managerial tie-ups and scope for a regional division of labour in the production of components.

As shown by Japanese industries exporting steel and home appliances, basing in foreign countries calls for policies that suit the local circumstances. Competition will become more and more severe and future market trends may rekindle US trade protectionism. From a global standpoint, the Japanese automobile industry has to construct a dual strategy of internationalization – one for areas like the USA, where the seeds have already germinated and grown from the sowing and another for areas like Asia where the seeds have yet to germinate or be sown. The problem is one of how to make effective use of the conditions in the Asian countries that have been industrializing in recent years. Measures for establishing such a network are now well underway. These areas will be closely watched as the key to future global strategy. As part of a global strategy the technological core is the Japanese automobile industry. The strategy also paves the way for the Japanese automobile industry which took up the challenge of de-maturity for itself and in so doing did the same for the world automobile industry.

AFTERWORD

Since the summer of 1991, coinciding with the editing work on this book, great changes have been underway in the Japanese automobile industry. Having led the world's automobile manufacturers in the 1980s the Japanese industry now finds its competitiveness and earning structure under a cloud.

Following the collapse of the so-called bubble economy in 1991, the Japanese domestic automobile market has declined two years in a row and, as a result, three of the eleven manufacturers ran into the red in the 1992 financial year. Even Toyota has experienced as sharp decline in its annual profits, down to just 40 per cent of those in its golden age. It is forecast that should this recession in the domestic market continue for another three years, at least half the Japanese automobile manufacturers will go into the red. Sales in the home market reached a peak of 7.8 million vehicles (minicars included) in 1990. In 1991 there was a decline and by 1992 the sales figure had slipped below the seven million mark. Nevertheless, it should be borne in mind that this level of domestic sales is till 1.1 million units higher than the 5.8 million or so which were sold in 1986. Why, then, have the profits of the Japanese car makers come under such pressure? Has the international competitiveness of the Japanese automobile industry really been lost for good, or is the set-back a temporary one? Has the apparent superiority of the Japanese lean production method been no more than an illusion?

In my opinion, it is unlikely that the Japanese automobile industry will be defeated in the world market, although the severe conditions manifest at the moment will persist for some time to come. To restore their competitiveness the Japanese automakers are having to make some drastic changes to their market strategies, a process of adaptation which will take anything between three and six years. Even supposing they do manage to restore their competitiveness, they are not likely to dominate the world industry as comprehensively as they did before. Much more plausible is the possibility that while still competing with the world's car manufacturers they will also seek a path of coexistence.

To take a look at the causes of the problems currently facing the Japanese automobile industry: while it is clear that the abrupt decline in profits was closely related to the contraction of the domestic market, it should also be noted that the huge investment burdens shouldered by manufacturers pushed their break-even points up to over 90 per cent. Thus they became vulnerable to even a slight reduction in sales. Investment in overseas facilities, not yet recouped, and in highly-advanced, automated factories at home, using vast low-interest funds raised while the economy ballooned, made up the bulk of this spending. A total of somewhere between sixty and eighty billion yen was put towards factory modernization in this period. Unfortunately for the car makers, production capacity as a result of these state-of-the-art facilities expanded just as the economic bubble burst and demand shrank.

The somewhat reckless diversification of model types, and the corresponding proliferation of parts, compounded the financial difficulties facing Japanese car makers. Ever-shortening lead times for new models were directly related to huge increases in research and development spending. Ironically, an excessive concern for model diversity and production flexibility resulted in the self-destruction of the 'lean system'.

Since 1992 Japanese automobile manufacturers have been pursuing a policy of reducing model types by 10 to 20 per cent and the number of different parts by around 30 per cent. Although approaching the problem in different ways, many have begun to review model-change cycles, prolonging the planned life span of some models in order to save on development costs. Some companies are undertaking restructuring by closing down old facilities and concentrating their activities, trying by this means to avoid having to lay off employees.

The rationalization measures being adopted by car makers, especially the policy of trimming the range of models, are bound to have grave repercussions for some parts makers. Among the small and medium-sized secondary and tertiary parts makers in particular, a process of natural selection has been triggered. The survivors will be those who can make best use of high technology in general. It is at this lower end of the automobile industry that the most radical restructuring will be carried out.

Mergers and acquisitions have already started among primary parts makers. Some of the car makers have also entered into co-operative relationships with each other. Isuzu, for example, a truck and diesel engine specialist, has begun to supply Honda with small trucks, receiving passenger cars in return. Mazda and Isuzu have plans for an exchange of diesel engines, and Nissan and Mazda intend to supply each other with small trucks. In the prevailing economic climate, this pattern of mutual supply is likely to be the dominant trend in relations between the Japanese car makers. Large-scale mergers involving high risks are likely to be avoided for the time being.

On balance, however, it is anticipated that the huge investments made by the Japanese car makers will prove their worth in the future, even though they have, for the time being, pushed up break-even points as a result of the inevitable increase in the associated fixed charges. The investments in automated factories are a necessary preparation to protect against the future shortage of young labour. The investments in research and development should bear fruit and are particularly necessary at a time when the industry must come up with measures to counter environmental problems.

The low-profit age for the Japanese automobile makers is set to continue for some time to come owing to the maturity of the domestic market and trade frictions in the economically advanced countries.

However, if, thanks to their rationalization policies, they manage to make it through this difficult period, and if they make the most of their overseas strategies, especially where local production bases are concerned, their heavy investment should pay dividends. Just when things will start to look brighter is, of course, dependent on domestic and overseas economic and trade trends.

# Notes

INTRODUCTION

1 Rae, J.B., *The American Automobile Industry*, (Twayne Publishers, Boston, 1984), 156.
2 Shimokawa, K., *Jidosha Sangyo Datsuseijyukuji-dai (The Dematured Age of the Automobile Industry)*, (Yuhikaku, Tokyo, 1985), 3.
3 Shimokawa, K., *Jidosha Sangyo Datsuseijyukuji-dai (The Dematured Age of the Automobile Industry)*, (Yuhikaku, Tokyo, 1985), 4.
4 Shimokawa, K., *Jidosha Sangyo Datsuseijyukuji-dai (The Dematured Age of the Automobile Industry)*, (Yuhikaku, Tokyo, 1985), 4.
5 Shimokawa, K., *Jidosha Sangyo Datsuseijyukuji-dai (The Dematured Age of the Automobile Industry)*, (Yuhikaku, Tokyo, 1985), 5.

1 THE JAPANESE AUTOMOBILE INDUSTRY: A BRIEF HISTORY

1 Shimokawa, K., 'The automobile industry', *Weekly Encyclopedia Alfa*, Nihon Mailorder Sha, 1972, 2666; Okumura, H., Jyunichi Hoshikawa and Kazuo Matsui, *Jidosha Kogyo (The Automobile Industry)*, (Toyokeizai Shimpo Sha, Tokyo, 1965), 54–8.
2 Iwakoshi, T., *Jidosha Kogyoron (A Study of the Automobile Industry)*, (Tokyo University Press, Tokyo, 1963), 248–52.
3 Okumura, H., Jyunichi Hoshikawa and Kazuo Matsui, *Jidosha Kogyo (The Automobile Industry)*, (Toyokeizai Shimpo Sha, Tokyo, 1965), 63–4.
4 Iwakoshi, T., *Jidosha Kogyoron (A Study of the Automobile Industry)*, (Tokyo University Press, Tokyo, 1963), 252–7.
5 Shimokawa, K., 'The automobile industry', *Weekly Encyclopedia Alfa*, Nihon Mailorder Sha, 1972, 2667.
6 Shimokawa, K., 'The automobile industry', *Weekly Encyclopedia*

Alfa, Nihon Mailorder Sha, 1972, 2667.
7  Shimokawa, K., 'The automobile industry', *Weekly Encyclopedia Alfa*, Nihon Mailorder Sha, 1972, 2667–8.
8  Shimokawa, K., 'The automobile industry', *Encyclopedia of Japan*, (Kodansha, Tokyo, 1983), 122.
9  Shimokawa, K., 'The automobile industry', *Encyclopedia of Japan*, (Kodansha, Tokyo, 1983), 122.


2   THE STRUCTURE OF THE INDUSTRY
1  Japan Automobile Manufacturers Association, *The Motor Industry of Japan*, 1992, 27, 28.
2  Shimokawa, K., *Jidosha (The Automobile)*, (Nihonkeizaishinbun-sha, Tokyo, 1987), 9–13.
3  Shimokawa, K., *Jidosha (The Automobile)*, (Nihonkeizaishinbun-sha, Tokyo, 1987), 13–4.
4  Shimokawa, K., *Jidosha (The Automobile)*, (Nihonkeizaishinbun-sha, Tokyo, 1987), 18.
5  Shimokawa, K., *Jidosha (The Automobile)*, (Nihonkeizaishinbun-sha, Tokyo, 1987), 18–19.
6  Shimokawa, K., *Jidosha (The Automobile)*, (Nihonkeizaishinbun-sha, Tokyo, 1987), 19–20.
7  Shimokawa, K., *Jidosha (The Automobile)*, (Nihonkeizaishinbun-sha, Tokyo, 1987), 21–2.
8  Shimokawa, K., *Jidosha (The Automobile)*, (Nihonkeizaishinbun-sha, Tokyo, 1987), 22–4.
9  Shokokumiai Chuokinko Chosabu, *Shitaukechushokigyo no Shin-kyokumen (New Apspects of Small Business Vendors)*, (Tokyo, 1983), 61–70.
10  Shimokawa, K., *Jidosha (The Automobile)*, (Nihonkeizaishinbun-sha, Tokyo, 1987), 25.
11  Nissan Motor Company, *Nijyuisseikieno Michi (Towards the Twen-ty-First Century)*, 1983, 87–8.
12  Nissan Motor Company, *Nijyuisseikieno Michi (Towards the Twen-ty-First Century)*, 1983, 89–90.
13  Shimokawa, K., *Jidosha (The Automobile)*, (Nihonkeizaishinbun-sha, Tokyo, 1987), 27–8.
14  Shimokawa, K., *Jidosha (The Automobile)*, (Nihonkeizaishinbun-sha, Tokyo, 1987), 28–9.
15  Shimokawa, K., *Jidosha (The Automobile)*, (Nihonkeizaishinbun-

sha, Tokyo, 1987), 30.
16  Shimokawa, K., *Jidosha (The Automobile)*, (Nihonkeizaishinbunsha, Tokyo, 1987), 31-2.
17  Shimokawa, K., *Jidosha (The Automobile)*, (Nihonkeizaishinbunsha, Tokyo, 1987), 33.
18  Shimokawa, K., *Jidosha (The Automobile)*, (Nihonkeizaishinbunsha, Tokyo, 1987), 34–5.


3   LABOUR RELATIONS AND WORKER PARTICIPATION
1   The Kanban system is known as the just-in-time production system.
2   Shirai, T., *Kigyobetsu Kumiai (The Company Union)*, (Chuokoronsha), revised edn, 4.
3   Shirai, T., *Kigyobetsu Kumiai (The Company Union)*, (Chuokoronsha), revised edn, 5.
4   Shirai, T., *Kigyobetsu Kumiai (The Company Union)*, (Chuokoronsha), revised edn, 7.
5   Shirai, T., *Kigyobetsu Kumiai (The Company Union)*, (Chuokoronsha), revised edn, 8.
6   Shirai, T., *Kigyobetsu Kumiai (The Company Union)*, (Chuokoronsha), revised edn, 10.
7   Shirai, T., *Kigyobetsu Kumiai (The Company Union)*, (Chuokoronsha), revised edn, 11.
8   Shirai, T., *Kigyobetsu Kumiai (The Company Union)*, (Chuokoronsha), revised edn, 44.
9   Shirai, T., *Roshikankeiron (Labour Relations)*, (Nihonrodokyokai, 1980), 51–2.
10  Shirai, T., *Kigyobetsu Kumiai (The Company Union)*, (Chuokoronsha), revised edn, 86–8.
11  Shimokawa, K., *Nihonkabushikigaisha no Outsider (Outsider of Japan Inc.)*, Nihonkeieishi Koza (4), 148.
12  Toyota Motor Company, *Thirty Year Company History*, 1968, 298–304.
13  Toyota Motor Company, *Thirty Year Company History*, 1968, 300–4.
14  Shimokawa, K., 'Entrepreneurship and social environmental change in the Japanese automobile industry', *Social Science Information*, (SAGE, London and Beverly Hills, 1982), 21–2, 284–5.
15  Yamamoto, O., *Mazda no Fukkatsu (Mazda's Come-back)*, (Jidosha Sangyokenkyusho, Tokyo, 1983), 33–42.

16  Shimokawa, K., 'Product and labour strategies in the contemporary Japanese automobile industry', *Keieishirin (Hosei Business Journal*, Vol. 21, 3), 43–4.
17  Federation of All Toyota Workers Union, *Union Activities at Toyota*, 1984, 14.
18  Shimokawa, K., 'Entrepreneurship and social environmental change in the Japanese automobile industry', *Social Science Information*, (SAGE, London and Beverly Hills, 1982), 284–5.
19  Shimokawa, K., 'Product and labour strategies in the contemporary Japanese automobile industry', *Keieishirin (Hosei Business Journal*, Vol. 21, 3), 44.
20  Ohno, T., *Toyota Seisanhoshiki (The Toyota Production System)*, (Daiamondsha, Tokyo, 1978), 64–6.
21  Shimokawa, K., 'Product and labour strategies in the contemporary Japanese automobile industry', *Keieishirin (Hosei Business Journal*, Vol. 21, 3), 47.
22  Shimokawa, K., 'Product and labour strategies in the contemporary Japanese automobile industry', *Keieishirin (Hosei Business Journal*, Vol. 21, 2), 47.
23  Shimokawa, K., 'Entrepreneurship and social environmental change in the Japanese automobile industry', *Social Science Information*, (SAGE, London and Beverly Hills, 1982), 284–5.
24  Shimokawa, K., 'Product and labour strategies in the contemporary Japanese automobile industry', *Keieishirin (Hosei Business Journal*, Vol. 21, 3), 47–8. Kazuo Koike, *Shokuba no Rodokumiai to san:a (Labour Union on the Shop-floor and Its Participation)*, (Toyokeizaishinposha, Tokyo, 1977), 199–200.
25  Shimokawa, K. and Y. Togai (eds), *Nihonkeieishio manabu, 3 (Japanese Business History, 3)*, (Yuhikaku, Tokyo, 1976), 91.
26  Abernathy, W.K., K.B. Clark and A.M. Kantrow, *Industrial Renaissance*, (Basic Books, N.Y., 1983), 74 and 85–6.
27  Shimokawa, K., 'Nichibei Jidoshasangyo no seisansei Kokusaihikaku' (Comparative study of productivity in the automobile industry in the USA and Japan), *Keieishirin*, Vol. 18, 4, 20.

4   THE AUTOMOBILE PARTS INDUSTRY

1  Sei, S., 'Structural characteristics of the automobile parts industry', *Statistics*, Vol. 80–10, 18.
2  The organization of parts makers at the bottom of the structure is

so complicated that it cannot be properly set out.

3 Takeuchi, A., 'Japan's automobiles supported by the base industry', *The Economist*, 17 February, 1981, 24.
4 Sei, S., 'Structural characteristics of the automobile parts industry, *Statistics*, Vol. 80–10, 21.
5 Shimokawa, K., 'Prospect and retrospect of 15 years of the automobile industry', *Automobile Journal*, July 1975, 19.
6 Sei, S., 'Structural characteristics of the automobile parts industry, *Statistics*, Vol. 80–10, 20.
7 Sei, S., 'Structural characteristics of the automobile parts industry, *Statistics*, Vol. 80–10, 20.
8 Oshima, T., 'Determinants of internal and external production in the Japanese automobile industry', in Yoshio Sato (ed.), *Management of Outside Production and Subcontracts in the Period of Low Growth*, (Chuo Keizai Sha, Tokyo, 1980), 190.
9 Ueda, T., 'Targets of the parts industry and new machinery promotion act in the future', *Automobile Journal*, July 1966, 20.
10 Sei, S., 'Research on the production structure in the automobile parts industry', *Kikai Keizai Kenkyu*, Vol. 8, 87.
11 Sei, S., 'Research on the production structure in the automobile parts industry', *Kikai Keizai Kenkyu*, Vol. 9, 58.
12 Sei, S., 'Research on the production structure in the automobile parts industry', *Kikai Keizai Kenkyu*, Vol. 9, 58–9; Ueda, T., 'Targets of the parts industry and new machinery promotion act in the future', *Automobile Journal*, July 1966, 21.
13 Sei, S., 'Research on the production structure in the automobile parts industry', *Kikai Keizai Kenkyu*, Vol. 9, 37–8.
14 Tomiyama, T., *The Automobile Industry in Japan*, (Toyo Keizai Shinpo Sha, Tokyo, 1973, 1973), 107–8.
15 Sei, S., 'Research on the production structure in the automobile parts industry', *Kikai Keizai Kenkyu*, Vol. 9, 46.
16 Sei, S., 'Research on the production structure in the automobile parts industry', *Kikai Keizai Kenkyu*, Vol. 9, 51.
17 Oshima, T., *The Automobile Industry*, (Toyo Keizai Shinpo Sha, Tokyo), 65.
18 Sei, S., 'Facts on the production rationalization and recession of subcontractors in the automobile industry', *Kikai Keizai Kenkyu*, Vol. 10, 59–60.
19 Oshima, T., 'Determinants of internal and external production in the Japanese automobile industry', in Yoshio Sato (ed.), *Management*

of Outside Production and Subcontracts in the Period of Low
Growth, (Chuo Keizai Sha, Tokyo, 1980), 226–7.
20  Abernathy, W.J., K.B. Clark and A.M. Kantrow, 'The new industrial competition', *Harvard Business Review*, Sept–Oct 1981, 75–6.


5   THE SALES AND DISTRIBUTION SYSTEM
  1  This part of the chapter is a summary of the author's two works, as
     follows:
     Shimokawa, K., 'Marketing and sales financing in the automobile
     industry: US and Japan', in Nakagawa, K. (ed.), *Marketing and
     Sales Finance in the Course of Industrialization*, (University of
     Tokyo Press, Tokyo, 1978), 135.
     Shimokawa, K., 'Marketing history in the automobile industry: the
     United States and Japan', in Okouchi, A. and Koichi Shimokawa
     (eds) *Development of Mass Marketing*, (University of Tokyo Press,
     Tokyo, 1983), 17–18.
  2  Shimokawa, K., 'Marketing and sales financing in the automobile
     industry: US and Japan', in Nakagawa, K. (ed.), *Marketing and
     Sales Finance in the Course of Industrialization*, (University of
     Tokyo Press, Tokyo, 1978), 136.
  3  Shimokawa, K., 'Marketing history in the automobile industry: the
     United States and Japan', in Okouchi, A. and Koichi Shimokawa
     (eds) *Development of Mass Marketing*, (University of Tokyo Press,
     Tokyo, 1983), 18.
  4  Toyota Motor Sales Co., *Motorization to tomoni (Our Years with
     Motorization)*, (Tokyo, 1970), 40–41.
  5  Osuga, H., 'Historical analysis of the Japanese automobile distri-
     bution mechanism: on the background of group specialization and
     scale enlargement', *Jidosha to sono sekai*, September 1975, 6.
  6  Toyota Motor Sales Co., *Motorization to tomoni (Our Years with
     Motorization)*, (Tokyo, 1970), 77–78.
  7  Shimokawa, K., 'Marketing and sales financing in the automobile
     industry: US and Japan', in Nakagawa, K. (ed.), *Marketing and
     Sales Finance in the Course of Industrialization*, (University of
     Tokyo Press, Tokyo, 1978), 136.
  8  Shimokawa, K., 'Marketing and sales financing in the automobile
     industry: US and Japan', in Nakagawa, K. (ed.), *Marketing and
     Sales Finance in the Course of Industrialization*, (University of
     Tokyo Press, Tokyo, 1978), 137.

9   Toyota Motor Sales Co., *Motorization to tomoni (Our Years with Motorization)*, (Tokyo, 1970), 114–7.
10  Shimokawa, K., 'Marketing and sales financing in the automobile industry: US and Japan', in Nakagawa, K. (ed.), *Marketing and Sales Finance in the Course of Industrialization*, (University of Tokyo Press, Tokyo, 1978), 137.
11  Toyota Motor Sales Co., *Motorization to tomoni (Our Years with Motorization)*, (Tokyo, 1970), 120–3.
12  Miki, Y., *Challenge of Nissan*, (Tokyo, 1967), 137.
13  Prince Motor Sales Company's organization had been in existence long after Nissan's acquisition.
14  Honda Motors, *The History of Honda*, (Tokyo, 1975), 64–5.
15  Honda Motors, *The History of Honda*, (Tokyo, 1975), 64–5.
16  Shimokawa, K., 'Marketing and sales financing in the automobile industry: US and Japan', in Nakagawa, K. (ed.), *Marketing and Sales Finance in the Course of Industrialization*, (University of Tokyo Press, Tokyo, 1978), 139.
17  Shimokawa, K., *Jidosha Senryaku Kokusaika no nakade: Kironi tatusu Dealer keiei (Internationalization of Automotive Strategy: Turning Point of Dealer Business)*, (Japanese Automobile Dealers Association, 1985), 19–21.
18  Shimokawa, K., 'Marketing and sales financing in the automobile industry: US and Japan', in Nakagawa, K. (ed.), *Marketing and Sales Finance in the Course of Industrialization*, (University of Tokyo Press, Tokyo, 1978), 21–4.
19  Shimokawa, K., 'Marketing and sales financing in the automobile industry: US and Japan', in Nakagawa, K. (ed.), *Marketing and Sales Finance in the Course of Industrialization*, (University of Tokyo Press, Tokyo, 1978), 25–6.
20  Shimokawa, K., *Jidosha Senryaku Kokusaika no nakade: Kironi tatusu Dealer keiei (Internationalization of Automotive Strategy: Turning Point of Dealer Business)*, (Japanese Automobile Dealers Association, 1985), 160.
21  Shimokawa, K., *Jidosha Senryaku Kokusaika no nakade: Kironi tatusu Dealer keiei (Internationalization of Automotive Strategy: Turning Point of Dealer Business)*, (Japanese Automobile Dealers Association, 1985), 161.
22  Shimokawa, K., *Jidosha Senryaku Kokusaika no nakade: Kironi tatusu Dealer keiei (Internationalization of Automotive Strategy: Turning Point of Dealer Business)*, (Japanese Automobile Dealers

168    *The Japanese Automobile Industry*

Association, 1985), 26.
23 Shimokawa, K., *Jidosha Senryaku Kokusaika no nakade: Kironi tatusu Dealer keiei (Internationalization of Automotive Strategy: Turning Point of Dealer Business)*, (Japanese Automobile Dealers Association, 1985), 27.
24 Shimokawa, K., *Jidosha Senryaku Kokusaika no nakade: Kironi tatusu Dealer keiei (Internationalization of Automotive Strategy: Turning Point of Dealer Business)*, (Japanese Automobile Dealers Association, 1985), 27.
25 Rae, J.B., *Nissan Datsun: A History of the Nissan Motor Corporation in the USA, 1960–1980*, (McGraw-Hill, New York, 1982), 39.
26 Shimokawa, K., 'Datsuseijyukeukajidai e muketeno Jidoshahanbai system no Katsuseika' (Revitalization of the automobile sales system toward a dematured age), JAMA, *Jidosha Kogyo* 22, Tokyo, July 1988, 20.
27 Shimokawa, K., 'Datsuseijyukeukajidai e muketeno Jidoshahanbai system no Katsuseika' (Revitalization of the automobile sales system toward a dematured age), JAMA, *Jidosha Kogyo* 22, Tokyo, July 1988, 20–1.
28 Sakamoto, K. (ed.), *Gijutsu Kakushin to Kigokozo (innovation and Corporate Structure)*, (Minerva, Kyōto, 1985), 137. To share the inventory burden between manufacturer and dealer various approaches are taken such as changing the ratio of inventory burden and increasing sales potential through emphasis on the sales of particular items. (137–9).
29 Shimokawa, K., 'Datsuseijyukeukajidai e muketeno Jidoshahanbai system no Katsuseika' (Revitalization of the automobile sales system toward a dematured age), JAMA, *Jidosha Kogyo* 22, Tokyo, July 1988, 21–2.
30 Shimokawa, K., 'Datsuseijyukeukajidai e muketeno Jidoshahanbai system no Katsuseika' (Revitalization of the automobile sales system toward a dematured age), JAMA, *Jidosha Kogyo* 22, Tokyo, July 1988, 22–3.
31 Sangyokenkyu-sho, *Wagakuni Jidosha Lease gyo no Genjo to Kongo no Kadai ni Kansuru Chosakenkyuhokoku-sho (Research Report on the Japanese Auto Lease Business)*, 1987, 13–47.
32 Shimokawa, K., 'Datsuseijyukeukajidai e muketeno Jidoshahanbai system no Katsuseika' (Revitalization of the automobile sales system toward a dematured age), JAMA, *Jidosha Kogyo* 22, Tokyo, July 1988, 23–4.

# Bibliography

## PUBLICATIONS IN JAPANESE

*Books*

Amaya, S., *Nihon Jidosha Kogyo no Shiteki Tenkai (Historical Development of the Japanese Automobile Industry)*, Aki Shobo, Tokyo, 1982.

Arisawa, H., *Nihon Sangyo Hyakunen Shi (100-year History of Japanese Industry) Parts I & II*, Nihon Keizai Shimbun Inc., Tokyo, 1967.

Fujisawa, T., *Taimatsu wa Jibun no Te de (Hold a Torch in Your Own Hand)*, Sangyo Noritsu College Press, Tokyo, 1974.

Fukuda, Y., *Jidosha no Marketing (Car Marketing)*, Toyo Keizai, Tokyo, 1974.

Furukawa, Y., *FMS: Seisan Kakumei no Shuyaku (FMS: Playing a Major Role in the Production Revolution)*, Nikkan Kogyo Shimbun Inc., Tokyo, 1983.

Hosei University Keiei Gakubu, *Nihon Jodosha Sangyo no Tenbo (Review of the Japanese Automobile Industry)*, Tokyo, 1983.

Ikari, Y., *Nihon no Jidosha Kogyo (The Japanese Automobile Industry)*, Nihon Noritsu Kyokai, Tokyo, 1981.

Iwakoshi, T., *Jidosha Kogyo Ron (A Theory on the Automobile Industry)*, Tokyo University Press, Tokyo, 1963.

——, *Jidosha Kogyo Ron (A Theory on the Automobile Industry)*, Tokyo University Press, Tokyo, 1968.

Jidosha Gijutsu Kai, *Nihon no Jidosha Gijutsu Nijunen Shi (20-year History of Japanese Automobile Technology)*, Jidosha Gijutsu Kai, Tokyo, 1969.

170     *The Japanese Automobile Industry*

Jidosha Kogaku Zensho, *Jidosha no Hanbai/Ryutsu System (Automobile Sales and the Distribution System)*, Sankaido, Tokyo, 1975.

Kageyama, K., *Gendai Jidosha Kogyo Ron (A Theory on the Modern Automobile Industry)*, Taga Shuppan, Tokyo, 1980.

Kajiwara, K., *Jidosha Daisenso (Motor Wars)*, Diamond-sha Inc., Tokyo, 1978.

Kamiya, S., *Asu o Mitsumete (Look to Tomorrow)*, Nihon Keizai Shimbun Inc., Tokyo, 1974.

Kanko Sangyo Kenkyusho, *Nihon no Motorization no Mirai (The Future of Japanese Motorization)*, Kanko Sangyo Kenkyusho, Tokyo, 1968.

Kato, H., *Nihon Jidosha Sangyo Ron (A Theory on the Japanese Automobile Industry)*, Horitsu Bunkasha, Yokohama, 1985.

Kato, M., *Zakkubaran (Be Frank)*, Nihon Keizai Shimbun Inc., Tokyo, 1981.

Kodaira, K., *Jidosha (Automobiles)*, Aki Shobo, Tokyo, 1968.

Koiso, K., *Kei-Jidosha Tanjo no Kiroku (Records on the Birth of Mini Cars)*, Zenkeikyo, Tokyo, 1980.

Konno, G. and Okano, Y., *Gendai Jidosha Kotsu Ron (A Theory on Modern Motor Traffic)*, Tokyo University Press, Tokyo, 1979.

Masamura, K., *Sengo-shi (Postwar History) Part II*, Chikuma Shobo, Tokyo, 1985.

Mito, S., *The Honda Management System*, Diamond-sha Inc., Tokyo, 1981.

Miwa, S., *America no Jidosha (American Automobiles)*, Nihon Keizai Shimbun Inc., Tokyo, 1968.

——, *Sozoteki Hakai (Creative Destruction)*, Chuokoron-sha Inc., Tokyo, 1978.

Morimoto, M., *Toyota no Dezain to tomoni (Toyota's Design)*, Sankaido, Tokyo, 1984.

Motor Fan Henshubu, *Kokusansha Hyakunen no Rekishi (100-year History of Japanese Home-Produced Automobiles)*, Sansei Shobo, Tokyo, 1978.

Murao, S., *Kamotsu Yuso no Jidosha-ka (The Motorization of Cargo Transportation)*, Hakuto Shobo, Tokyo, 1982.

Nakamura, S., *Gendai Jidosha Kogyo Ron (A Theory on the Modern Automobile Industry)*, Yuhikaku, Tokyo, 1983.

———, *Nihon Jodosha Kogyo Hattatsushi Ron (A Theory on the Historical Development of the Japanese Automobile Industry)*, Kaiso Shobo, Tokyo, 1953.

Nihon Jidosha Buhin Kogyo Kai, *Jidosha Buhin Kogyo Hatten Shoshi (The Historical Development of the Automobile Parts Industry)*, Nihon Jidosha Buhin Kogyo Kai, Tokyo, 1969.

Nihon Jodosha Kogyo Kai, *Kogata Jidosha Hattatsu Shi (The Historical Development of Compact Cars)*, Nihon Jodosha Kogyo Kai, Tokyo, 1968.

———, *Nihon Jidosha Kogyo Shi (A History of the Japanese Automobile Industry) Parts I, II and III*, Nihon Jidosha Kogyo Kai, Tokyo, 1965, 1967, 1969.

*Nihon Jidosha Kogyo Kojutsu Kiroku Shu (Collection of Transcriptions of the Japanese Automobile Industry)*, Jidosha Kogyo Shinko Kai, Tokyo, 1975.

*Nihon no Jidosha Sangyo no Tenbo (A Review of the Japanese Automobile Industry)*, Hosei University Press, Tokyo, 1983.

Ogawa, E., *Gendai no Seisan Kanri (Production Control in the Modern Age)*, Nihon Keizai Shimbun Inc., Tokyo, 1982.

Ohara, S., *Toki wa Nagareru (Time Passes): Parts I and II*, Kenbunsha, Tokyo, 1983, 1985.

———, Munden, Y., *Toyota Seisan Hoshiki no Shin-Tenkai (New Developments in the Toyota Production System)*, Nihon Noritsu Kyokai, Tokyo, 1983.

Ohno, T., *Toyota Seisan Hoshiki (The Toyota Production System)*, Diamond-sha Inc., Tokyo, 1978.

Okamoto, T., Osawa., Y., and others, *Jidosha Juyo no Yosoku (An Estimate of Car Demand)*, Nihon Seisansei Honbu, Tokyo, 1968.

Okumura, S., *Sekai no Jidosha (Automobiles around the World)*, Iwanami Shoten Publishers, Tokyo, 1964.

Oshima, F. and Kuazono, S., *Nihon Kotsu Seisaku no Kozo (The Structure of Japanese Traffic Policy)*, Nihon Keizai Shimbun Inc., Tokyo, 1975.

Oshima, T., *Gendai Nihon no Jidosha Buhin Kogyo (The Automobile Parts Industry of Modern Japan)*, Nihon Keizai Hyoronsha, Tokyo, 1987.

———, *Jidosha Sangyyo (The Automobile Industry)*, Toyo Keizai Shimpo, Tokyo, 1980.

Ozaki, M., *Kiichiro Toyoda*, Jikensha, Tokyo, 1955.

Ryusenkeisha, *Ryusenkei (Streamline)*, Ryusenkeisha, Tokyo, 1937, 1942.

Sakitani, T., *Honda Cho-Hasso Keiei (Honda's Super-Idea Management)*, Diamond-sha Inc., Tokyo, 1979.

Sanei Shobo, *Jidosha Hyakunen no Kiseki (100-year History of Automobiles)*, Sanei Shobo, Tokyo, 1978.

Shibata, K., Omichi, Y., Ishiro, K., *Jidosha (Automobiles)*, Nihon Keizai Shimbun Inc., Tokyo, 1986.

Shimamura, H. and others, *Jidosha Haigasu Kogai (Motor Exhaust Gas Pollution)*, Kagaku Kogyosha, Tokyo, 1971.

Shimokawa, K., *America Jidosha Bunmei to Nippon (American Motor Civilization and Japan)*, Bunshindo, Tokyo, 1981.

Shimokawa, K., *Beikoku Jidosha Sangyo Keiei Shi Kenkyu (Historical Research on the Business History of the American Automobile Industry)*, Toyo Keizai Shinposha, Tokyo, 1977.

Shimokawa, K., *Jidosha Sangyo Datsuseijuku Jidai (The De-Matured Age of the Automobile Industry)*, Yukaikaku, Tokyo, 1985.

Shimokawa, K., *Jidosha Senryaku Kokusaika no Nakade (The Internationalization of Automobile Strategy)*, Jihanren, Tokyo, 1981.

Shimokawa, K., *Sekai Jidosha Sangyo no Kobo (Rise and Fall of the World Automobile Industry)*, Kodan-sha, Tokyo, 1992

Shimokawa, K., Sakaguchi, A., Matsushima, H., Katsura, Y., and Omori, H., *Nihon no Kigyoka (4) Sengo-hen (Japanese Entrepreneurs (4) Postwar edition)*, Yuhikaku, Tokyo, 1980.

Tanaka, T., *Sakichi Toyoda Den (A Biography of Sakichi Toyoda)*, Toyota Motor Corporation, Tokyo, 1955.

The Mainichi Newspapers, *Showa Jidosha Shi (A Motor History of Showa)*, The Mainichi Newspapers, Tokyo, 1979.

Tomitsuka, K., *Autobicycle no Rekishi (A History of Motor Cycles)*, Sankaido, Tokyo, 1980.

Tomiyama, K., *Nihon no Jidosha Sangyo (The Japanese Automobile Industry)*, Toyo Keizai, Tokyo, 1973.

Toyoda, E., *Ketsudan (Decision)*, Nihon Keizai Shimbun Inc., Tokyo, 1985.

Tsusan-sho, *Tenkanki no Jidosha Sangyo (The Automobile Industry at its Turning Point)*, Nikkan Kogyo Shimbun Inc., Tokyo, 1976.

Tsusan-sho Jodosha-ka, *Nihon no Jidosha Kogyo (The Japanese Automobile Industry) 1960–1*, 1965 Tsusho Sangyo Kenkyusha, Tokyo, 1961, 1965.

Tsusan-sho Jukogyo-ka, *Nihon Jidosha Kogyo no Mirai (The Future of the Japanese Automobile Industry)*, Jidosha Shuhosha, Tokyo, 1957.

Yaesu Shuppan, *Kokusan Motor Cycle no Ayumi (The Historical Development of Japanese Home-Produced Motor Cycles)*, Yaesu Shuppan, Tokyo, 1972.

Yamamoto, H., *Kotsu/Unyu no Hattatsu to Gijutsu Kakushin (Development and Technological Innovation of Traffic and Transportation)*, United Nations University, Tokyo, 1986.

Yamamoto, N., *Nihon no Jidosha: Toyopet Seicho-shi (Japanese Automobiles: The Historical Development of Toyopet)*, Tokyo Sogensha, Tokyo, 1959.

Yamamoto, O., *Mazda no Fukkatsu (Honda's Comeback)*, Jidosha Sangyo Kenkyusho, Tokyo, 1983.

——, *Honda no Genten (Honda's Origin)*, Jidosha Sangyo Kenkyusho, Tokyo, 1977.

Yamamoto, S., *Nihon no Jidosha Kogyo wa donaru (What will Become of the Japanese Automobile Industry?)*, Keizai Oraisha, Tokyo, 1951.

Yamazaki, K., *GM (General Motors)*, Chuokoronsha, Tokyo, 1969.

Yanagida, K., *Jidosha Sanjunen Shi (30-year History of Automobiles)*, Sansuisha, Tokyo, 1944.

Yanagihara, S., *Jidosha Kogai to sono Taisaku Gijutsu (Motor Pollution and Counteracting Technology)*, Natsumesha, Tokyo, 1971.

*Company History*

Aichi Toyota Jidosha Shashi Hensan Shitsu, *Aichi Toyota Nijugonen-shi (25-year History)*, Aichi Toyota Jidosha, 1969.

Aishin Seiki Shashi Henshu Iinkai, *Aishin Seiki Nijunen-shi (20-year History)*, Aishin Seiki, 1985.

Arakawa Shatai Kohyo Shashi Henshu Iinkai, *Arakawa Shatai Nijugonen-shi (25-year History)*, Arakawa Shatai Kogyo, 1972.

Atsugi Jidosha Buhin Shashi Hensan Shitsu, *Atsugi Jidosha Buhin Shashi (Company History of Atsugi Jidosha Buhin) Part I*, Atsugi Jidosha Buhin, 1977.

Daihatsu Kogyo, *Moete, Kakete-Hachijunen no Ayumi (Historical Development for 80 years)*, 1977.

Daihatsu Kogyo Shashi Henshu Iinkai, *Nanajunen-Shoshi (70-year History)*, 1977.

174     *The Japanese Automobile Industry*

Daihatsu Kogyo Shashi Henshu Iinkai, *Gojunen-shi (50-year History)*, Daihatsu Kogyo, 1957.
Daihatsu Kogyo Shashi Henshu Iinkai, *Rokujunen-shi (60-year History)*, Daihatsu Kogyo, 1967.

Fuji Jukogyo, *Fuji Jukogyo Sanjunen-shi (30-year History)*, 1984.
Fuji Jukogyo Shashi Hensan Iinkai, *Fuji Jukogyo Sanjunen-shi (30-year History)*, Fuji Jukogyo, 1984.

Hino Jidosha Hanbai Shashi Hensan Iinkai, *Hino Jidosha Hanbai Nijunen no Ayumi (Historical Development for 20 Years)*, Hino Jidosha Hanbai, 1968.
Hino Jidosha Hanbai Shashi Hensan Iinkai, *Hino Jidosha Hanbai Kabushikigaisha Sanjunen-shi (30-year History)*, Hino Jidosha Hanbai, 1978.
Hino Jidosha Kogyo Shashi Hensan Iinkai, *Hino Jidosha Kogyo Yonjunen-shi (40-year History)*, Hino Jidosha Kogyo, 1982.
Honda Giken Kogyo, *Honda no Ayumi (The Historical Development of Honda)*, 1984.
Honda Giken Kogyo Somubu, *Honda no Ayumi (Historical Development)*, Honda Giken Kogyo, 1975.
Howa Kogyo Henshu Iinkai, *Howa Kogyo Rokujunen-shi (60-year History)*, Howa Kogyo, 1967.

Isuzu Jidosha, *Gaikyo (Outlook)*, 1985.
——, *Sanjunen no Ayumi (Historical Development for 30 Years)*, 1967.
——, *Shashi Sowa (Company History with Episodes)*, 1979.
——, *Yonuunen no Ayumi (Historical Development for 40 Years)*, 1977.
Isuzu Jidosha Shashi Hensan Iinkai, *Isizu Jidosha-shi: Nijunen-shi (20-year History)*, Isuzu Jidosha, 1957.

Kanto Jidosha Kogyo Shashi Hensan Iinkai and Others, *Kanto Jidosha Kogyo Yonjunen-shi (40-year History)*, Kanto Jidosha Kogyo, 1986.
Kayaba Kogyo Shashi Henshu Iinkai, *Kayaba Kogyo Gojunen-shi (50-year History)*, Kayaba Kogyo, 1986.

Mazda, *Asu o Hiraku Toyo Kogyo-Toyo Kogyo Gojunen-shi (50-year History)*, 1970.

———, *Kaisha Gaikyo (Company Status)*, 1985.

Mitsubishi Jidosha Hanbai, *Mitsubishi Jidosha Hanbai Kabushikigaisha-shi (Historical Development)*, 1986.

Mitsubishi Jidosha Kogyo, *Kaisha Gaikyo (Company Status)*, 1980, 1981, 1984, 1985.

Mitsubishi Jidosha Kogyo Shashi Hensan Shitsu, *Mitusbishi Jidosha Hanbai Kabushikigaisha-shi (Historical Development)*, Mitsubishi Jidosha Kogyo, 1986.

Mitsubishi Jidosha Kogyo Tokyo Jidosha Seisakusho Shashi Hensan Shitsu, *Fuso no Ayumi (The Historical Development of Fuso)*, Mitsubishi Jidosha Kogyo Tokyo Jidosha Seisakusho, 1977.

Mitsubishi Jukogyo Shashi Hensan Shitsu, *Mitsubishi Jukogyo Kabushikigaisha-shi (Historical Development)*, Mitsubishi Jukogyo, 1956.

Nihon Denso Shashi Henshu Iinkai, *Nihon Denso Nijugonen-shi (25-year History)*, Nihon Denso, 1974.

———, *Nihon Denso Sanjugonen-shi (35-year History)*, Nihon Denso, 1984.

Nihon Jidosha Hanbai Kyokai Rengo-kai Shashi Hensan Iinkai, *Nijunen-shi (20-year History)*, Nihon Jidosha Hanbai Kyokai Rengokai, 1979.

Nihon Jidosha Kaigisho Henshu Iinkai, *Jidosha Sogo Nenpyo: Jidosha Gyokai Nijunen no Ayumi (Comprehensive Chronological Table of Automobiles: Historical Development for 20 Years)*, Nihon Jidosha Kaigisho, 1967.

Nihon Jidosha Kogyo-Kai Henshu Iinkai, *Junen no Ayumi (Historical Development for 10 Years)*, Nihon Jidosha Kogyo-kai, 1978.

Nissan Diesel Hanbai, *Sanjunen no Ayumi (Historical Development for 30 Years)*, 1985.

Nissan Diesel Kogyo, *Kaisha Annai (Company Guide)*, 1984.

Nissan Jidosha Chosa-bu, *Niju-issesiki e no Michi: Gojunen-shi (The Way to the 21st Century: 50-year History)*, Nissan Jidosha, 1983.

Nissan Jidosha Shashi Hensan Bukai, *Nissan Jidosha Shashi: Gojunen-shi (50-year History)*, Nissan Jidosha, 1985.

Nissan Jidosha Shashi Hensan Iinkai, *Nisan Jidosha Shashi: Yonjunen-shi (40-year History)*, Nissan Jidosha, 1975.

Nissan Jidosha Shashi Henshu Iinkai, *Prince Jidosha Kogyo Shashi (Historical Development)*, Nissan Jidosha, 1968.

Nissan Jidosha Somubu, *Nissan Jidosha Sanjunen-shi (30-year History)*, Nissan Jidosha, 1965.

Nissan Shatai Shashi Henshu Iinkai, *Nissan Shatai Sanjunen-shi (30-year History)*, Nissan Shatai, 1982.

Osaka Nissan Jidosha Shashi Hensan Iinkai, *Osaka Nissan Jidosha Sanjunen-shi (30-year History)*, Osaka Nissan Jidosha, 1973.

Suzuki Jidosha Kogyo, *Kaisha Annai (Company Guide and Outlook)*, Kaikyo, 1979, 1985.

Suzuke Jidosha Kogyo Shashi Hensan Iinkai, *Yonjunen-shi (40-year History)*, Suzuki Jidosha Kogyo, 1960.

Suzuki Jidosha Kogyo Shashi Henshu Iinkai, *Gojunen-shi (50-year History)*, Suzuki Jidosha Kogyo, 1970.

Tokyo Nissan Jidosha Hanbai Shashi Hensan Iinkai, *Kokyo Nissan Nijunen no Ayumi (Historical Development for 20 Years)*, Yokyo Nissan Jidosha Hanbai, 1964.

Tokyo Toyopet Shashi Hensan Iinkai, *Tokyo Toyopet Sanjunen-shi (30-year History)*, Tokyo Toyopet, 1983.

Tokyo Toyota Jidosha Shashi Hensan Iinkai, *Tokyo Toyota Jidosha Yonjunen-shi (40-year History)*, Tokyo Toyota Jidosha, 1986.

Toyo Kogyo Shashi Hensan Iinkai, *Toyo Kogyo Gojunen-shi (50-year History)*, Toyo Kogyo, 1972.

———, *Toyo Kogyo Yonjunen-shi (40-year History)*, Toyo Kogyo, 1960.

Toyota Jidosha Hanbai, *Toyota Jihan no Ayumi (The Historical Development of the Toyota Automobile Sales Company)*, 1964.

Toyota Kyohokai Henshu Iinkai, *Kyohokai no Ayumi (Historical Development)*, Kyohokai, 1967.

Toyota Seihokai Henshi Iinkai, *Seihokai no Ayumi (Historical Development)*, Seihokai, 1966.

Toyota Shashi Henshu Iinkai, *Sozo Kagirinaku: Toyota Jidosha Gojunen-shi (50-year History)*, Toyota Jidosha, 1988.

Toyota Shashi Henshu Iinkai, *Bunmei ni totte Kuruma to wa: Toyota Jidosha Yonjunen-shi (40-year History)*, Toyota Jidosha Kogyo, 1978.

———, *Motorizaation to Tomoni: Nijunen-shi (20-year History)*, Toyota Jidosha Hanbai, 1970.

———, *Sekai e no Ayumi: Sanjunen-shi (30-year History)*, Toyota Jidosha Hanbai, 1980.

———, *Toyota Jidosha Hanbai Kabushikigaisha no Ayumi: Junen-shi (10-year History)*, Toyota Jidosha Hanbai, 1962.

——, *Toyota Jidosha Nijunen-shi (20-year History)*, Toyota Jidosha Kogyo, 1958.

——, *Toyota Jidosha Sanjunen-shi (30-year History)*, Toyota Jidosha Kogyo, 1967.

——, *Yonjunen-shi (40-year History)*, Toyota Jido Shki Seisakusho, 1967.

Toyota Shatai Shashi Henshu Iinkai, *Toyota Shatai Yonjunen-shi (40-year History)*, Toyota Shatai, 1985.

Yamaha Hatsudoki, *Keireki-sho (Historical Development)*, 1985.

*Associations and Government*
Jidosha Gijutsu Kai, *Jidosha Gijutsu (Automobile Technology)*, Jidosha Gijutsu Kai, annually since 1965.

——, *Nihon no Jidosha Gijutsu Nijunen-shi (20-year History of Japanese Automobile Technology)*, Jidosha Gijutsu Kai, 1969.

Jidosha Kogy Shinko Kai, *Jidosha Guidebook (Automobile Guidebook)*, Jidosha Kogyuo Shinko Kai, 1976–1985.

——, *Nihon Jidosha Kogyo-shi Kiroku-shu (Collection of Historical Records of the Japanese Automobile Industry)*, Jidosha Kogyo Shinko Kai, 1973, 1975, 1979.

Jidosha Sangyo Keieisha Renmei, *Jidosha Sangyo Keieisha Renmei Nijunen-shi (20-year History of the Automobile Industry Managers' Federation)*, Jidosha Sangyo Keieisha Renmei, 1967.

Kankyo-cho, *Kangyo-cho Junen-shi (10-year History of the Environment Agency)*, Kankyo-cho.

——, *Kankyo Hakusho (White Paper on the Environment)*, annual editions, Kankyo-cho.

Kogata Jidosha Shimbunsha, *Kogata Jidosha Gyokai no Ayumi (The Historical Development of the Mini Compact-Car Industry)*, Kogata Jidosha Simbunsha, 1961.

Kotsu Kogaku Kenkyukai, *Kotsu Kankyo no Sho-Monbdai (Traffic Environment Problems)*, Kotsu Kogaku Kenkyukai.

Nihon Jidosha Buhin Kogyo Kai, *Jidosha Buhin Kogyo Hatten Shoshi (The Historical Development of the Automobile Parts Industry)*, Nihon Jidosha Buhin Kogyo Kai, 1969.

Nihon Jidosha Hanbai Kyokai Rengo Kai, *Nijunen-shi (20-year History)*, Nihon Jidosha Hanbai Kyokai Rengo Kai, 1979.

178     *The Japanese Automobile Industry*

Nihon Jodosha Kaigisho, *Jidosha Nenkan (Automobile Yearbook)* 1954–85 editions, Nihon Jidosha Kaigisho.

——, *Nihon Jidosha Sogo Nenpyo (Comprehensive Chronological Table of Japanese Automobiles)*, Nihon Jidosha Kaigisho, 1967.

——, *Rikuun Tokei Yoran (Statistical Handbook on Land Transportation)*, annual editions, Nihon Jidosha Kaigisho.

Nihon Jidosha Kenkyusho, *Senshinteki Jidosha Gijutsu Chosa (Survey of Advanced Automobile Technology)*, Nihon Jidosha Kenkyusho, 1986.

Nihon Jidosha Kogyo Kai, *Jidosha Kogyo (The Automobile Industry)*, Nihon Jidosha Kogyo Kai, annually since 1967.

——, *Jidosha Kogyo ni ikeru Kikai Setsubi Donyu no Doko nistite (Trends in the Introduction of Mechanical Facilities in the Automobile Industry)*, Nihon Jidosha Kogyo Kai, 1970.

——, *Jidosha Sangyo Kanren Tokei (Statistics of Industries Related to the Automobile Industry)*, Nihon Jidosha Kogyo Kai, annually since 1971.

——, *Jidosha Tokei Nenpyo (Chronological Table of Automobile Statistics)*, Nihon Jidosha Kogyo Kai, annually since 1953.

——, *Junen no Ayumi (Historical Development for 10 Years)*, Nihon Jidosha Kogyo-kai, 1978.

——, *Kogata jidosha Hattatsu-shi: Soseiki yori Showa Nijunen madeno Kiroku (The Historical Development of Compact Cars: From Their Inception to 1945)*, Nihon Jidosha Kogyo Kai, 1968.

——, *Motorization to Doro Taisaku no Kadai (Motorization and Problems in Road Construction Policy)*, Nihon Jidosha Kogyo Kai, 1969.

——, *Nihon Jidosha Kogyo Shi (Historical Development) Parts I, II and III, Nihon Jidosha Kogyo Kai, 1965, 1967, 1969.

——, *Nihon no Jidosha Kogyo (The Japanese Automobile Industry)*, Nohon Jidosha Kogyo Kai, 1952, 1978, 1979, 1980, 1983.

——, *Nihon no Kotsu Taikei niokeru Jidosha no Chii (Position of Cars in the Japanese Traffic System)*, Nihon Jidosha Kogyo Kai, 1970.

——, *Seisan Setsubi jono Kokusai Kyoso-ryokku Hikaku no Kenkyu (A Comparative Study of International Competitiveness in Production Facilities)*, Nihon Jidosha Kogyo Kai, 1969.

——, *Shuyo Koku Jidosha Tokei (Statistics of Automobiles of Major Countries)*, Nihon Jidosha Kogyo Kai, annually since 1972.

——, *Taiki Osen to Jidosha (Air Pollution and Cars)*, Nihon Jidosha Kogyo Kai, 1979.

——, *Taiki Osen to Jidosha Gyokai no Taisaku (Air Pollution and Countermeasures by the Automobile Industry)*, Nihon Jidosha Kogyo Kai, 1972.

Nihon Jidosha Shatai Kogyo Kai, *Shatai Kogyo no Ayumi (The Historical Development of the Car Body Industry)*, Nihon Jidosha Shatai Kogyo Kai, 1971.

Nihon Jidosha Yunyu Kumiai, *Gaisha no Ayumi (The Historical Development of Foreign Cars, Part II)*, Nihon Jidosha Yunyu Kuiai, 1986.

Tsusan-sho, *1953 Jidosha Tokei Nenpyo (Chronological Table of Automobile Statistics 1953)*, Tsusan-sho, 1953.

Tsusan-sho, *Nihon no Jidosha Kogyo (The Japanese Automobile Industry)*, Tsusan-sho, 1963–8.

Tsusan-sho Jidosha-ka, *Nihon no Jidosha Kogyo (The Japanese Automobile Industry)*, 1958–61 editions, Tsusan-sho Jidosha-ka.

Zenkoku Kei-Jidosha Kyokai Rengo Kai, *Kogata-/Kei-Jidosha Kai: Nijunen no Ayumi (The Historical Development of the Compact and Minicar Industry for 20 Years)*, Zenkoku Kei-Jidosha Kyokai Rengo Kai, 1979.

*Yearbooks and Statistics*

Keizai Kikaku-cho, *Keizai Hakusho (White Paper on the Economy)*, Keizai Kikaku-cho.

——, *Sekai Keizai Hakusho (White Paper on the World Economy)*, Keizai Kikaku-cho.

Nihon Jidosha Buhin Kogyo Kai, *Nihon no Jidosha Buhin Kogyo (The Japanese Automobile Parts Industry)*, Auto Trade Journal-sha.

Nihon Jidosha Gijutsu Kai, *Jidosha Gijutsu (Automobile Technology)*, Nihon Jidosha Gijutsu Kai.

Nihon Jidosha Kogyo Kai, *Jidosha Tokei Nenpyo (Chronological Table of Automobile Statistics)*, Nihon Jidosha Kogyo Kai.

——, *Nihon no Jidosha Kogyo (The Japanese Automobile Industry)*, Nihon Jidosha Kogyo Kai.

Nikkan Jidosha Shimbunsha, *Jidosha Nenkan (The Automobile Yearbook)*, Nikkan Jidosha Shimbunsha.

Nissan Jidosha, *Jidosha Sangyo Handbook (Handbook of the Automobile Industry)*, Nissan Jidosha.

Tsusan-sho, *Tsusho Hakusho (White Paper on International Trade and Industry)*, Tsusan-sho.

## PUBLICATIONS IN ENGLISH

*Books*
Abernathy, W.J., *The Productivity Dilemma: The Roadblock to Innovation in the Automobile Industry*, Johns Hopkins University Press, 1977.
—— and D.H. Ginsburg, *Government, Technology, and the Future of the Automobile*, McGraw-Hill, 1980.
——, K.B. Clark, and A.M. Kantrow, *Industrial Renaissance*, Basic Books Inc., 1983.
Altshuler, A. and D. Roos, *Future of the Automobile*, MIT Press, 1984.

Banker, T., *The Economic and Social Effects of the Spread of Motor Vehicles*, Macmillan Press Ltd., 1987.

Chandler, A.D. Jr., *Strategy and Structure: Chapters in The History of the Industrial Enterprise*, MIT Press, 1962.
——, *Giant Enterprise: Ford, General Motors and the Automobile Industry*, Harcourt, Brace & World, Inc., 1964.
——, *The Visible Hand: The Managerial Revolution in American Business*, Harvard University Press, 1978.
Cusumano, M.A., *The Japanese Automobile Industry: Technology and Management at Nissan and Toyota*, Harvard University Press, 1985.

Duncan, W.C., *US–Japan Automobile Diplomacy*, Ballinger Publishing Co., 1973.

Edwards, C.E., *The Dynamics of the American Automobile Industry*, University of South Carolina Press, 1965.

Ford, H., *My Life and Work*, Doubleday & Company, Inc., 1922.

Halberstam, D., *The Reckoning*, William Morrow and Company, Inc., 1986.

Keller, M., *Rude Awakening: The Rise, Fall, and Struggle for Recovery of General Motors*, William Morrow and Company, Inc., 1989.

——, *Collision: GM, Toyota, Volkswagen and the Race to Own the 21st Century*, Doubleday, 1993.

Mito, S., *The Honda Book of Management*, The Athlone Press, 1990.

Odaka, K., K. Ono and F. Adachi, *The Automobile Industry in Japan: A Study of Ancillary Firm Development*, Kinokuniya Company Ltd./Oxford University Press, 1988.
Okochi, A. and K. Shimokawa, *Development of Mass Marketing: The Automobile and Retailing Industries*, University of Tokyo Press, 1981.

Rae, J.B., *American Automobile Manufacturers: The First Years*, Chilton, 1959.
——, *The American Automobile Industry*, Twayne Publishers, 1988.
——, *The American Automobile*, University of Chicago Press, 1965.
Rothschild, E., *Paradise Lost: The Decline of the Auto Industrial Age*, Random House, 1973.

Sloan, A.P., *My Years with General Motors*, Doubleday & Company, Inc., 1972.
Sorensen C., *My Forty Years with Ford*, Collier Books, 1962.

Tolliday, S. and J. Zeitlin, (eds), *The Automobile Industry and Its Workers*, Polity Press, 1986.

White, L.J. *The Automobile Industry Since 1945*, Harvard University Press, 1971.

Yates, B., *The Decline and Fall of the American Automobile Industry*, Empire Books, 1983.

*Company History*
Kamiya, S., *My Life with Toyota*, Toyota Motor Sales Company Ltd., 1976.

Rae, J.B., *Nissan/Datsun: A History of the Nissan Motor Corporation in the USA, 1960–1980*, McGraw-Hill, 1982.

*The First Twenty Years in the USA*, Toyota Motor Sales, USA, 1976.

*Toyota: A History of the First 50 Years*, Toyota Motor Corporation, 1988.

Yamaha Hatsudoki, *Yamaha Today: 25th Anniversary*, 1980.

# Index